# The Impossible Document: Photography and Conceptual Art in Britain 1966 - 1976

The Impossible Document:
Photography and Conceptual Art in Britain 1966 - 1976
edited by John Roberts

A **Camera*words*** publication
Series edited by Camerawork, Volume 1

First published in 1997 by
**Camerawork**
121 Roman Road
London E2 0QN



Printed in Great Britain by Spiderweb Ltd.


British Library Cataloguing in Publication Data
A catalogue record for this book is available from the British Library

ISBN 1 871103 10 X

## THE IMPOSSIBLE DOCUMENT

Contents:



All interviews by John Roberts; interviews with Keith Arnatt, Alexis Hunter and David Lamelas in response to written questions

## ACKNOWLEDGEMENTS

Camerawork would like to thank all the artists for their unstinting support of the show and The Lisson Gallery and The British Council for lending works. Thanks also to Geoff Cox, Di Leech, Lynda Morris, Sandy Weiland.

## PREFACE

There is now a rich and complex history of debates on culture, representation and technology, of which Camerawork's engagement with photographic theory and practice has played a small, but significant part. *Camerawork*, the magazine, was one of the leading photographic publications of the late 70's and early 80's. Today the old slogan 'the politics of representation' has become commonplace; and theory itself, has become an intoxicating and apprarently bewildering profusion of options. Yet, in many ways the uses of theory in the production of visual culture remain very much under-examined.

In *Camerawords*, a new imprint from Camerawork, we seek to address this legacy, encouraging critical reconsideration and reappraisal of artistic and cultural debates. This publication accompanying the Camerawork exhibition *The Impossible Document: Photography and Conceptual Art, 1966-76* (April-June 1997) is the first in this series.

Conceptual art is currently under widespread re-evaluation. In the 1990s there have been major historical shows of conceptualism at ARC in Paris and MOCA in Los Angeles. *The Impossible Document* sees itself as contributing to this historicisation. However, what distinguishes this publication is its primary focus on photography. As John Roberts argues, looking at the presence of photography in conceptual art draws out many of the major disputes around the uses of the visual in art over the last twenty years, even if photography itself went largely untheorised as a medium in the early years of conceptualism. In this respect photography in conceptualism focuses on problems that remain central to contemporary art: how is it possible to produce images without rejecting that scepticism about the primacy of the visual that analytic conceptualism so effectively pursued? Roberts sees the legacy of conceptual art and the history of the avant-garde itself as part of deeper cultural conflict with roots in the Enlightenment: the struggle between iconophobia (the fear of images) and iconophilia (the love of images). Today the culture of art has swung unapologetically towards iconophilia in its embrace of the pleasures of popular culture. But if art now takes its challenges and values from a very different cultural space to that of conceptual art, faced with the problems of making *art* it still remains neurotically attached to the legacy of iconophobia. It is the continuing historical problems attached to art's pursuit of critical autonomy, and its cultural marginality, which is addressed by *The Impossible Document.*

# PHOTOGRAPHY, ICONOPHOBIA AND THE RUINS OF CONCEPTUAL ART

John Roberts

Conceptual art continues to underwrite the art of the present, as if what it discovered about power and aesthetics is the unspoken challenge of all serious art. But this challenge, of course, has no uniform inheritance, just as conceptual art itself has no stable set of positions. If conceptual art lives on today it is not because of the transmittance of any orthodoxy, but through its aporias, mistakes and misrepresentations. This is why it continues to fascinate: for all its megalomanical and messianic tendencies it destablised certain conventional expectations about making and talking about art which remain the shared cognitive ground of advanced art today. As such, it is no surprise that twenty years after it imploded and reassembled itself as a diverse range of disaffirmative practices, it should currently be the object of so much critical attention and dispute. Since 1990 a wide range of publications and exhibitions have sought to historicise its challenges, bringing its intellectual allure into some kind of workable alignment with the problems of contemporary art.[1] That some of this writing and curatorship is either fuelled by

1. For example the exhibitions 'L'art Conceptual, une Perspective', ARC, Paris 1989, 'Reconsidering The Object of Art: 1965-1975', Museum of Contemporary Art, Los Angeles 1995, organised by Ann Goldstein and Anne Rorimer, 'You are Now in the Middle of a N.E. Thing Co. Landscape', UBC Fine Arts Gallery, Vancouver 1993, organised by Nancy Shaw and William Wood. See also Joseph Kosuth, *Art after Philosophy and After: Collected Writings, 1966-1990*, MIT 1991, Charles Harrison, *Essays on Art & Language,* Basil Blackwell 1991, Terry Atkinson, *The Indexing, The World War I Moves and the Ruins of Conceptualism*, Circa publications, Corner House, Irish Museum of Modern Art, 1992, *Artists Think: The Late Works of Ian Burn*, Power publications, Sydney 1996, Thierry de Duve, *Kant after Duchamp*, MIT 1966, Benjamin Buchloh, 'Conceptual Art 1962-1969: From The Aesthetic of Administration to the Critique of Institutions', *October* 55, Winter 1990, Michael Newman, 'Conceptual Art from the 1960s to the 1990s: An unfinished project?', *Kunst & Museum Journal*, volume 7, number 1/2/3 1996, David Green, 'Between Object and Image', *Creative Camera*, number 340, June/July 1996.

nostalgia or by the business-as-usual packaging of the culture industry, does not alter the fact that the neuroses of conceptual art continue to speak to us, and as such remain open to ideological contest.

What *was* conceptual art, has therefore become the major site of dispute of the new writing? This has brought all the old conflicts and wounds out into the open again as conceptual art's leading disputants and supporters are given new vigorous identities or marked off as irrelevant or mere curiosities by the professional historians. Moreover, the disputants themselves have not been far behind the historians in wanting to derogate conceptual art as mere curiosity or defend its founding ideals. In these terms, there are three discernable positions on conceptual art: those who see it as a vast waste of time and energy, yet another example of sixties counter-cultural indulgence; those who want to defend some version of its founding critique; and those who want to pay tribute to the ambition of its mistakes; and put that tribute to work in the reflexive spirit of conceptual art itself. This latter position is what defines the tone and intellectual concerns of *The Impossible Document*, and what carries forward any serious historical work on that which continues to arrest our attention from the past. That is, it is easy to feel nostalgia for conceptual art in a period where much of what it stood for politically has little life beyond academic art history. It is harder to treat it as something which might contain energies and insights that allow certain ideals to remain, if not practically possible, then at least intellectually defensible.

Beyond this melancholic work of redemption though there are immediate problems of interpretation. To pay tribute to the instructive mistakes of conceptual art is at the same time is to open up the question of what such a tribute might actually mean. Or, in other words, if conceptual art is worth defending in terms of its mistakes and aporias, then what is it which underlies such things in the first place? Hence the concern of this publication: *photography*. With photography we arrive at one of the paradoxes of conceptual art. Linguistic or analytic conceptual art was largely an attack on the primacy of the visual, yet the majority of the forms which went under the heading of conceptual art were photographic, just as analytic conceptual art was mediated through photographic reproduction. This can be construed in one way as a failure of analytic conceptualism to make its claims tell, but in another way it reveals what many artists wanted out of conceptual art's critique of Modernist orthodoxy: a new *reading* of the pictorial. That this was to carry analytic conceptual art before it as well by 1975, points, I would argue, to the subfusc function of photography within conceptual art. Photography was the means by which conceptual art's exit from Modernist closure was made realisable as *practice*. Yet photography itself was of little interest to most conceptual artists, producing a situation in which critical agency is given to the photographic image without photography becoming theoretically self-conscious as a medium. Photography, then, had an indirect function: it allowed conceptual art to reconnect itself to the world of social appearances without endorsing a *pre*-Modernist defence of the pictorial.

But if the history of conceptual art needs to be opened up to the disruptive presence of photography, this does not mean we have somehow explained conceptual art or accounted for what made conceptual art so damaging and exciting in the first place. For there is a tendency at the moment in the revisionist histories to use conceptual art's relationship with photography as an excuse to 'tidy up' conceptual art in the interests of making it more palatable to administrators and critics. Thus in emphasising photography at the expense of analytic conceptual art, some writers have wanted to 'save' conceptual art from what they take to be its descent into bureaucratic theoreticism, that is, 'save' it from Art & Language. The reduction of Art & Language's analytic conceptualism to a caricature of reified reason maybe a convenient way of attacking the theoretical prolixity of conceptual art as a whole, but as empirical evidence about what made Art & Language's practice so compelling as a contribution to conceptual art it is inadmissable. What also needs to be brought back into the historical frame is how humorous and sardonic much of their early work was; and how this impulse is what distinguishes the place of theory within conceptual art from Modernism. This is important because the perlocutionary force of much of their writing against the 'sins' of others was actually satirical. Consequently in opening up conceptual art to the unconscious place of photography it is necessary to keep in mind that the dominant theoretical voice of conceptual art was also, in a sense, not to be 'trusted', was not what it seemed to be. And to insert myself and my own intellectual formation into this history, this is what had the greatest appeal for me about conceptual art reading *Art-Language* in the late seventies and early eighties. The mixture of theoretical exactitude and playfulness, political rectitude and irresponsibility, the language of the seminar and the pub, produced a highly toxic brew. Indeed it was seductive to the point of wanting to be like that; for to be rude and rigorous, artist and philistine seemed the best of all possible worlds. Thus as analytical conceptual art is rightly opened to criticism and the countervailing arguments of photography we need nevertheless to keep in mind what made conceptual art's theoretical excursions so liberating: that seriousness and ambition in art might also be a form of deliquency and malingering.

In the late sixties conceptual art gave Modernism a "nervous breakdown".[2] It did this by subjecting Modernism to a thorough-going epistemological and ontological demolition job.

---

2. Mel Ramsdan, 'Ian Burn's Excellent Adventure', *Artists Think: The Late Works of Ian Burn*, op cit p23

As if caught in the interrogative glare of both the psychoanalyst and detective, Modernism's claims to self-knowledge were shown to hide the symptoms of the repressive personality. Modernism's disinclination, or resistance, to examine what it understood as value and quality meant that the new art was continually forced to test its ambitions against what it perceived as arbitrary and authoritarian criteria. Consequently, the idea that incontestable quality in art was identifiable with certain kinds of 'optically vivid' abstract painting and sculpture was judged to be based on prejudice rather than reason. Moreover, such justifications could be exposed non-cognitively as connected to vested art-market interests. As a result what conceptual art set out to reclaim was the identity of the artist as a conceptual thinker, as someone whose judgement on art and culture was not to be governed by unexamined notions of 'good taste' and aesthetic sensitivity. This meant a very different sense of the modern *in* art than Modernism was prepared or able to imagine; that is, conceptual art rejected Kantian self-criticism in favour of a reindentification of self-criticism with the negative critique of the avant-garde. Thus whereas Modernism could only conceive of aesthetic transformation in terms of the internal modification of a restrictive set of formal contents (abstract painting), conceptual art questioned the very coherence and legitimacy of these contents. In these terms the critique of the language of art was brought to bear on Modernism as a critique of art's historical identity. This involved shifting the primary function of the artist as the producer of discrete objects to the producer of ideas about ideas; or rather, in order for the artist to feel historically confident about producing objects or events as art the artist had to become their own best critic and historian. Hence the emergence of conceptual art in 1966 lies in the self-education of a generation of artists as a practical reassertion of the demands of artistic autonomy. It makes little sense to talk about conceptual art as artists doing theory-as-art, as if conceptual art had the theory in place which they then designated as art. The theory took on a prominence because that is what artists necessarily had to do - fitfully, pathologically even - in order to clear away a workable space for practice.

In Britain and the USA in the late sixties the focus of this clearance was a philosophical enquiry into art's *conditions of possibility*. A number of artists began to use the tools and categories of analytic philosophy (and only later Marxism and Situationist theory) to detach art from presuppositions about what art *is*. This meant that there could be no talk of art but only 'art' insofar as the activity of art making could not be derived from what was taken to *be* art at a given historical moment. Thus the intellectual and aesthetic work of art out of which the art object or event is made is logically and ontologically prior to any pregiven supposition about the essence and unity of art. This rejection of any a priori identity of the artwork is the shared problem of the writing of all the early British and American conceptualists that concern me here: Michael Baldwin, Terry Atkinson, Ian Burn, Mel Ramsden, Dave Bainbridge, Harold Hurrell, Philip Pilkington, Joseph Kosuth, Victor Burgin, John Stezaker. However, if the problem is shared the response to it is very different in a number of the writers; and importantly it is these initial differences that come to define the development, fissure and dissolution of conceptual art. For the critique of artistic a priorism is merely the substratum upon which debates about art and capitalist culture, language and art, image and text, the retinal and anti-retinal, get fought out in conceptualism. It is the dispute over what this critique of a priorism entails, therefore, which forms the fundamental ideological split in conceptual art between analytic conceptualism and so-called stylistic conceptualism.

I first want to look at three founding statements of analytical conceptualism, one by Joseph Kosuth, and two by Ian Burn and Mel Ramsden, before they joined Art & Language.

One of the most notorious and quixotic statements of analytic conceptual art is Kosuth's - now well known - 'Art After Philosophy', first published in 1969. As a contribution to the philosophy of aesthetics or cultural theory it is to say the least confused, but as a manifestation - and manifesto - of what analytic conceptualism demanded of art it is beautifully symptomatic. In a grandiose echo of Hegel's thesis about the necessary subsumption of modern art under philosophy Kosuth argues that since Duchamp art has failed to meet the exacting requirements of the truth of the ready-made: with Duchamp, art and aesthetics are finally seen to be different orders of experience, and therefore, art does not need to identify itself with an aesthetic experience of the visual in order to be classified as art. With Duchamp art's focus of cognitive engagement changes from the morphological to the functional. The historical and teleological importance of conceptual art, then, is that it makes visible and completes this process by dissolving art into the analysis of the concept 'art'. Thus whereas Hegel talked about the end of art as the beginning of art's philosophical identity as intellectually revealed truth, Kosuth talks about the end of aesthetics as the beginning of art's virtuality as art-idea about art-idea. As he says: "Works of art are analytic propositions. That is, if viewed within their context - as art - they provide no information what-so-ever about any matter of fact. A work of art is a tautology in that it is a presentation of the artist's intention, that is, he is saying that a particular work of art *is* art, which means, is a *definition* of art".[3] In effect analytic conceptual artworks should be self-referring as art, for all other references (to the world of human desires and social relations) are extraneous to the truth of the enquiry. With this he concludes that the operations of art are similar to the proce-

3. 'Art After Philosophy', *Art after Philosophy*, op cit p20

dures of logic, mathematics and science.

Beyond raising the seriousness of what artists do to the level of a 'research programme' it is not clear what this actually means practically. For faced with the internal contradictions of art as an abstract method of deduction about its own conditions of possibility, he is confronted with the immediate and ineradicable problem of how such propositional content is to be presented. He 'resolves' this by recognising the necessity of the production of ideas in visual form but not as an 'art experience'! His use of photostats in *One and Five Clocks*, for instance, (1965?)[4] is, he contends, merely a temporal home for the work's content. The photostat could "be thrown away and then re-made".[5] This allows him then to claim that the art remains separate from its actual form of presentation.

This separation of art from aesthetics by intellectual fiat is expanded upon in the following year in 'Introductory Note to *Art-Language*'. Here though he is more explicit about what constitutes an adequate mode of presentation for analytic conceptualism. "Many artists working outside (deserts, forests, etc) are now bringing to the gallery and museum super blown-up colour photographs (paintings) or bags of grain, piles of earth and even in one instance a whole uprooted tree (sculpture). It muddles the art proposition into invisibility".[6] Or, in other words, work which incorporates bits of the world through the process of mechanical reproduction is pre-conceptual, a residuum of traditional forms of pictorialism, and therefore a subsumption of art (propositional con-

4. Kosuth's dating of this work as 1965 is certainly open to contention. 1965 predates all the substantive writing on analytic conceptualism.

5. Joseph Kosuth, ibid p31

6. Joseph Kosuth, 'Introductory Note to *Art-Language* by the American Editor', *Art after Philosophy and After*, op cit p39. First published in *Art-Language,* Vol 1, No 2, 1970

tent) under the judgements of aesthetics. In order to firm this up as a model of 'good practice' he makes the distinction between the 'why' artist who works with ideas and the 'how' artist who adopts a traditional craft base to production and identifies art solely with the morphological. Kosuth's model is different in certain respects to other analytic conceptualists, but this binary opposition between 'making' and 'thinking' is certainly something that marks the early period of conceptual art, and as such defines the ideological boundaries of the debate on the possibilities of art. The power of 'thinking' is what distinguishes the 'good' (historically iconoclastic) from the 'bad' (historically unreflective).

Whilst Kosuth was finding good ways in New York of distinguishing 'how' from 'why' the journal *Art-Language* in England was pursuing a similar process of philosophical adjustment, or "radical surgery".[7] Before Art & Language emerged as a coherent group out of the collective organisation of the journal, *Art-Language* became the intellectual home for the new writing on analytic conceptualism. Two artists and later members of the group, Ian Burn and Mel Ramsden (Ramsden is still a member) who, like Kosuth, were, sympathetic to the journal set up The Society for Theoretical Art in New York. In a number of co-authored papers they address themselves to a similar set of questions to that of Kosuth. I want to look at two papers in particular, 'Stating and Nominating' (1970)[8] and 'The Grammarian' (1970)[9]. As with Kosuth they are indicative of what was being brought to bear on the visual, photography and Modernism during this period.

In 'Stating and Nominating' we are presented with a compa-

7. Joseph Kosuth, '1975', *Art after Philosophy and After*, ibid p135
8. Unpublished paper, The Society for Theoretical Art, New York, 1970
9. Unpaginated pamphlet, The Society for Theoretical Art, New York, 1970. Later published in *Analytical Art*, Number 1, 1971

rable split between work which acts on and analyses the propositions of art, and art which reworks a received propositional content. Burn and Ramsden refer to this distinction as between art which *states* and art which *nominates*. Analytic conceptualism is art which reveals the propositional content of the work as a requirement of its making, and stylistic conceptualism simply points to things in the world as worthy of aesthetic legitimation. In contrast to analytic conceptualism stylistic conceptualism has been concerned with expanding an "observable range of non-propositional qualities without being required to provide any conceptual account of this art-work's stated nature". In this regard conventional practices are the result of acting without knowing what the elements or grammar of the language being employed signify, practice is 'blind' to its own determinates. Thus like Kosuth, in distinguishing analytic conceptualism from the mere nomination of things in the world, Burn and Ramsden argue that the content of the work must be stated linguistically. However, unlike Kosuth, this remains *syntactical* rather than semantic. That is, it is the linguistic content embedded in the internal relationship between signs which forms the analytic content and not the externalised linguistic demonstration of that content (as in Kosuth's *One and Five Clocks*). This obviously introduces a somewhat different understanding of the relationship between aesthetics and art. Whereas Kosuth sees his art-as-propositional content as lying beyond reference to any aesthetic precedents, Burn and Ramsden see their analytical conceptualism as consistent with the intentions of the best of abstract art: as in Modernism, advanced art must make transparent to the spectator its own rules of operation. However, if this locates their analytic conceptualism in an actual formal tradition, distinct from Kosuth's ahistoricism, this does not mean Burn and Ramsden are any more favourable to the morphological bias of Modernism. Like Kosuth they see analytic conceptualism as authoring a radical enquiry into the formal boundaries of art. As they declare in 'The Grammarian', because an artwork may need not be a denoted physical object, "the object simply becomes "less self-important". Hence the inquiring framework of proposition-based art should be linked to making moves from *of* questions to *for* questions (the securing of functional premises)".

This move from *is* to *why* derives its content initially from two related sources: linguistic philosophy's emphasis on matters of truth as matters of sense and context, and minimalist sculpture's recognition of the importance of context as a means of 'seeing' the artwork. In this regard 'The Grammarian' points to one of the key ethical and cognitive demands of analytic conceptualism in its attack on the morphological and visual: the production of new conditions of dialogue between artists and their audience, or as Burn and Ramsden put it, "new spectator requirements". It is easy to idealise this politically, particularly when the move from *is* to *why* does not in itself entail any commitment to analysing matters of sense as matters of ideology, just as it is easy to forget how indifferent Kosuth was to anything but an audience of learned artists. Yet it was these "new spectator requirements" that provide analytic conceptual art with its self-esteem and binds it to the future. Thus the whole point of shifting attention away from art-as-nomination to art-as-stating was to release the spectator from what was seen as the 'sleep' of Modernist spectatorship. To think about the artwork in terms of the premises that govern its propositional content is to rewaken the viewer as intellectually attentive. Consequently, it was not just Modernism's aesthete which was the target here, but stylistic conceptualism's would-be creatively imaginative spectator, the spectator as free-associating libertarian. The liberal mantra of "make of it what you will" was not something that analytic conceptualism felt provided any stable conditions for self-emancipation.

The production of the ideal spectator as reader and intellectual interlocuter and critic is eventually what brings Burn and Ramsden into Art & Language in 1970, and which sustains Art & Language's later understanding of the social implications of analytic conceptualism. However, analytic conceptualism's ideal spectator, in either its 'pure' or 'active' forms, brings with it certain costs. And it's these costs as they bear on the position of photography that I now want to discuss.

Despite Kosuth's early writing, analytic conceptual art was not a rejection of the visual as such (philosophically defeasible anyway), but a rejection of its unthinking historicisation as 'truth', 'pleasure' and 'beauty'. Modernism, therefore, was viewed as an historical blockage of the multivalent functions, applications and uses of the 'visual'. But nevertheless, this does not answer the very real sense of disembodiedness which analytic conceptualism brought to bear on thinking about the visual. In the bid to extract artist and spectator from the sleep (and charms) of the aesthete it set cognition against bodily needs and desires. Separating 'stating' from 'nominating', 'why' from 'how', it turned sensual appearance into an enemy of knowledge. However, this is not an argument about how 'thinking' suppresses 'feelings' or how 'concepts' suppress bodily pleasure. Analytic conceptualism rightly demolished the positivistic philosophic basis of these oppositions. But an acknowledgement that analytic conceptualism's - shall we say - distrust of the 'visual' was part of a deeper philosophical and cultural dialectic that went largely unrecognised by its participants: the conflict between iconophobia and iconophilia. Iconophobia, or the fear of images, and iconophilia, or the love of images, ground Western's philosophy's approach to epistemology. That is, images are either perceived as deceitful and leading to the promotion of untruth, or they are held to provide a truthful connection to an object or state of affairs. In matters of philosophy it can be argued with some justification that analytic conceptualism held images to be deceiving, and as such aligned itself with the anti-empiricism of modern linguistic philosophers such as W.V.O. Quine, Nelson Goodman and Wittgenstein - the "heyday of meanings" to quote Ian Hacking.[10] Wittgenstein's concern with *how* language describes, and his later anti-mentalist philosophy, undoubtedly underwrites conceptual art's re-thinking of perception and meaning, although the *Philosophical Investigations* themselves were not available in their complete version in English until 1974.[11] Wittgenstein like Marx is treated as part of the intellectual foundations of conceptual art's programme. But if the connection between conceptual art and Wittgenstein is much cited, as if the philosopher was a conceptual artist avant la lettre, the iconophobic implications of his philosophy are rarely discussed in detail.

Wittgenstein was important for early conceptual art because of one thing: his unswerving rejection of the notion that meaning is equivalent to something coming unbidden before one's mind. For Wittgenstein this mentalist theory of meaning is defeasible precisely because it puts a sensation of understanding before an awareness of a sign's use. Recognising a picture of a washing machine does not dictate an understanding of what a washing machine might be used for. Thus, understanding a sign is to have an ability to understand, to be a master of a technique, to possess a skill, and not a spontaneous process in which a image of a thing can be called on to give meaning to that thing. Abilities of comprehension are not interior, hidden performances. Moreover -

10. Ian Hacking, *Why does Language Matter to Philosophy?*, Cambridge University Press 1975

11. Ludwig Wittgenstein, *Philosophical Investigations*, Basil Blackwell 1974. An earlier version had been published in 1953, and reprinted in 1958 and 1963 by Blackwell's, *Zettel*, which contained notes on the *Investigation,* was also published by Blackwell's in 1967. This was certainly read by Art & Language on its publication.

and this is characteristic of Wittgenstein's philosophical naturalism - understanding as a matter of rule-following and the application of concepts is not a conscious intellectual process. What Wittgenstein calls 'seeing-as' (comprehension) is involuntary; understanding is coterminous *with* 'seeing-as'. In Wittgenstein then, the 'moment of spontaneity' could be said to shift from the production of meaning to its application.

This argument was obviously a powerful theory to attack the occultist and magical theories of spectatorship and meaning in Modernism. For what Wittgenstein's anti-mentalist account of meaning demonstrated was the essential temporal nature of understanding, that is, a sign only comes to 'speak' once it has been subject to a process of use through time. The act of understanding may be spontaneous but the process is not. This very simple - and now philosophically commonplace - point had enormous ramifications for art in the late sixties and early seventies, because it allowed artists to theorise "new spectator requirements" in ways that divested judgements of the 'visual' from the requirements of aesthetic immediacy. Clement Greenberg's and Michael Fried's Modernism is largely inherited from an Enlightenment account of the separate and autonomous characteristics of the arts, in particular those arguments used by Gotthold Lessing in the *Laocoon* (1776)[12] to distinguish painting from literature. Lessing argues that literature is an essentially temporal art, whereas painting is a spatial art. The reading of literature occurs in time; the apprehension of painting is instantaneous.

12. Gotthold Lessing, *Laocoon: An Essay on the Limits of Poetry and Painting*, Farrar, Straus and Giroux, 1969. For a wide ranging discussion of this essay in relation to iconophobia and the iconophobic tradition, see W.J.T Mitchell, *Iconology: Image, Text, Ideology*, University of Chicago 1986. In conclusion to his book Mitchell asks a question that could be quite easily brought to bear on conceptual art: : "How can the rhetoric of iconoclasm serve as an instument of cultural critism without becoming a rhetoric of exaggerated alienation that imitates the intellectual despotism it most despises" (p204)

The visual arts are confined to corporeal beauty, and spiritual significance is confined to literature. Although this is not a hard and fast distinction for Lessing - he talks about certain kinds of painting representing temporal action indirectly - the distinction does hold as a matter of what is essential to painting and literature. Thus painting may allude to the temporal but it is not its proper realm because it is not up to the task. Hence the would-be literariness of painting, for Lessing, offends natural law, producing a kind of monstrousness and arbitrariness. For Lessing the worst kind of painting is that which is allegorical. These "speaking picture(s)" are a mere "arbitrary method of writing".[13] In short they are forced. Thus whereas Modernism sought to shore up Lessing's space-time differentiation of the arts, conceptual art was intent on breaking it down. Indeed conceptual art's turn to the extended presentation of non-painterly forms severely tested the idea that the visual was anything but spatial. The identification of art's spectatorship with reading, the incorporation into the cognitive space of art the expanded time of serial photography, and as such the self-conscious expansion of the experience of art into interactivity-through-time, are evidence of a radical new temporality. In effect, the demands of linear and non-linear scanning, retrodiction, memory and physical interactivity produce a spectator who is never at rest, who is always being called to account for things in terms of what they do or do not know, where they are standing and where they have just been standing, like and unlike.

If this obliteration of the distinction between looking and 'reading', knowing and feeling, produces an alertness in the spectator not seen since the avant-garde of the 1920s, it also brings with it an enormous amount of unconscious intellectual baggage. For the historical irony of conceptual art's attack

13. Lessing, *Laocoon*, op cit, pX

on spatiality in the name of temporality and textuality is that Lessing himself favoured literature above painting on strict iconophobic grounds. Whatever painting might make of itself formally, its sensuality was always potentially deceiving. The sensual rendering of bodies in motion in painting always had the power to inflame the imagination, and distract it from art's spiritual quest. Translated into the politics of the spectacle of the late sixties the distrust of the visual in analytic conceptualism introduces a similar radical or even revolutionary iconoclasm. The cognitively attuned spectator and critical collaborator of conceptual art judges Modernism (and pictorial art) to bring about a degeneration of weakening of critical self-awareness. The spectator is seduced by forms that are not in the interests of his or her autonomy as a thinking and acting subject.

It is no surprise therefore, that Wittgenstein's own prejudices against the 'visual' should fill-out the iconophobic-iconophiliac dialectic during this period. For Wittgenstein's anti-mentalist subject is the perfect candidate for analytical conceptualism's ideal spectator: the spectator undistracted by the potential illusions of images. This is to say that Wittgenstein's anti-mentalist account of meaning in the use of ordinary language enabled the processes involved in perception to be given a basis in conceptual description rather than 'mere' sensual identification. Yet it is problematic to think that processes of identification do not play a determinate part in the reconstruction of meaning. For instance on occasions the perception of an object coming before one's mind can play an important role when the subject draws on his or her powers of reasoning.[14] When someone mentions BSE for instance, I might think of the image of a Friesian cow. Clearly the image won't help me in understanding BSE or even the biology of Friesian cows, but it might prompt me

14. For a discussion of Wittgenstein and anti-mentalism see Colin McGinn, *Wittgenstein on Meaning*, Basil Blackwell 1984

to think of various physiological factors that might then stir my stored knowledge on the subject. But because Wittgenstein's anti-mentalism treats any image coming before the mind as a sign (as mere interpretation), there is little space in his philosophy of perception for mental images as relays to understanding. Thus although it is axiomatic that being able to point to or recognise something is not sufficient for understanding to take place, perceptual experience acts as input to the subject as a concept-applying entity. As such the important point is that our powers of recognition (of nomination) occur within the context of a range of concept-applying abilities, and therefore is a necessary part of a complex-range of meaning-producing skills. As Gareth Evans has argued in *The Varieties of Reference*, in relation to the issue of knowledge by acquaintance: "when the subject wishes to make absolutely sure that his judgement is correct he gazes *again at the world...* he does not in any sense gaze at, or concentrate upon, his internal state. His internal state cannot in any sense become an *object* to him."[15] The powers of recognition then may be fallible outside of understanding use, but the retrieval of perceptual information functions as a constitutive part of our conceptual abilities.

The reason I mention all this is that the idea of knowledge through perceptual acquaintance is what haunts the debate on the visual in conceptual art, despite the construction of an ideal spectator trained to resist the lures of empiricism. Thus all the moves made through photography against analytical conceptualism endorse some account of pictures as providing a means of connecting the spectator's cognitive skills to the naturalistic world of appearances, rather than simply to the philosophical categories of art. And it is this sense of photography as bringing art into re-aquaintance with the physical world that defines the work of those who see con-

15. Gareth Evans, edited by John McDowell, *The Varieties of Reference*, Oxford University Press 1983, p227

ceptual art as an opportunity to re-theorise art as a social practice. By this I mean that photography brought back from the critique of artistic a priorism a different set of expectations on knowledge and pleasure than analytic conceptualism. In a crucial way it reconnected art to the 'ordinary' and 'everyday'.

In 1966-67 there was no discourse on photography to speak of in avant-garde art. What discussion on photography there was in the culture remained confined to the professional institutions who were still fighting for photography to be recognised as an art in itself. John Szarkowski's tenure as the head of the Museum of Modern Art's photography department during the late sixties was driven by the need to displace the functionality of photography and create a great canon of American and European art-photographers. This Modernist aggrandisement of photography was, however, of no or little interest to avant-garde artists using photography during this period. Indeed the majority of artists (in the USA and Britain) had no knowledge of the history of photography. What they were interested in was the very fact that photography was commonplace, as much at home with the amateur as the professional and therefore something that fitted quite readily into conceptual art's anti-aesthetic and disaffirmative ethos. Thus in Ed Ruscha's photographs for example - considered to be a precursor of conceptual photographic activity - there is both an expulsion of the photojournalist's 'significant moment' through the repetition of everyday objects and an indifference to qualities of presentation subscribed to by the fine art professional. The effect is to create a form of attention which is as 'ordinary' or unassuming as looking at a family album or in an estate agent's window. This 'anti-professional' use of photography clearly feeds into early conceptualism's rejection of fine-art pictorialism. For what was of concern for artists such as Bruce Nauman, Robert Barry and Douglas Huebler in the late sixties was for the use of photography to be distinguished from its location within the history of photography. In this the fundamental difference between the uses of photography in early conceptual art and the concurrent development of photographic Modernism under the aegis of Szarkowski, is that conceptual art openly embraced photography's functional and anti-aesthetic character, whereas Modernism actively suppressed this through aestheticism. As such this re-introduces the distinction between Modernism as a practice of self-reflection on the formal limits of a medium and the avant-garde as a theory of positional negation. Nauman, Barry and Huebler and others were using the photographic document or snapshot in order to negate dominant artistic notions of taste and sensitivity and not as an advanced form of photographic practice. This means that the very thing that Modernism in painting and photography found so problematic - photography's indexicality and ubiquity - becomes one more resource to question the hierachies of taste and genre which prop up conservative ontologies of art. In this respect, we see a familiar avant-garde move being made on the part of these artists: the indexicality and infinite reproducibility of the photograph becomes a source of the 'primitivistic renewal' of the artist's autonomy. There are many complex registers of 'primitivism' in conceptual art. Art & Language's intellectual deliquency, for instance, can be read as a good example of how a number of the tropes of the 'primitive' (the ugly, the philistine, the behaving-badly) seek to distinguish the official and received, as managed and homogeneous, from the unofficial as the awkward, incompetent and heterogeneous. But what unites most conceptual art in its disaffirmation of official Modernist taste is the valorization of the amateur, and this is particularly evident in the use of photography. As such the 'primitivistic' use of the photographic document carries with it the same message that many other 'primitivist' moves in art have carried this century: the idea that the work of art is closer to 'ordinary' labour and the 'ordinary' skills of the artistic amateur than the dominant, professional institutions of art would have us believe. The use of the photographic in early conceptual art, then, serves one overiding function: to question the concept of artistic skill enshrined in Modernist and traditional accounts of taste and sensitivity. Thus we need to be clear that the use of photography in early conceptual art is part of a continuing dialectic concerned with art and the division of labour that stretches back to the Russian revolution of 1917. Conceptual art's amateur is the direct descendant of Productivism's dissolution of aesthetics into artistic functionality.

But what is striking, however, is that until the mid-seventies in Britain in particular, this legacy played no part in the self-understanding of these artists and other artists using photography 'against the grain'. Consequently, the social content of early conceptual art's use of photography has to be seen as very different in implication than the early avant-garde. Although Nauman et al may identify demotically with the skills of the amateur and the non-specialist, the artists were not interested in replicating the social reportage of post-Revolutionary culture. There is no interest in turning the camera on social subjects in order to say something about social power etc. At no point did the early conceptualists want to return to, or want to be confused with, the social documentarists. This changes, and of course can be subject to counterfactual evidence in the work of some artists (Dan Graham for example), but overall, the opening period of conceptual art embraces the culturally disruptive function of photographic reportage only to withdraw it from the social world. This is because photography is soon submitted to an internal critique. In turning away from the ethical demands of photojournalism and the aesthetic ambitions of Modernism, the indexical function of photography undergoes a process of re-alignment. In his essay '"Marks of Indifference"' for the MOCA conceptual art show

'Reconsidering the Object of Art 1965-1975', Jeff Wall refers to this as a process of *subjectivisation.*[16] The reportorial capacities of photography are turned on the activity of the artist and his everyday social relations. But if this subjectivisation is widespread we need to get from the fact of this shift to why it took place and with what ends in view. Wall overlooks most of the details of this shift because he is more concerned with dealing with the impact of performance on conceptual art.

I would argue that the turn to photography as a means of documenting the art event is a readjustment of the space of the 'real' within photography, and as such presages the idea, so prevalent in the 1980s, of the staged photograph as constructed biography. Thus it is not good enough to say that Bruce Nauman, for example, was using photography simply to document what he was doing in the studio as a 'sculptor', and therefore was only concerned with transfering the studio activity into an image of that activity. Rather, Nauman's early photographs (*Self-Portrait as a Fountain*, 1966) present a re-adjustment in perception about where the photographer might situate himself or herself within the photographic process of 'truth-telling'. To enact something as an event for the camera, something as banal as spitting out a fountain of water, is not merely to produce a photograph of a 'performance' but to opt for the possibility that photography might have established a very different relationship to the 'real' than conventionally supposed. These are photographs which also represent the externalisation of states of consciousness. They therefore disrupt, in casual, humorous and at times inane ways, the privilege given to certain high-serious identities in art and photography, in particular the idea of the anonymous author in Modernism (as a rejection of the bad-form of self-description and autobiography) and the idea of

16. Jeff Wall, '"Marks of Indifference": Aspects of Photography in, or as, Conceptual Art', in *Reconsidering the Object of Art*, op cit p253

the photographer as objective witness. Both these identities presume a relationship to truth which stands outside, or athwart, the representation of the everyday as 'microscopic' and pathological. As Nauman himself says: "It... had to do with trying to make a less important thing to look at".[17]

This pointing at things that photography had inevitably overlooked extends photography's powers of ostension. Ostension is to show someone something by directing their attention to it. Now of course photography is the ostensive medium par excellence. It's indexical relationship to the world of objects and events is no more nor less a form of 'pointing'; and pointing necessarily contributes to our knowledge of the world. But as I have explained analytic conceptualism tended to separate the ostensive act of 'showing something' from 'meaning something'. If I have shown how difficult this is to accept once we acknowledge the part perceptual acquaintance plays in our conceptual abilities, this becomes clearer once we understand the singularly important part ostension plays in human communication. An ostensive act is always an inferential one. That is, to point something out is to make a claim on its significance or value. Thus someone who engages in ostensive behaviour makes manifest a number of assumptions about his or her actions. Consequently it can be argued that the pointing out of something always entails the recovery of the intentions behind the act even if information about such intentions are minimal initially. From this we might argue that even where the recognition of intentions are weak some recovery of meaning nevertheless does take place based on the ability of the subject to infer meaning from the available evidence. Thus, for instance, the illocutionary force of a gesture might provide the possible direction in which the relevance of the gesture is

17. Bruce Nauman quoted in Joseph Kosuth, 'Information 2', *Art after Philosophy and After*, op cit p59

sought. 'Showing forth' and the recovery of meaning, therefore, are always part of the same cognitive act. In their work on ostensive communication Dan Sperber and Deidre Wilson draw on the implications of this to argue for a revaluation of human communication. In a suggestive commentary on linguistic theory they argue that verbal communication is never principally about the mutual understanding of intentions or the decoding of signs. "Human intentional communication is never a mere matter of coding and decoding. The fact is that human external languages do not encode the kind of information that humans are interested in communicating. Linguistically encoded semantic representations are abstract mental structures which must be inferentially enriched before they can be taken to represent anything of interest".[18] From this perspective processes of decoding are never autonomous they are always positioned within an inferential framework, particularly when those decoding processes are involved in forms of communication where information about intentions are not manifest, such as art. The implications of this for photography are obviously enormous. The photographic document is not so much an inert nomination of things in the world, but a source of inferential complexity. I would argue therefore that subjectivisation in early conceptual photography involves a recognition of this at the level of how it organizes its materials in front of the camera. To photograph yourself spurting out water is to draw on the ostensive powers of photography in ways that are overtly allegorical rather than descriptive. As such this refusal to invest in the would-be objective truth of photography or its aesthetic validation has important implications for the debate on iconophobia in conceptual art. To nominate the 'pathological' and 'trivial' as the subjects of snapshot photography clearly shows that iconophobia is not only internal to analytic conceptualism; photo-conceptualism and analytic concep-

18. Dan Sperber and Deidre Wilson, *Relevance: Communication and Cognition*, Basil Blackwell 1986, p174

tualism are permeated by it in various ways and to various degrees. Nauman, Huebler and Barry all produce images, which in their resistance to pictorialism and spectacularization, take up a distance from an easy sensuality.

Overall what unites the early American photo-based conceptual art and analytic conceptualism is an ethics of amateurism. The absolute disregard for Modernist notions of high-seriousness and professionalism positions them in a similar kind of D.I.Y. space. Both treat the issue of art's autonomy as a matter of disabling the link between aesthetic performance and artistic value. This is why it is important to recognise that the American photo-conceptualists expressed their disregard for photographic history as avant-garde artists, not as avant-garde photographers. What counted above all else was that the work looked as if it could be made by anyone; and this was the last thing that professional photographers wanted to be identified with.

This disregard for photography as a medium, however, is very different in Britain during the late sixties and early seventies. In fact, it is Britain during this period that photographic conceptualism undergoes a widespread social reevaluation. We can point to precedents in the USA (for instance Dan Graham's *Homes for America*, 1966-67), but it is in Britain where photography and conceptual art takes a qualitatively different direction. The reasons for this are complex, but suffice it to say, the development of a sophisticated indigeneous Marxist culture, the rise of film studies, the importation of French structuralism, and the energy of a popular counter-culture produced a context in which many kinds of interesting work on the social meanings of art could be pursued. In this respect from 1970-76 we see a very different sense of how photography in art might distinguish itself from Modernism and photojournalism. Armed with a stronger sense of the historical development and contingency of the avant-garde than the Americans, avant-garde photography positions itself as a critique of the avant-garde itself. This leads to a more thoroughgoing assessment of how photography stands in relation to its wider conditions of production and consumption.

In 1969 John Stezaker and Victor Burgin were both working with photography within the framework of analytic conceptualism, although Burgin never strictly adopted the voice of the philosopher-as-artist. His aversion to this was there from the start. Nevertheless in his early *Photo Path* (1969) (a photographic trompe l'oeil of the gallery floor) there is a Kosuth-like play with different orders of reference and questioning of the formal boundaries of sculptural identity. Does a photographic representation of a section of the gallery floor constitute a sculptural 'event' or is the photograph just a photograph of the floor? John Stezaker, however, is more direct about the need for an art of propositional critique. In photo-texts and essays between 1969 and 1971 he takes on the voice of the self-scrutinizing Wittgensteinian. As he argues in 'The Necessity of Categories' (1971) "Art activity must...house theoretical conjectures concerning its own identity in the absence of a priori concepts of art. Thus discovery and construction must be reconciled within a single activity".[19] In a photo-text book completed in 1971, like Kosuth and Burgin, he deals with the non-identity between photography and its referents. At one point he writes: " 1) Series of photographs each representing 1/1000 sec of the history of a fountain. 2) 1 photograph representing 1 sec of the history of a fountain".[20] This sense of the instability of

---

19. John Stezaker, 'The Necessity of Categories', *Beyond Painting & Sculpture*, works bought for the Arts Council by Richard Cork, Arts Council 1973, p29. See also 'Introduction to 'categories'', in *A Survey of the Avant-garde in Britain*, Vol 2, Gallery House, London, 1972. "We cannot hope to forward at this point a precise and well defined concept of the concept of art as this is logically subsequent to first developing some concept of art" (p10)
20. John Stezaker, *Works 1969-71*, unpublished and unpaginated

photographic representation is explored through the book in a series of images engaged reflexively with like and unlike. By 1973 though both artists had dropped the work on propositional content in order to open out a space for discussion of the social production of meaning. Burgin to a large extent got there 'first', with less investment in analytic conceptualism he began to look at photographs as a source of connection to order of knowledge governed by the social function of photography under capitalism. As he was to say in 'Margin Note' written for *A Survey of the Avant-garde in Britain in 1972*: "As the domain of art therefore is the domain of those sign systems by whose means social reality, that is to say *ideology*, is constituted and disseminated then it cannot be 'value-free'".[21] Hence art (photography) is "useful" to the degree it "disarticulate(s)" social codes and contradicts ideological norms.[22]

This is a very different kind of language (borrowed principally from Barthes' *Elements of Semiology*) and proposes a different kind of critical function for photography. Photography is for the first time since the 1920s and 30s inserted into an explicitly politically counter-hegemonic space. As such this issue of use-value is something that the American photo-conceptualists and analytic conceptualists had great difficulty squaring with their negation of the professional categories and aspirations of art. Burgin's alignment of photography with a semiotic critique of the rhetorics of mass culture appeared to restore an unacceptable faith in the social function of art, even if Burgin was at pains to talk about the need for artists to act 'as if' art was socially effective. This precipitated another ideological struggle within conceptual art as Burgin (and later Stezaker) began to use photography not just as a way out of analytic conceptualism

21. Victor Burgin, 'Margin Note', in *A Survey of the Avante-garde in Britain*, op cit p18
22. Victor Burgin, ibid p18

but the idea of the avant-garde itself. Indeed in Britain in the early seventies the debate on photography moves overwhelmingly into a discussion of popular culture and mass culture.

If semiotics provides the initial point of theoretical access to this, it is the wider impact of Situationist theory (Debord's *Societé du Spectacle* had been translated in 1967), and the students' movement and the new counter-culture that provides the political framework. Situationism, with its emphasis upon the destablisation of the sign as a political act, provided photography with a further set of interrogative tools. This in turn established a route back to the cultural debates of the 1920s and 1930s, although the serious genealogical work on the early avant-garde wasn't done until the late seventies. One artist who pursued the Situationist turn was John Stezaker. But if Stezaker shares with Burgin a desire for a practice which rejects the iconophobia of the avant-garde, he does not share Burgin's - or the Situationists - faith in the political use-value of photography. That is, he argues, that the political option of semiotic-practice reinvests art with the rhetoric of artistic exclusion and therefore continues to support an isolationist view of artistic practice and cultural politics. Touching on issues in the early seventies that now overwhelmingly preoccupy a younger generation of artists, he demands a practice which engages with the forms and images of popular culture as a shared realm of meaning, of pleasure and alienation. As he outlined in 1973 the job of a post-avant-garde art is, "to expose social values inherent in modes of communication without using the avant-garde convenience of separating the form of exposure from the realm of social ideology".[23] In other words, the artist must drop his or her fear of the stereotype, cliche and worn-out in order to open out to the social world as lived by most people. As a

23. John Stezaker, Statement, *Arte inglesse oggi 1960-76*, British Council/Comune di Milano, Palazzo Reale, Milan 1976, p399

consequence, it is the appropriated or found image which is at the centre of Stezaker's concerns, for it is the appropriated or found image which allows direct access to the realm of social ideology by virtue of the fact that such images are embedded within previous uses and histories. Hence particular forms of appropriated imagery such as advertising or the picture postcard, are highly suitable as triggers for collective experience. Thus what the appropriated image allows Stezaker to do is narrow the cognitive and social gap between an experience of the popular in art and specialist forms of artistic attention. The result is that the rhetorics of popular forms of representation - the way images position the subject ideologically - are exposed *through* the process of re-contextualisation and manipulation.

In these terms Stezaker's turn to found imagery as a common source of myth and desire extends the debate on the ethics of the amateur within conceptual art. For what Stezaker becomes is a collector of the photographic image and therefore, by implication, an archivist of the industrially produced image. This collecting of what has been lost or remaindered through consumption is systematic in its endeavours in a way that the early American photo-conceptualists transformation of the found photograph into a 'ready-made' is not. In Ruscha, Huebler and Barry, in particular, there is a greater preoccupation with the interchangeable and repeatable possibilities of the found image. For what counted for those artists was how the minimalist principles of repetition and quantification might undermine issues of good taste and composition. They were not interested in the found image as a social resource. Moreover, despite their antipathy to professional categories of photography, they also remained *photographers,* at some level. Stezaker, on the other hand, only worked with found images. This naturally is not advantageous in itself, but the important issue, as regards the development and crisis of conceptual art, is that as a collector and archivist of images Stezaker establishes a very different kind of subject position for the anti-Modernist and post-traditional artist. As with all artists working under the mantle of conceptual art, Stezaker's adoption of the voice of the amateur at this time is that of the anti-aesthete. But whereas analytic conceptualism substituted the critical nay-sayer and amateur philosopher for the connoisseur and sensitive 'emoter', Stezaker takes on the position of the 'fan' and memorialist. This of course owes something to Benjamin and the Surrealists; and interestingly it is the younger British conceptual artists using photography who reintroduce this idea of the artist-as-rag-picker into the avant-garde arena in the early seventies. But more significantly this derives from the idea of 'fan-knowledge' as a form of cultural capital which is not determined by academic standards of success. By this I mean that in the early postcard pieces and montages Stezaker places a priority on his own immersion in the popular culture of the image. Thus the crucial issue for Stezaker's post-avant-garde artist is about how the artist might find a working relationship to the photographic image which is not intellectually superior to the culture which produced it. This is not to substitute Marx's or Wittgenstein's sceptic for Peter Winch's anthropologist, but a recognition - as with Art & Language - that radicalism in art invariably comes with the privileges of education and class.

In this respect concern about "new spectator requirements" becomes a debate about what relationship the artist is to have to what kinds of artistic materials. As such what Stezaker's archivist sets out to do is re-write the ideological contest between 'stating' and 'nominating' in the interests of common identifications. But rather than treating nomination as the avant-garde photo-conceptualist might as the transformation of the 'everyday' into *art*, he treats the incorporation of the found image into art as co-extensive with the pleasures of popular culture itself. Naming and identifying does not operate as the imprimatur of avant-garde brinkmanship, but as a relay to shared pleasures and knowledges. For Stezaker, at least, this had as much to do with his own perception of himself as a 'book artist' as a gallery artist. Working as an archivist of the 'culturally remaindered' his relationship to the image led him inevitably to organise his material as readable sequences and series' and therefore to the problem of the most appropriate form in which to display the material. In this light Stezaker's interest in the book form is no different from many other artists using photography and text during the period. As Germano Celant boomed at the time: "the book becomes the most accessible medium... for creating art".[24] Of course it didn't, but as a means of collating the work of the image-archivist it at least proved very successful at undermining the Modernist preoccupation with the singular aesthetic experience.

This opening up of conceptual art through the found image to the insubordinate and seductive pleasures of popular culture had a radical effect on the use of photography in conceptual art in Britain from 1973. A clear cultural reorientation takes place as a number of younger artists identify with photography not just as a negation of Modernist taste, but as the source of a wider debate on the social function of the artist and the social production of meaning. In the work of John Hilliard and Alexis Hunter, for instance, by 1973-4 there is a recognition that a critical understanding of the use of photography within popular culture might offer a way out of both Modernist aestheticism and the ironic forms of nomination of West-coast photo-conceptualism. Thus what distinguishes Hilliard's and Hunter's work is the actual extension of the photographic document into an engagement with popular representational practices (advertising, fashion photography, photo-romans) and popular genre derived from film and lit-

24. Germano Celant, *Book as Artwork, 1960/72*, Nigel Greenwood 1972

erature (romantic drama, horror). In its view that the dominant forms of the culture industry demands from the artist something other than Frankfurt-school disengagement or populist replication, this is close in spirit to Stezaker and Burgin. The post-avant-garde artist should, in a sense, work from inside the alienated materials of the dominant culture, and therefore trust the forms of art to their powerful collective focus. But unlike Stezaker, in particular, Hilliard and Hunter appropriate popular representional practices for their narrative seductions and literary inclusiveness. In effect their passage through conceptual art is as oblique story-tellers.

Story-telling would seem to proscribe much discussion of conceptual art. Nevertheless if we recognise the allegorical base of the story-teller's art we can trace its presence through the whole debate on photography in conceptualism. Nauman's early photographic studies are no more no less than autobiographical fragments. Similarly Keith Arnatt's work from 1969 offers an extraordinary subjectivization of the photographic document. From *Self-Burial* (1969) through to *Portrait of the Artist as a Shadow* (1971), he uses his presence or absent presence in a series of masochistically inflected studies on artistic alienation. In *Self-Burial* his gradual disappearance into the ground from one panel to the next is a pointed commentary on the thesis of art's so-called dematerialisation under conceptualism. Here we see the artist quite literally enacting his own cultural marginalisation. As Arnatt was to say in 1973: " I see no reason why the range of experiences that an artist can deal with should not include the difficulties he experiences as an artist".[25] For Arnatt the use of photography was primarily a means of reflecting back on the pathologies of the artistic subject; and it is these pathologies as a story-board of the 'everyday' that so obviously divides the ostensive powers of photography from its critics. Arnatt's

25. Keith Arnatt, Statement, *Beyond Painting & Sculpture*, op cit p38

photography fills out the de-differentiated subject of analytic conceptualism with all kinds of messy emotions and feelings that from the position of a strict rational critique of artistic a priorism would appear to be illicit.

Both Arnatt and Hilliard began their careers as sculptors, and like many artists of their generation first turned to photography to document the temporal nature of their work. This idea of the photograph as a marker of the impermanent was initially a critical response to minimalism. The would-be sensitivity to the contextual reading of the artwork in minimalism was in fact belied by the restrictive monumentality of its geometric forms and its gallery-based location. The photographic document then offered a way of bringing back information about sculptural activities from contexts that were not restricted to the gallery. The photograph became an inseperable structural component of the art-experience. However, this turn to the photograph as a first-order artwork was soon subject to a process of internal aestheticisation. Richard Long and Hamish Fulton were happy to settle for a kind of conceptual-pictorialism; a perfect example of photographic nomination as the reinscription of tradition painterly forms. Hilliard though, like Arnatt, broke with the incipient pictorialism of the photo-as-sculptural-document by incorporating his self-image into a commentary on the conditions of photographic production itself. In a series of moves reminiscent of developments in structuralist film-making at the time, Hilliard drew attention to the produced nature of photographic truth-telling by photographing himself photographing, or photographing the same object at different exposures and on different papers (*7 Representations of Colour*, 1972). The work from this period (1970-73) is perhaps the only photo-based conceptual art which is actually discursively engaged with the mechanics and chemistry of the photographic document.[26]

26. Roger Cutforth's work from the late sixties also needs to be recognised as a contribution to these moves.

By 1973, to return to previous comments, this singularly materialist emphasis on the construction of photographic-truth had been incorporated into the broader area of the social function of photography. Hilliard extended his concern with the potential misreading of images inherent in all photographic perception, to a concern with the narrative suggestiveness of image and text, reminiscent of photo-love stories. This produced a shift in the context of conceptual art in Britain, which was as significant in its way as Stezaker adopting the role of the archivist: that is, the production of the photograph becomes a matter of its 'filmic' staging. Of course the staged photograph is nothing new; and early photo-conceptual art's turn to self-representation has a direct route back to the domestic photographs of the Surrealists, in particular Claude Cahun. But in this instance staging becomes a matter of employing and disarticulating the dramatic forms of popular culture, of arraigning and simulating them. To stage the image, essentially, means staging the conditions of the photograph's mass consumption. As such it also means addressing issues of sexuality and sexual difference. The implications of this were not lost on Alexis Hunter in 1973, as the increasing dissolution of conceptual art as the first generation of anti-Modernists, is helped on its way by the emergence of the first generation of feminists into art. In *Voyeurism* (1973), for instance, there is a qualitative transformation in the role of the staged figure, insofar the cinematic sequencing of Hunter disguising and revealing herself becomes self-consciously attached to issues of social and sexuality identity, prefiguring the whole development of late conceptual art into the photo-conceptualism and identity politics of the 1980s. In essence, the staging of photographic and filmic genres is further evidence of the embodying of conceptual art at the expense of its ideal spectator. The series of works Hunter made in 1976, *Approaches to Fear*, is a vivid example of the cultural tensions being played around this. Although Hunter's work is indebted to the alignment in the early seventies between conceptual art, Marxism and feminism, *Approaches to Fear* derives its primary source of engagement with questions of gender and identity from the seductions and fascinations of popular culture. The burning of a high-heeled shoe in front of the camera is clearly the work of someone keen to align critical consciousness in art with non-specialist forms of attention. As a result it was characterized as the worst kind of capitulation to iconophilia. For by 1975 the iconophobic impulses of early conceptual art had passed into the feminist critique of popular culture as evidence of one of the principle sites of women's self-alienation. There was little space for work which commandered some of the allure of popular genres such as the horror film. Thus, it is the turn to the conditions of consumption of images that contributes to conceptual art's final crisis in 1975-76, as a whole number of demands about the re-embodiment of the spectator and the need for the re-positioning of the artist within the culture fill out the conceptual programme of cultural disaffirmation and artistic reflexivity, and prepare the ground for a series of other struggles about the ethics of representation.

One artist who also represents this final playing out of the iconophobic-iconophilia dialectic in conceptual art is David Lamelas. Lamelas worked in London at the height of conceptual art, arriving from Argentina in 1968. Like Hilliard he moves from a materialist engagement with photographic truth - in his early urban photographs of Brussels and Dusseldorf he deals with the instability of the representation of the photographic event - to treatment of the photograph as part of an imaginary film script or projection of his own fantasies of omnipotence, (*Rock Star*, 1974). For example *The Violent Tapes* (1975) is a sequence of 10 black and white photographs of a fictional chase, borrowed in its *mis en scene* from the seventies TV cop show. The man and woman are being chased by mysterious (corporate?) assailants who are intent on retrieving a film tape the couple are carrying. This tape consists of sensitive documentary material of a violent nature. We assume that the couple have either stolen the tape or have made it. The play with the unstable truth-conditions of the photographic event is still evident, but this is directed outwards to the conditions under which the dominant relations of capitalist culture exist: censorship, a prurient interest in the victims of violence, and the violent denigration of the culture's critics. What we see therefore is the threat of violence as the threat of censorship or even death. Thus, unlike TV Cop shows the violence is implied, leaving the representation of actual violence outside of the frame. What this presents, I would suggest, is the iconophobic inclusion of the representation of violence within the iconophilic framework of a post-avant-garde art, an art which in sense can no longer avoid the cultural evidence of such violence. For the question of violence is more than a simple matter of Lamelas's own artistic concerns; it traverses the whole historical period. Conceptual art began out of violence, the violence of American imperialism and the Vietnam war. To say that conceptual art saw itself in resistance to the cultural effects of American imperialism does not thereby mean that conceptual art was thereby concerned with the problems of political representation in textual form (although politics and the value of propaganda of course became a central point of dispute about the direction of analytic conceptual art around 1972). Rather the politics of anti-imperialism were inscribed in the forms of iconophobia itself, as if the spectacle of violence could only be challenged by de-aestheticising the visual. This may sound contentious in the light of analytical conceptualism's scepticism about the social function of art, but conceptual art's rejection of the discourse of the aesthete was also, I would contest, a negation of the social 'blindness' of the aesthete's sensitivity: the fact the aesthete can never tolerate the social fact of violence, even as he or she is consuming it as an image.

Furthermore the end of conceptual art coincides with the beginning of the women's movement and the 'beginning'of the recognition - in public, legalistic, moral and cultural terms - of actual and symbolic violence against women. The representation of violence, therefore, hangs over conceptual art, extending the iconophobic-iconophilic dialectic into areas where it never ventured before. Lamelas's *The Violent Tapes* is a product of this constellation of forces, turning to violence as the secret code of the image under capitalism, but rejecting in good iconophobic terms its actual representation. The pressures to do otherwise, of course, is the history of the last twenty years, as the embodied spectator of art has come to share the same place as the embodied consumer of popular culture.

If this kind of work presages fundamental changes in the uses of photography, neverthless it is around this time that Art & Language begin to attack what they describe as 'Semio-art'. In *Dialectical Materialism* (1975) and *Above Us the Waves* (1976) they use photographic reproductions of Armenian Socialist Realist paintings and WWII illustrations respectively with ironic texts about the social claims of 'Semio-art', their specific target being the journal *October*. Although the group invariably use the skills of the graphic artist (particularly around this period) the use of photo-text here is clearly designed to embarass or 'see-off' what they perceive as the idealism and managerial tendencies of photo-based conceptualism. In his history of the group and conceptual art *Essays on Art & Language*,[27] Charles Harrison re-endorses this position. But there is a world of difference between the necessary rejection of the idealist claims of those who assume that photography is more democratic than painting, or that art can be a direct extension of ideological struggle, and reduction of all photographic practices to some

27. Op cit

amorphous 'Semio-art'. In doing this Harrison can then conveniently identify this mythical 'Semio-art' with the crudity of advertising and propaganda, and therefore the suppression of reflected thought. The satirical voice of the work is not served by the comparison of 'Semio-art' to the "falsehoods of journalism".[28] Art & Language have argued that they were not attacking photography *as such*; but this deflation is the kind of shibboleth which produces a history of photography and conceptual art without any dialectical self-consciousness. It is no surprise therefore that Art & Language experienced its own internal crisis over the identity of photography, image and text, at the same time Terry Atkinson left in 1974. When Atkinson departed in dispute over the future of the group and the role of the *Index*, a vast 'language community' of shared and disputed ideas presented in the form of index cards, he produced a series of photo-texts pieces, *The Bridging Works*, combining historical images (WWI and the Commune) with long satirical captions mimicing the operations of the *Index* itself. If this was Atkinson's own version of Art & Language's "black propaganda",[29] unlike Art & Language at the time Atkinson was to risk exploring the social possibilities of an ironised representational post-conceptual practice. As Atkinson was to write fifteen years later: "This bridging work appropriated A&L motifs from the Indexing and grafted onto them, capriciously and brutally, motifs which I took to be anti-A&L".[30] The ideological fallout from this, however, has been to turn the shared iconophobic-iconophilic conditions under which the initial dispute was played out into a matter of personal positioning. That is, both Art & Language and Terry Atkinson were far more embedded in a wider cultural argument about the challenges of representation than they both could or were prepared to admit in 1974 and 1975.

28. ibid, p139
29. ibid, p139
30. Terry Atkinson, *The Indexing...*, op cit p12

Thus far from reducing the conceptual art to an inert pictorialism, photography actually opened out a range of working possibilities for art during the period 1966-1976. In this I agree with Jeff Wall. "It could be said that it was photography's role and task to turn away from conceptual art, away from reductionism and its aggressions".[31] The history of conceptual art, therefore, will be traduced if the complex positioning of the photograph is not given its due. Because if we need to address the social and political contexts in which the iconophobic-iconophilic dialectic is embedded this in turn cannot be separated from the recurrent place and function of the photographic document within the twentieth century avant-garde. Through Constructivism, Productivism and Surrealism, photography has served to disinvest the voice of the aesthete in the name of the 'ordinary' user and spectator. This same sense of aesthetic disinvestment through the indexical and ostensive resources of photography passed through conceptual art, although with the bearest historical consciousness of what this disinvestment had stood for. As Benjamin Buchloh points out with some accuracy: it was precisely "the utopianism of earlier avant-garde movements... that was manifestly absent from Conceptual art".[32] If this is what constitutes the sorrows of conceptual art, it also points to the fact that the artists who were involved were young - sometimes very young - and were mostly winging it. The problem with writing about conceptual art, therefore, is that the moves it made, the strategies it adopted - across a range of artistic positions - were contingent and messy responses to shifting and sometimes unfocussed questions and issues. This is why it is mistaken to hold conceptual art as somehow responsible for the collapse of Western cultural values and cultural continuity, as Thierry de Duve does in *Kant After Duchamp.* Although for opposite reasons to Charles Harrison, like Harrison he flattens out the hetero-

31. Jeff Wall, "Marks of Indifference", op cit p266
32. Benjamin Buchloh, 'Conceptual Art 1962-1969', op cit p141

geneity of conceptual art in his defence of what he believes to have been eroded by its idealisms. He does this by conveniently eliding conceptual art with Kosuth's suppression of aesthetics. So the failure of conceptual art becomes the inability to suppress aesthetics in the name of art. As such Kosuth's fantasy of exclusion is made to stand for a position that few other conceptual artists actually held. The failure of conceptual art is simply the disappointment experienced knowing that artworks cannot avoid being subject to aesthetic appraisal. This is to judge conceptual art as if its only value is as a contribution to the philosophy of aesthetics. De Duve barely addresses conceptual art as an *artistic* culture, as a conversation between specialist and non-specialist knowledges, and when he does acknowledge this he demeans it. "Those were the days my friend, enthralling days, liberating days, and yet, in the long run, sterile".[33] Thus it is particularly revealing when he says "conceptualism remains unsatisfactory",[34] as if conceptualism claimed to offer anything other than its own lack of "satisfaction". On the contrary conceptualism embraced dissatisfaction as a matter of principle. In this it provided a range of forms and strategies that opened up how art might make sense of its historical dysfunctionality; hence the importance of photography, particularly in the light of the art of the last twenty years. For the emergence of a reflexive photography out of the iconophobic strategies of analytic conceptualism, made it possible to produce a representational art that avoided many of the problems of iconophilia. As such, far from conceptualism's unruliness delivering the absolute negation of art, it demanded that the artist (and critic) be attentive to their own conditions of production in the face of the increasing professionalisation of the modern art institution. In this, its deliquencies continue to demand our attention.

---

33. Thierry de Duve, *Kant After Duchamp*, op cit p300
34. Thierry de Duve, ibid

Keith Arnatt

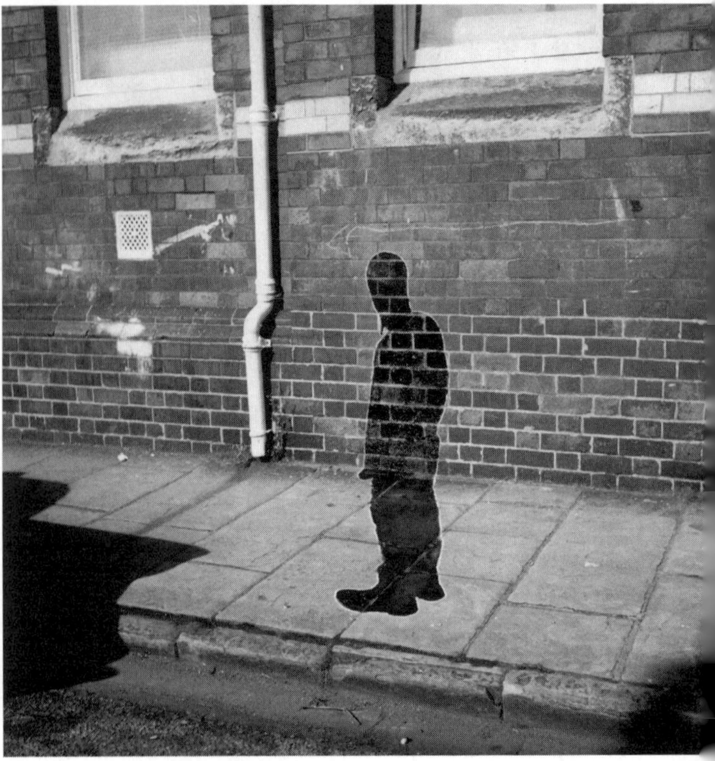

*Portrait of the Artist as a Shadow of his Former Self*, 1972

## INTERVIEW WITH KEITH ARNATT

*In a good deal of early conceptual art which emerged out of sculpture photography became a structural component of the work. Photographic evidence functions in a first-order way as the art object itself. Richard Long is the obvious candidate here. In your early work, however, there is a primary commitment to the instability of perception. Your hole diggings and play with mirrors set out to destroy any straightforward confidence in photography's truth-telling powers. Did you conceive these initial works as quasi-experiments in perception?*

Though the earlier work certainly involved "the instability of perception", I did not think the work was about that. A question I had in mind when I did some of this work was: how visual does visual art have to be? Originally I thought of the work as being the 'objects' photographed - *not* the photographs themselves - their function I simply regarded as 'evidence'. However, they *were* taken with the idea of showing that what was photographed - the mirror works particularly - would pose difficulties for a viewer. That is, the viewer would need to investigate the object in order to comprehend it. Of course, the photographs, more often than not, did not make at all clear what was photographed, but rather, presented the viewer *of the photograph* with precisely the same difficulty, i.e. that of making sense of the photograph! I suppose I was beginning to become aware of the unreliability of photographic evidence and began to play with that feature. I felt that what a photograph could not tell or show might be just as significant as what it could.

*The sense of being tricked, of not knowing what it is one supposedly looking at and how to evaluate it, also has the gentle humour of English absurdism (Lewis Carroll's love of paradox for instance). This humour and love of the uncanny reap-*

*pears in your photographs, and distinguishes your work on the gap between 'looking' and 'knowing' from much other work in Britain at the time. Did you see your 'conceptualism' as made out of other things than the post-minimalist debate on sculptural form and art's analytic linguistic turn?*

You are on target mentioning Lewis Carroll in connection with my work. I am fond of paradox - though equally attracted to perversity. If my work has connection with the post-minimalist debate it would be because of my focus on its seemingly reductive stance. The logic of that stance seemed to call for an escalating negativity - no material form, no content and ultimately no artist. It all seemed like a scenario for a Beckett play. My feelings about this were rather ambivalent and it posed the problem for me just *how* to show that I did feel this way. Resort to "gentle" humour and self-deprecation seemed one way of showing that I was not really one of *them.* I have never been quite sure whether my attitude, then, was one of bemused attachment or bemused detachment. Looking back, I feel that my work could be likened to 'asides' from the wings.

*Early photo-based conceptual art looked to the 'least event' or 'small event' for its content: everyday gestures and activities. These were also the cognitive and semantic building blocks of Anglo-American analytic philosophy (Donald Davidson, John Searle, W.V.O.Quine) in its hey-day in the sixties and the seventies. The connection between the post-Wittgensteinian inquiry into the meaning of meaning and conceptual art's reflexiveness was of course something that many artists at the time were keen to defend. How did you see the relationship between art and philosophy during this period?*

Later work did gravitate towards the mini-event or action - it seemed a natural progression from the object. Unlike 'process' art I preferred not to leave a residue - other than the photograph of the action. I think it had something to do with the fact that I always found photos of Pollock *making* his paintings more interesting than the paintings themselves. I now realise that my understanding of contemporary art came in some measure from seeing photographs of work rather than from seeing the work itself. A brief flirtation with moral philosophy in the late fifties left me with an interest in the philosophy of language and I later went on to read, Austin, Grice and Searle. However, in my work I did not think *my* use of language had much to do with "analysing the propositional content of art". I did believe though, that some areas of academic philosophy did have a bearing upon my interest in 'art behaviour'. Again, I do remember feeling that so much writing by artists of analytic persuasion seemed tedious and onerously serious. I think I was attracted to a more ludic oriented activity.

*I want to extend this issue of the 'everyday'. In your work, as in a number of other artists' work, there is a good deal of evidence of labour. In the early photographs (*Earth Plug, Invisible Hole, Inside Out, Self-Burial*) you are digging. The foregrounding of the production of the work as an act of realist disclosure was, of course, very much in the air at the time via the industrial aesthetics of minimalism and Brecht's dramaturgy. But what was particular for you about being 'close to the earth' and needing to photograph it?*

The idea of "being close to the earth" or "needing to photograph it" could not have been further from my mind! The whole digging phemonenon, so prevalent in the late sixties, did interest me I felt my own digging activity to be, in a sense, a comment on that mode of behaviour. The hole, for me, was important - it allowed me to 'hide things'. Holes, of course, have to be holes in something, and it is relatively easy to make holes in the earth. I wonder how your notion of "the work as an act of realist disclosure" applies to my *Invisible hole revealed by the shadow of the artist.* That hole was made with the intention of obscuring the fact it was made. You were not meant to see it - though you could fall into it! Perhaps this could be understood as a metaphor for dangers of reductivism. Also, it struck me as the ultimate in perversity to laboriously construct the hole so that you were unable to distinguish it from the environment. The notion of it being the product of work or banausic effort simply does not arise unless you do realise it is there.

*Entering the space of the photograph yourself in* Self-Burial *(with its obvious allegorical references to artistic marginality and masochism) your work shifts focus onto the identity of the artist. Self-images as 'shadows' and 'cyphers' appear, enacting a crisis of the artist as self-present author and originary creator of meaning. You were one of the few artists at the time in Britain who was actually addressing the* subjectivity *of this crisis. Did you see it like this, them, or subsequently?*

When I did *Self-Burial* I did not have "artistic marginality or masochism" in mind. I did it because a writer/critic made the suggestion - in connection with the notion of the dematerialisation of the art object, that *if* the art object disappeared then it followed that the artist would disppear. So I disappeared! However, I did recognise that the series of photographs could be 'read' in other, but related, ways. The potential for playing with the mutability of meaning attracted me and I went on to use the series in different contexts thus making the same series function in different ways - the TV interference in Germany being but one example. Of course, you are quite right in seeing my shift of focus onto the artist himself and my work did become increasingly concerned with what I felt to be a predicament, rather than a crisis. My fascination with the idea of the 'ultimate gesture' had got me into quite a hole!

*Most conceptual artists using photography learnt to work with photography as they went along. In fact photography as a practice with a critical history and technical trouble-spots wasn't really an issue for artists. Most artists learnt their history retrospectively. When, and how, did you begin to see photography as a set of specific issues with a history of their own?*

In 1970 I met David Hurn, a Magnum photographer, who was asked to set up a new course in Documentary Photography at the college where I was teaching. It was through him that I became aware of the history and practice of photography. What struck me forcibly was the range of concerns that that history encompassed. I also felt that many of those concerns overlapped and paralleled those of practioners in other media. I never felt the need to question the *status* of photography. I regarded it as simply another medium to be used when the job required it. A consequence of holding this view and the way it inflected my own work led some to accuse me of becoming a photographer!

*One school of thought has it that conceptualism failed because its rational self-reflexiveness ended up replicating the bureaucratic structures of capitalist administration. Others have condemned it on the grounds that there is only so much you can do - or is worth doing - analysing the propositional content of art. How do you see the demise of conceptual art now?*

I do not think of conceptual art as something that either suceeded or failed. And to talk of the demise of conceptual art, seems to me, to be rather odd. For to say what it *was* is really rather difficult - it was so many things. However, I do think that its legacy has been to 'admit' an increasingly broad spectrum of subject matter for the artist to deal with and given the licence to deal with it through any means that seem appropriate. I feel that the most interesting art of the present would not have happened without it.

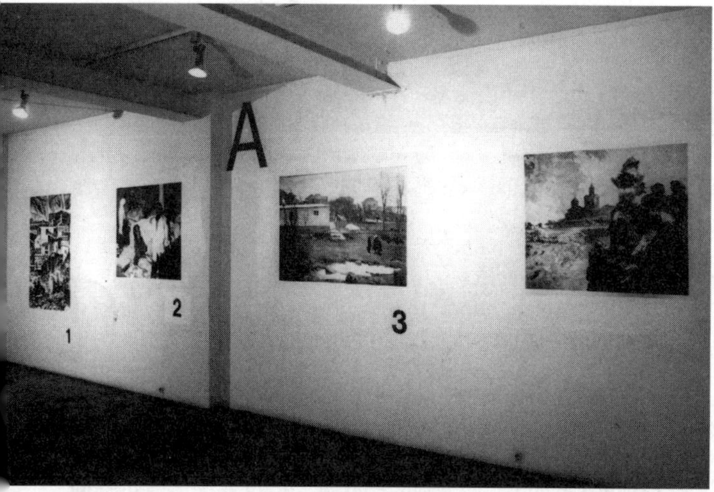


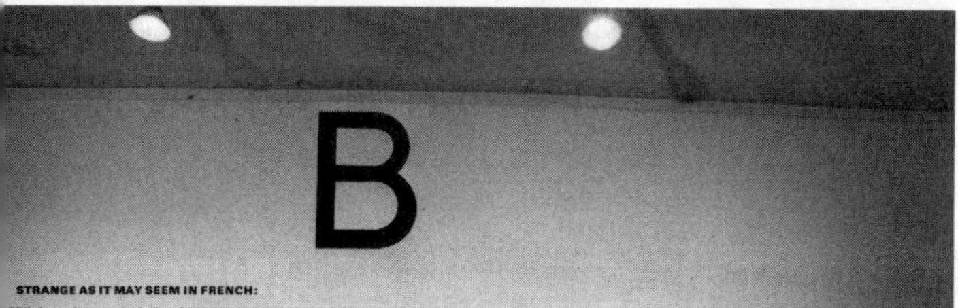


*Dialectical Materialism (Armenian Socialist Realism)*, 1975

## MOTI MEMORIA

Art & Language

Not for the first time we are being asked to remember conceptual art. Not for the first time we are tempted to mischief - or at least to that sense of civil disobedience which might attend making the whole thing up.

Remaking our memory as mischievous fiction might be some sort of service to the truth. Insofar as memory under headings which purport to trace and individuate some sort of practice go to matters of self-patronage and self-curation, we might argue that a Gödelian memory style has a lot to recommend it. Might this be because conceptual art, or rather some conceptual art, represented a gross inconvience - indeed - and internal untruth to the curatorial mechanisms which it eventually encountered, or might it be because our rememberings are little more than apostrophes?

Our recollection is at best an attempt at a rescue which is highly vulnerable to irony. More vulnerable, however, are those who engage in such exercises without any sense of the absurdity of their rhetoric. It's a long time now - and while we may want to recognise, do want to reject, self-patronising whiggery - we are *stuck* with the task of remembering and writing.

What would a truly false and harmful text be like? Would it be one which departed from the premise that there is unfinished business?

It might be best to try not to engage with the narrative of the often odious curatorial category of conceptual art and talk about a project which occured in one form or another to some in the 1960's following the deflating challenge which was faced by late high Modernism. Many who had been students in the late to mid 1960's had concluded that recent European developments from Pop art to various forms of kinetic art and sculpture were without critical virtue and certainly without vividness. What was vivid was a set of puzzles, questions Jasper Johns' had reworked *via* Duchamp, which Frank Stella's black paintings had posed for abstraction (emptying it of its high Modernist aesthetic while seeming to preserve the letter of the Modernist law), which Judd and Morris had posed for painting in general. The avant-garde didn't come from Europe, its critical potential came from the possibility of the break up of the finally attenuated Abstract Expressionist Empire. The territory to be contested was the manipulative and constituting power of Modernist criticism and the surfaces (including the uncrusty 'optical' surfaces) to which that criticism assigned virtue.

It can of course by said that at the time the various appropriations of Pop Art stood in some opposition to high Modernist precepts, were infected with an imperialistic triumphalism less subtle and more manifestly fetishistic than later writers would associate with Abstract Expressionism. The Pop icon - the picture - in the sense of the relatively transparent image of consumption and half-hearted criticism was associated with a quasi-modernity. This was the mirror image of Modernity's high clerisy. It was associated with a slightly Americanised tee-shirts and basketball boots appearance cultivated by certain art school teachers keen to regard the Americanisation of the world with unambiguous gratitude. Similarly, the various high-tech developments of Pop Art which attached themselves to a burgeoning sense of youth culture seemed to be no more than a trendy submission to the absurdly celebratory analogisms of Marshall McLuhan and other would-be providers of a self-image for the age.

The idea of an 'image' or 'icon' as a loaded cultural entity was almost never considered in the (fabulous) heyday of conceptual art. Was this because they were seen as occupying a region of popular culture, as 'coming from' Pop art and therefore transcended in the high purposes of Stella and neutralised (or de-popularised) by Johns? The target for our assault was not (well not obviously) the imagery of Pop art, but the cultural imagery, the *power* of high Modernist sanctity, its critics and its *weltanshauung* of metaphysical and moral assurance and exclusivity. Those who had been essentially *celebrators* of the popular image (they saw themselves as iconoclasts of the hand-knitted) had, by the mid-1960s, been sidelined as utter provincials - and for that matter reactionary, fetishistic and uncritical, save in a sadly *enfant terrible-iste* sense.

What Stella had done (he more than anyone) was to save us the trouble of having recourse to popular imagery (as cultural critical material or as a badge of aggression) by *outdoing* the dumbness (or emptiness or exhaustedness) of eg. a Warhol or a Lichtenstein with a far more telling critical device. The factural face of high-born painting had been confronted (spat in) in terms which it could almost recognise as its *own*. It was shamed by its own means and *in its own image*. But Stella's subversive black paintings were themselves subverted in being transformed into neurotic spectacle easily co-opted and finally *subject* to the very cultural heritage which they had immediately confronted. It was necessary therefore to confront that culture with an ontological impossibility - something unconsumable and consequently un-mappable into the discourse. The project was to displace the whole - both paintings and discourse.

The *first* consideration was the thought that 'a text' (a set of symbols intrinsically incapable of bearing the predicates which ascribe such things as expressive power to paintings) could colonise a space (a physical and cultural space) previously occupied by non-textual material. Now was this not a way of doing a very reduced Frank Stella with a kind of collage? The difference maybe is that the *reading* of the text was intended to supplant the psychologically loaded business of recovering formal expressive detail. The text thus rendered the reader *qua* painting 'reader' homeless - his or her intentionality or mode of seeing were thereby challenged. (Pictures as information together with texts were often employed. Any marginally 'aesthetic' virtue possessed by such pictures was usually regarded as trivial. Relations with texts mattered.)

We're discussing texts this way because it would be wrong to say that conceptual art was univocal - or consistent. (There is a phase in Art & Language from the mid to late 1960's which might be called formally aggressive. This was to be supplanted by 'indexing' and related activities. But indexing was a dialectical or dialogical development; it is not *the* story of conceptual art or of Art & Language.

What grew in part as a critique of Land Art and other outward-bound tendencies which were developing in the mid to late 1960's was a conviction that, insofar as language was a 'representation', and since reference could be very precisely determined, a verbal or 'theoretical' specification could be used to represent kinds of objects or specific objects. The referential relation involved was without the unreflected baggage - the aesthetic penumbra (or essence) of a picture. The close and simultaneously distant relative of such a resource is the diagram - which is pictorial - but sevely limited to its iconic purport, often to some explanatory or heuristic purpose. Enter, however, opaque or intensional 'logics', modality, 'general' entites, 'possible walls', and the fun-to-operate Polish notation for modal logic. It was this fiddling around with quantification (or not) into intensional contexts and the theory of such (pronounced sinful and worse by W.V.O.

Quine) that led to an interest in the complexities, pragmatical or semantic or logical, of the very language we used, and in a question of what we used it to do, however inexpertly.

Wherewith images then? Can we say that *all* texts used by us were not images? Insofar as these texts supplanted something which might have retained certain iconic vestiges, then they might be thought of as anti-images - and thereby the bearers of some 'general' trace. there's another sense of 'image': *viz,* that texts were reproduced from negatives photographically, were enlarged etc. In other words, they shared certain technical or physical features of photographic images generally, although they were not iconic. The naming of things - the use of verbal representation in the form of declaration that certain visible or invisible things were art works (or anyway, of interest) was a deliberate strategy, requiring the suppression of the viewer's response *vis à vis* any concrete specificity which remained to the text and which ran counter to its being conceived as a message, or something like one.

Of course, there is something called 'photoconceptualism' which is an influential and workable genre. (There are others more qualified to speak of this than us). The use of photographs as documentation was widespread in some kinds of conceptual art by 1968-9. It has persisted because there remains something to distribute, some kind of record - an ontological stability to point to.

What if one tries hard to identify some Art & Language work under some technical type description? We have suggested that some of it was *indexical* in character. Would this tell us that it consists of merely ghostly traces of other art and other events? Would this tell us that it involves displacement - that it is something other than what it *is,* or looks like, appears to be, or appears to be like? It is of course representational in some way but then, so are other kinds of images and documentation. A picture, a photograph, a painting, a sculpture - all have more or less fixed ontological margins. They are identified as a media rather than as 'work'. They may be *of* things other than what they are made from, but there is almost always some steady consensus as to their identity, their relative autonomy and their edges and boundaries. One familiar way of identifying conceptual art is to assume that it is readily described according to these conventions. 'A text' or 'words on a wall' is a sufficient description of conceptual art conceived as a kind of public presentation. 'Words or 'texts', not 'paintings' or 'photographs' or 'installation'. This is only plausible as a matter of curatorial or journalistic decorum. The idea of conceptual art as something a bit intellectual, a bit dematerialised is decidedly from the 60's and 70's, however. The term is now used to refer to anything that is a bit de-skilled and theatrical - sort of neo-dada plus advertising technique.

If the middle sized dry goods type of genre description and self-identification doesn't work or is trivial, then it follows that some *story* as to the origins and causes of some conceptual art must be necessary. (But we must nevertheless make sure that we know that any such story is curatorially fake).

Conceptual art was in some of its forms ontologically recalcitrant and needs describing thus. It removed a ratifiable 'presence' - and ended up with what? With some kind of 'absence'? Perhaps this is too strong. Perhaps there was some kind of de-materialised or ultra-minimal 'presence'. This was the kind of description favoured by some during the late 1960's. 'Invisible art', 'post-object art', were labels posted by people who were intoxicated by the thought of the final reduction. But some forms of ultra-minimal conceptual art were like Man Friday footprints. You couldn't identify the work unless you found out about what caused it, a bit about what it was embedded in, a bit about what it stood next to, a bit about what it was *of* - the things which were *not* present as much as things which are present. An exertion was required of the beholder (who was also the reader), in acceeding to a dialogical possiblity and a continuing demand that work be done. This means that some conceptual art may depend for its identity in being forever contested. In this sense some conceptual art is 'told' in myth or in narrative - is a story told and retold, contradicted, destroyed but never (or almost never) amenable to the imposition of a curatorial dignity. The ethical upshot of this maybe a commitment to a present - or present work - conceived as having more of a future than a past. This is work that is *refigured* and only barely remembered, work that lacks telelogical symmetry.

There was much in Art & Language's practice of the late 1960s and early 1970s that decidedly lacked grandeur, much that was inexpert or amateurish or sat in the shadows with the malingerer. Here was a non-transcendental world of contingencies and daft proposals, of models and lists, of undiscisplined talk, of meetings and tape recordings and messy transcripts.

We are suggesting that if Art & Language's conceptual art 'appearance' is pinned down to 'texts', 'words' or even 'absence' then it is ready to be assimilated into a historiography of conceptual art analogous to the State Department's account of the Vietnam War. It has no narrative, no place, in a word it has no circumstance. And since some conceptual art can perhaps be best described as *only* circumstantial: there's not much hard evidence, there's no body (or if there was a body it was made of apertures). It had no home but didn't lack one, it was homeless and not very sure of the negative of that.

In the face of failure of an ontologically normal description we must attempt a highly vulnerable narration of, or exemplification of, or picture of, the origins of conceptual art. (This *is* dangerous territory. Policing the origins of all conceptual art has become a full time occupation for some.)

We have suggested that there is no reason to argue with the notion that early conceptual art was infested with quite simplistic sense of ultra-minimalist de-materialisation. But the urge to make minimal art even more minimal, to damage its insolent literalism with a kind of virtual absence to be specified in theoretical or 'invisible' objects as neither a simplistic reduction nor puristically reductive moment. There are images here, pictures here, representations, icons, allegories, symbols, aesthetics, but they were *ghosts*. Consider also, the now defunct picture theory of ideas. This was an important though not overwhelming background theory - a theory that somehow our ideas are what they are about because they picture (or resemble, icons of) their objects. This view was available to licence internal pictoriality. We're not sure that anyone in Art & Language actually subscribed to this view, but it was decidedly on the go. The point here is that we did consider pictures in various guises. The difference which seemed important was a) the 'use' to which any item was put - a picture could be flat (ie. diagramatic) or 'transparent' information and nicely (or usually not nicely) presented - or broken, or put in logical or operational jeopardy qua picture - whatever. What it had to resist was first-order artistic interpretation or aestheticisation. This led to b) the rejection of surface treatment or production which could confine or interrupt the first objective. In other words, we took a view of depiction which might be called Satrean. Leaving aside diagrams and maps, which are self-effacing in another way, we were concerned (insofar as we were concerned at all) with pictures which had little physical presence - were transparent, in the sense that our interest did not rest on the surface of the picture.

What was finally reached by (some) ultra-minimalism was not purity nor reduction but *paradox*. And that is what's somewhere in the black-box of (some) conceptualism, a virus within the business-as-usual of art and a pointer beyond it- perhaps. It may have had as its impetus a kind of cultural hygiene, a purge of the vestiges of the image similar to that begun by minimalism - a purge which finally had to include minimalism itself. But instead of a new metaphysical category of 'idea Art' it opened art to what is now (un)fashionably called its 'context' - brought it to reflect upon its real circumstances or its real institutions. It promised as a consequence to let the world come mewling and pissing in and often, admittedly, mewling and pissing out.

In approaching a kind of entropic exhaustion, an experiential transformation and even mystical conversion took place. The head was neither challenged nor invigorated; it was, rather, turned around.

Let us consider as 'images' the early Art &Language 'Mirror' works for a moment. They are blank, they have no pictorial structure of their own but they are inflected by whatever they reflect. Is the mirror the Modernist surface so reduced that it transforms itself into what? Into a camera? The interest in mirrors rested in the fact that the mirror produced the perfectly 'transparent' image - its medium is, *pace* Panofsky, physical reality itself - something other than its surface - but this does not mean that you cannot be aware of the surface of the mirror itself however difficult that is (as Ian Burn pointed out).

And consider what to do with other 'material' from this period: columns of air, chemical constituents, ice, fog banks, water, etc? Are these (pre?) conceptual, ultra minimal *devices*, or are they *in* the black-box of conceptualism? These invisible or theoretically specified 'objects' must be identified somehow. How? They must be spoken about, written about, even photographed. This can be discursive or social activity. The identification of the 'invisible' entity might involve the circumstance through which it is identified. Here, doubt is thrown on the divisions between 'artist' and 'critic', 'participant' and 'spectator'. The implication is that a lot of artworld protocols wre rendered provisional at least and endanged at most. In the middle was *confusion*. This seems to be the paradoxical consequence of the urge to drive the literalism of minimalism literally into absence and then into a paradoxical virtually - a virtuality of 'theory' - if it was 'virtual' or if it was even 'theory'.

The possibility here is that the author or the artist is no longer alone; that a socialised base of art just might be developed not from a sentimental notion of commonality but as a necessary internal development of 'the work' itself, a queer consequence of speculation or conversations about 'invisible' or de-materialised objects. Such talk made for itself the requirement that it be not *just* overexcitedly neological but turn sometimes towards some kind of epistemic adequacy or at least be conversationally sustainable. It demanded of itself that its character should not be art-wordly and knowing but somehow ordinary and dialogically substantial even if that ordinariness compassed a high degree of wildness and absurdity. Grammatical and legislative conditions might be described and prescribed. The conversational and collaborative and 'language' base of (some) conceptual art starts here and the stabilised identities of 'artist', 'critic', 'theory', 'practice' start pulling apart.

And this has been the burden of, as well as the emancipatory potential of conceptual art. It is what's in the black(ish)-box of conceptual art. Never mind 'texts' or 'language' or 'philosophy'. It doesn't have to matter if, and it may be important that, painting or sculpture or photographs are also involved. There is no purity to lose.

There was, however, a romantic dream somewhere - it attached to a practice of teaching in which the founder members of Art & Language were engaged in - a dream which was a moderately close relative of the Nietzschean idea that art, at its most Romantic disappears into philosophy. But what philosophy? The idea is, of course, absurd- but also paradoxical. But the setting of speculative and necessarily impossible goals - extreme models which could only be approached asymtotically - or not at all as they may have been merely provocative slogans - were a part of the transforming culture of oppostion. This was a world where the rapidity of their self-inflation of theory-like things was matched by the rapidity of their self-deflation. Our talkative teaching confronted the mystification that the teacher was *never* corrigible in possessing some mysterious property or power. The power to validate or to reject supervened over the teacher ('artist') who was not called upon to function save in the realm of authenticity. But this realm - the 'thereof we must keep silent' which was the stock in trade of the artist, was nevertheless manipulated (and spoken of) in the division of labour between artist and critic. This division of labour required the artist to play his or her part in the preservation of the mysteries (in not being discursively uppity) and for the critic to play his or hers in ratifying this or that work on ineluctably mysterious aesthetic grounds. In short, to take part in an economy of barbarism.

The possibility of oppostion to this mystification, this complaissance of the radical sundering of theory from practice seemed to lay in the tranformation of the surface of painting itself, in its being invaded or syndicalised by its *other* - the surface-less text. But once you have decided that this is possible, you have to decide on the text. Will *any* text do? For some this was the case - in which case the transformation would have been at best partial and readily absorbed by the prevailing system. The text *qua* any text would rise to the surface as a more or less extreme form of collage. To prevent this, the text had to possess (or to demonstrate or to call into consideration) a level of intentionality or 'meantness' - whatever it took to achieve a level of transparency - of referentiality (analogous some might say to a possible tranparency metaphorically ascribed to some pictures) which abolished entirely the aesthetic possibilities of the surface. (It would be wrong to suggest that in reading *qua* reading we attend to the surface upon which the linguistic representation is distributed, but it would also be wrong to say that we cannot attend to it when we actually do read. The recovery of the meaning for a concrete surface *qua* surface, but we might be aware of it and recover another sort of significance from it. This is more than obvious. To talk of the complete effacement of the surface from the complex psychological occurence would be wrong, but to produce a text for *reading* is necessarily to produce something more or less neutral in respect of its medium of production and transmission.

Texts, then, were of necessity to be directly meaningful otherwise they would not perform their invasive and expropriating function. What do we mean by 'meaningful'? Nothing all that clear. What happened is that the transformation of surface into non-surface (text) produced by mechanical and/or photographic means was also an invasion of the critical/discursive space. In order to effect such an invasion the text had to have some sort of critical power, or virtue, however small or attenuated. Indeed, some texts were stuck somewhere between found object and assertoric text: and the actual business of identifying a text and of discovering one's place (or lack of place) in its production was often at issue. We were not philosophers but former art students. Texts as art had acquired in the confusion a curious status as *critical discourse*. In various ways, 'things' escaped or were bound back to text. Art & Language was a site for these transformations to take place - a land of exile from the walls. And from time to time the texts within that site began (to seem to be) used like more or less conventional critical texts. But there was always that marginal possibility of escape - of their being transformed - of their getting out to the walls and living a different life. Later, the circumstances which had generated these texts became complex, talkative, discursive.

They had started to mark points of reference in a collaborative (dialogic) practice. But the texts generated therein were theoretical just in case they were art object-like, and art object-like just in case they were theoretical.

One of the clearest essays in this connection is Charles Harrison's 'Art Object and Artwork' in the catalogue *L'art Conceptuel, une Perspective* (1989) at A.R.C. He reflects upon the problem of the public and the question of the transformation of spectactor into participant. He argues that the changes in the sense of public and of spectator which the Art & Language *Indexes* entrain were not a matter of tendentious managerial correctness but a technical requirement that it generate the possiblity of a changed sense of artist and a changed sense of public. According to Harrison:

"Conceptual Art was an attack on the boundaries of 'artist', 'reader', 'spectator', 'audience', 'consumer'. An attack on the standard form of relationship of artist to public"

A set of technical questions were imprisoned in moral and political questions and vice-versa, a kind of rupture both inside and outside of questions of style and medium. That's why some of the early essays in *Art-Language* are so occupied with what's an 'internal' and what's an 'external' question - or what's a first- order and second-order question).

It didn't (much) matter what the work 'looked like' or what medium was used. It could be or could have been a photograph, an image, a painting or a text. The real conceptual problem was linked to the genuine possibility of social production and organised work. For some this was the dangerous and frightening potential of the *Indexing* work. It is instructive to note that this particular essay of Harrison's has been subject to serious misrepresentation. Screwing up the protocols or rendering provisional and contingent the roles of 'critic' and 'artist' continues to be the position from which to drive the business of art *mad.* Some critics have seen this professional danger. There is a passage from the essay which has been doing the rounds of late. It has been quoted out of context.

"Realistically, Art & Language could identify no actual alternative public which was not composed of the participants in its own projects and deliberations."

This passage has been quoted by Rosalind Krauss, Thomas Crow and others. Krauss seeks to demonstrate that Art & Language is a hopeless and disreputable brainwashing sect dominating the media but simultaneously failing to understand it. Crow seeks to show the severe lack of critical reach of Art & Language's early work into the larger social world. Both authors have their own agendas. The question is why this quotation attracts misrepresentation? It is because it is close to the essence of what makes some conceptual art have emancipatory potential and consquently what makes it such a nuisance for self-ratifiers, art historians and other consumers? Here's what Harrison actually wrote:

"The requirement of realism to which any image of the public must submit is that it should be the self-serving product of a liberal (or other) fantasy. Realistically, Art &Language could identify no *actual* alternative constituency which was not composed of the participants in its own projects and deliberations - whoever they might be. Insofar as there was a *potential* public, it was composed not of dispassionate spectators, but of interested readers and learners. The implication of this circumstance was not that the members of Art & Language constituted the only and sufficient audience for Art & Language work. It was rather that no secure principle existed whereby a body of members or teachers or authors could be divided off from the larger world of learners or readers."

The substantial point of this quotation is always missed: here is a threat to the profession. Here are no positivistically healthy moves. The participants are not necessarily beneficiaries - they might be victims. It might be bad for business. Harrison continues:

"Assumptions about the status of artist as author connected both to the object character of the work of art... and to presuppositions about audience. Conventionalisation of the relations between audience and author tends to stabilise the technical categories of art. In turn, insofar as the critical self-image of the cultural depends upon the plausibility of the aesthetic, the idealisation of a patrician public and of its experience necessitates a commensurable image of the artist as author."

This is a project which remains incomplete. The work of art was at best provisional and often cast as incidental. Whether they were paintings or photographs or texts, such things were the contingent products of a discursive activity not the non-discursive products of a passive regard.

We conclude that a history of conceptual art cannot be concieved in the soul of the sage. In remembering, we write semi-autonomous texts whose modes are either spatial or temporal displacement. And these are texts which go blind as soon as they leave for the empirical world, to pervert Paul de Man's phrase. We are stuck with the dialectical premise which the two modes create. These, combined with the various forms of representation either stand in need of unprejudiced investigation or else are themselves the products of temporal or spatial displacement. It should not be necessary either to caution against self purism or patronising whiggery - which can take a Spenglerian turn in seeking to submit to whatever are supposed to be the necessities of the epoch - as the radical homelessness and inchoateness of conceptual art's representational forms should make such distinctions more or less impossible. But historical narratives are often made by artists and by critics on the back of a claim *pro domo* which is supposed to make their account (Whiggish, purist, Spenglerian) the only one possible and necessary. We can only try to murder the sleep of these professionals.

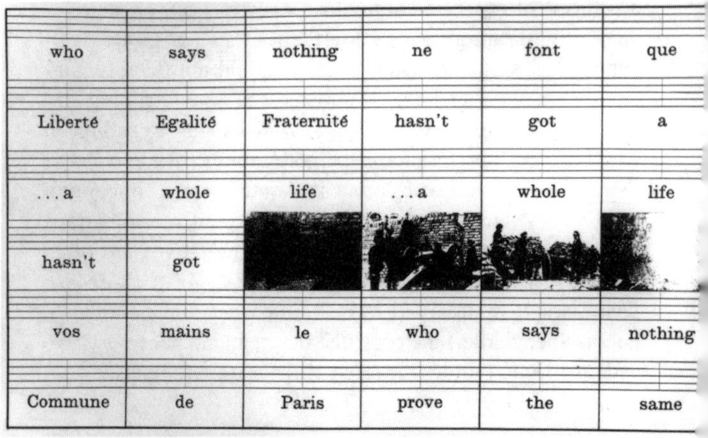


*Bridging Work 1: 'vos mains le who'*, 1974

A first move to caricature what I, by this time, considered to be the overdetermined historical construction Terry (AL). An attempt to make a kind of Art-Language nonsense verse. (The lined base of the print is a sequestered piece of Art & Language graphics designed about this time for an Art & Langage real project.) The fatuous mixing of French and English was, I think, trying to unpick some strands of Terry (AL). Onto this I grafted the images of the Paris Commune. The third image from the left is the same image as the one used singly in Bridging Work 12. The move here was all betting and trying - with Rimbaud-me howling in the studio background, whilst the Art & Language wind beat on the shutters. At this stage, the first Bridging Work, I still had the feeling of being beseiged by my own Art & Language loyalty. "Le Who" seemed, at the time, a suitably grimacing stab at a successor-name to Terry (AL). There was also some obscure resonance here - It was rumoured that Keith Moon owned a pub in Chipping Norton - Michael Baldwin's home town.

## USING PHOTOGRAPHS circa 1974

Terry Atkinson

*The Bridging Works* (hereafter BW) were a first move, and a far from clear one, away from the pictorialism of a text-based practice. Insofar as these works were a move away from something then, obviously, they were a move to somewhere else - to a more photobased practice might be one loose-ish way of characterising the place. The works were named retrospectively in the later seventies. They were also a bridge out of Art & Language (hereafter A&L). The kind of work the BW turned out to be was a kind of first sidestep, a sidestepping of the pictorialism of the text, through gropingly embracing some notion of a possible alternative pictorialism - hence photobase. At least that was the plan - insofar as there was one. By the time BW were completed it seemed clear that a sidestep was not enough, something nearer a volte-face - whatever that might turn out to be - seemed to be required. Hence the move to drawing, the World War I works, made in the years following 1974. This latter is a story for another essay. Here I want to try and discuss the relation between the BW, photography and some aspects of conceptualism.

Perhaps the first point should be to state the obvious. At no point during the making of the BW did I use a camera. Where the use of a camera was required (eg. BW11, where the requirement was to photograph a chunk of A&L text) I employed a photographer. No sense of skill, or the re-skilling or de-skilling of photographic competence, was a concern to me in these works. Often I used photographs I found. I also used montage. I guess, then, my interest in using photographs in the BW turned on the notion of the photograph as historical record, therefore some notion of reportage was a concern, but the use amounted to appropriating some other photographer's reportage and recontextualising it. But all this presupposed photography's depictive function. In retrospect, around a year or so later, I did come to see the use of photographs in the BW as striving to make some link between the photograph as a device to resist pictorialised text and the photograph as a device of historical record. This was punctuated throughout the BW by attempted acts of ventrioquising, spoofing, imitating, plagiarising etc; and in the case of processes such as these, photographs seemed an accessible ally. The act of having someone photograph a chunk of A&L text/graphics fitted some notion of historical record (if only one's own) as much as did the selecting of some photograph of an event in the Paris Commune and World War I. There is implicit in the BW the notion of faking a historical record (the possibility that the future A&L historical record might be faked) as well as the historical recording of a fake. The attraction of the photographs of events in the Paris Commune and of events in World War 1 was their positioning as part of encoding a historical record which might well be full of fakes and staged scenarios.[1] A second point of attraction was that both the Paris Commune and World War I were group events, historically grandiose in relation to A&L as a group event, but group events with a certain resonance vis à vis my view of how A&L history was working out in 1974. The Paris Commune was a group event where it could be claimed that the nation-state was imploding (implosion was a favourite A&L motif throughout the indexing); World War I was a group event of nation-states expanding, in the end inevitably, at the cost of other nation-states contracting and, in some cases, disappearing. As such, these devices have not worked out as altogether inappropriate allegories of presently running A&L history wars. At the

1. One that came to mind whilst I made the BW was Robert Capa's famous picture of the falling Republican soldier in the Spanish Civil War. It is reputed to be staged. BW 6 and 14 use a photograph of an event in the Paris Commune which is apparently a fake.

time of their making the BW cleaved to an idea that photographs (someone else's photography) provided a medium through which various historical fragments, some such as including fragments of photographs (montage), photographs as fragments of the history of photography, and photographs of authentic A&L texts, photographs of quasi-A&L texts and photographs of pseudo-A&L texts, would be uniformly presented as the material of art work. The hope was that the photograph of the text in this context raised the question of the text, vis à vis its position at that time within conceptualism, as a form of the pictorial. Thus the BW were conceived as wall works. People read wall notices all the time, walls are awash with notices, graffiti, instructions, etc. But whether the reading of texts (as artworks) on the walls of conventional art environments (galleries, art museums) required some notion of idealised reader seemed then, 1974, to me, to be a moot point. Certainly at that time there remained within the art milieu an anxiety about language in general - what else would such an anxiety be manifest in except through linguistic agency? - and specifically texts as art presented in conventional art environments. the general anxiety about language remains widely in place in the art milieu today - but texts as art seem to have become conventionally pantheonised as part of 'the pictorial'. Insofar as these works, the BW, were driven, then they were driven by the notion that reading in such contexts as conventional art environments seemed complex, and contentious enough, especially in matters of history recording, to be engaging. But, to repeat, the use I tried to make of photographs in the BW was not at all that of seeing myself as a photographer.

Whilst I did feel some unease in using a photobased practice since, in the end, the controversies, if that is what they were, of the prioritising of the text over some such as the pictorial, had not been taken lightly in A&L during the years 1966-1974, it still seemed to me the sidestep necessarily involved some risk of historical incongruity - as it turned out photo-based practice was not historically incongruous enough, by 1974 it was too conceptually respectable. Hence the turn in starting to look for practices which Western avant-gardism would consider to be intellectually despicable and ideological death, such as Soviet Socialist Realism, and hence, in late 1974 after the BW, starting to try and figure out the making of the World War I works.

If now we were to subscribe to what I take to be some of Jeff Wall's criteria for marking out the functions of photography in conceptualism in '"Marks of Indifference"'[2] then the use of photographs in BW took over, commandeered, some other photographer's reportage. I am presuming, and presuming it may be risky, that one of the points Wall is arguing is that without using a camera no artist can be held to engage in "the photographer's complex social engagement (his or her assignment)."[3] Thus whatever else I may have been doing in using photographs in the BW I was not involved in a photographer's complex social engagement. At best, I was appropriating in some sense the original photographer's reportage, of say, an event in the Paris Commune. But this use also reported a relation between the present context (1974) of the appropriator and an earlier context of his history, text based practice - this much seemed obvious making work as a continuation of/reaction to earlier work is conventional. And something like the art practice equivalent to Kuhn's paradigm shift[4] may be difficult to sort out in such contexts. In 1974 getting a clear demarcation between my ongoing work

2. Jeff Wall, '"Marks of Indifference": Aspects of Photography in, or as, Conceptual Art', *In Reconsidering the Object of Art: 1965-75*, eds. Anne Goldstein and Ann Rorimer, Museum of Contemporary Art, Los Angeles, MIT Press, Cambridge, Massachussetts, 1995 (hereafter MI)

3. ibid. p250

4. Thomas Kuhn, *The Structure of Scientific Revolutions*, University of Chicago Press, 1962

and work I had previously contributed to as a member of a group was perhaps easier to intend than to achieve. Disconfirmation in art may not quite work out the way it does in science. In any case it wasn't simply a case of disconfirming something called conceptualism, disconfirming is not the same thing as rejecting, it was more figuring out what of its achievements and failures remained useful - i.e. what might consitute an ongoing critical practice given the gains, or otherwise, of some conceptualist practices.

Thus the use of photography in the BW was imbedded in this general set of judgements and positions. Whether or not these concerns would count to qualify as '... Aspects of Photography in, or as, Conceptual Art' (the last part of Wall's essay title) I'm not sure, but nonetheless some categories of Wall's analysis are perhaps worth dwelling upon in respect of the use of photographs in the BW. The notion of skilled production versus the artist as a consumer of picture-making gadgets (see Wall's comments on Warhol)[5] did not seem to be at all at stake in BW. Whilst the photographs used in the BW which were found could, in a sense, be seen to conform to some crude logic of the readymade, obviously they were chosen for what they depicted (e.g. an event in the Paris Commune). In this sense their mentor, if there was one, was Benjamin rather than Duchamp or Warhol; and not Benjamin the collector per se, but Benjamin the weigher of historical fragments. This is a retrospective judgement by four years or so, I did not come to study Benjamin's work until I arrived in Leeds in the late seventies.[6] Nevertheless a

---

5. '"Marks of Indifference"', op cit, p263

6. I knew a little of Benjamin's work during the time I was a video artist-in-residence in a city centre school in Coventry (1975-77), but it was when I started at the University of Leeds in late 1977 that I came to seriously study Benjamin's work. This was not, paradoxically, as a result of my contacts within the Fine Art dept. at Leeds University but through Cliff Slaughter, whom I met through my friend Geoff Teasdale who taught at Leeds Polytechnic. (continued overleaf).

narrative of not only a continuum of high and low culture was present in the photographs of the events, say, in the Paris Commune, but the event of the Paris Commune itself fiercely exemplified a lethal clash between one particular model of high culture, the aristocratic model,[7] and low culture. Using Thomas Crow's term "the dip down" from high into low culture, but inverting it, the Paris Commune was a lethal 'dip up', and anti-aristocratic modernists such as Courbet were up to their cultural ears in dipping up, with equally formidibly cultural irrascible figures like Rimbaud cheering the successes of the Commune from the provinces.[8] Fine Artz, the first group I helped found in 1963, was an ideological failure, but the sentiment of championing and defending a 'low' culture (rock 'n' roll) against the pretensions of an aristocratic culture (The Slade School of the early sixties) is what drove the initial start of the group.[9] Although its technological utopianism was crude, the historical record of which is, likely to be unforgiving, Fine Artz was a reflection of the emergence of the complexity of early '60s pocket cultures threatening the boundary of low/high culture formations. Again, in the BW, another of the things I had in mind in using some of the photographs, especially those of events in the Paris

---

Cliff Slaughter eloquently articulated many of Benjamin's texts, and was particularly insistent and instructive upon the importance of 'The Work of Art in the Age of Mechanical Reproduction'. In the nineties I have read Robert Hullot-Kentor's essay 'What is Mechanical Reproduction?'. This essay seems an important juncture in Benjamin studies. Thanks to Robert Linsley in Vancouver for directing me to Hullot-Kentor's writing.

7. See for a powerful account account of earlier culture wars between aristocratic cultures and various populist cultural aspirations, John Carey, *The Intellectuals and the Masses: Pride and Prejudice among the Literary Intelligensia, 1880-1939*, Faber and Faber, London and Boston, 1992.

8. In 1974 Rimbaud became an important studio figure for me. I invented a studio presence called Rimbaud-me, ostensibly something like an alter-ego through which I might talk myself out of old reflexes of loyalty to A&L. See, Terry Atkinson, *Rimbaud-me, The Indexing and the Phantasmagoria of the World War I Works*, unpublished. In the late eighties a book which came to uncannily resonate upon the aspirations and failures of the BW was Kristin Ross' book, *The Emergence of Social Space: Rimbaud and the Paris Commune*, McMillen, 1988.

Commune, was a deployment of their depictive functions as a registering of culture wars, aristocratic versus street scum. Fine Artz, brief and as ideologically misguided as its management was, was an attempt to champion the street scum against the brokers of the European Treasure House version of culture. the BW photographs represented some kind of yearning for what we failed to do in Fine Artz.[10]

At any rate, it seemed clear that by 1973 'the conceptualist photograph' could be, and was becoming, "integrated into the regime". And that text, which in a strong sense was also becoming "integrated into the regime", was still the most secure purchase for re-contextualising the photograph, and again, this was to cleave to, what in retrospect I saw as a tradition of Adorno and Benjamin rather than Duchamp and Warhol. Whilst Duchamp may be constructed as a central figure in a critique of what I have called the 'European Treasure House' version of culture, and Warhol as a figure who championed the cultural gains of the 'technologically consuming proletariat', if the BW forward scanned to anything it was an art practice centering upon Adorno and Benjamin rather than Duchamp or Warhol. When I came to write the last version of the text notices for the BW in 1992, I wrote this in the text of BW3, "These kinds of works look to me now (1992) like some kind of historical alluvium of that space where I suppuratingly hung between being in and out of A&L. Some notions of flailing and veering-off a seemingly proscribed course. A bit like, having missed the turn you required, banging your head on the dashboard when you're sitting in the traffic jam you have inadvertently

10. The technological utopianism, not least because we read Marshall McLuhan very glibly, was always overdetermined. Fine Artz though, at least for me, was to provide resources for examining the culture wars, and David Bainbridge and Harold Hurrell, both at this time, 1963-65, at St. Martins School of Art, closely observed Fine Artz's short incandescence and demise from their own technological concerns in sculpture (cybernetics, etc.), the further developed resources of which they were to bring into A&L later.

become stuck in - not that you had a tight schedule on your original assignment, but since you're stuck in the car you want to get moving".[11] Thus whether you turned to the text or photograph the going was heavy - by 1973 "the regime", in one way or another, controlled all the familiar routes. Sidestepping from route to route still kept you on the marked out roads. The BW were an attempt to sight forward, but I was uneasy with their resources, with photographs as much as text. For better or worse, I kept a studied distance from getting behind a camera, this is not to say that I have no interest in notions such as artist-photographer.

11. The BW texts have been revised two or three times since 1974, the last revision being 1992. This last version was provoked by having found the negatives in 1991 after their having been missing since 1979. I had given them up. But we moved our youngest daughter into what had been our studios in the house in Leamington up until 1991. This entailed a radical refurbishment, the builders ripped out cupboards from where emerged the negs in the pristine wrappers which Ted Harrison had furnished them back in 1974.

Victor Burgin

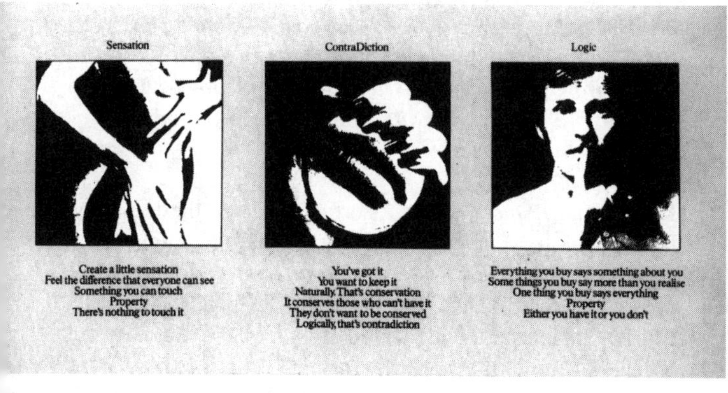


*Sensation*, 1975

## INTERVIEW WITH VICTOR BURGIN

*I want to open this conversation by drawing attention to the main concern of 'The Impossible Document', the fact that the show opens out a 'hidden' history of conceptual art and photography. By this I mean that although a large number of artists who were engaged with what is now known as conceptual art, were using photography and the photographic document, there was very little discourse on photography as such, from 1966 through to the early seventies. Maybe we could start then by looking at your own particular involvement in this period, the work that you were doing from the late sixties through to the early seventies, when you yourself shifted from largely text based activity to photography itself. Perhaps we could start with* Photo Path. *How did you see that early moment?*

I think that *Photo Path*, is a sort of hinge in the transition from a mainly Modernist trajectory to what you might retrospectively call a Post-Modernist trajectory. It sounds more pretentious that I intend it to sound, but to spell it out a little: I was a student in the graduate Art and Architecture School at Yale in the mid sixties. I went to Yale in the heyday of minimalism, and amongst the people who were teaching there were Donald Judd, Robert Morris, Ad Reinhardt, Helen Frankenthaler and so on. I remember Donald Judd saying to a class I was in that he believed that a form that was neither organic nor geometric would be a great discovery. For him, this was a formal problem in sculpture: a problem of how to liberate yourself from the constraints of, on the one hand, a sort of baroque tradition, and on the other hand, a classical tradition. What occurred to me, and no doubt occurred to a lot of other people at the same time, because later we had the first wave of conceptualism, was that the only such form that you could think of would have to be a mental form or it wouldn't actually make sense to say that it was neither geometric nor organic. 'Roundabout the same time Robert Morris was teaching there, and he published his 'Notes on Sculpture', a two part article in *Artforum*, leaning very heavily on the phenomenological philosophy which was prevalent in art circles at the time. And Morris, in the course of this article, said that he wanted his work to be no more or less important than any other 'term' in the room. Now by other 'terms' in the room I understood him to mean moulding, window frames, radiators... you know, anything in the room that has an objective presence. He said that he wanted his, for example, 'grey cube', archetypal of Morris's minimalist work of that period, to sit in the gallery and to draw no more or less attention than any of the other objects. And when he came to Yale I referred to his article and said, "Well that raises the question, why have sculpture at all, if it's no more or less important than anything else? What's to stop us walking in there and looking at the radiator?" And he said, "I never wrote that". Well, I knew he had written it because I had the magazine but I didn't dwell on the point because I thought, well this is it, I've hit upon the important question to be answered by the next generation.

Now, the idea that there is an important question to be answered by your generation and your generation alone is peculiarly Modernist. Greenberg spoke that way, and Greenberg got it from Vasari, who had a cyclical view of history. Painters of each generation, he argued, faced a problem that was then solved by the following generation, but in solving it they raised another problem. In his case of course he was talking about the development of linear perspective and the move towards an illusionism in painting. In Greenberg the argument becomes an argument about the perfection of painting as painting, that is, from generation to generation the Modernist artist succeeds in shedding any reference other than to painting itself. But in both cases there is a progressivist and historicist view of the problems internal to art, some unified goal that the artist is working towards unquestioningly. Well I thought, here's the problem: how do you recognise something which isn't 'there', how can you get people to walk into a gallery and adopt the same forms of behaviour that they adopt when they walk into a gallery which obviously has a piece of sculpture in it. Can I get them to bring the same forms of perceptual behaviour and cognition to something which is not sculpture? How do you do that? And the photograph *Photo Path* was one answer to that question I set myself. How do you draw attention to the floor, but without altering the form of the floor? The photographs of the floor were a convenient way of doing this. Now, at the Camden Arts Centre in 1970 I produced a similar kind of work for a large room. When you first walked into the room, it looked like there was nothing there at all, for instance there was nothing on the floor, but then you realised that on the wall there were these typewritten sentences - you wouldn't call them statements because they weren't really statements - and these sentences focused your attention on the condition of being in the room and adopting a mode of cognition which is traditionally rooted in the spectatorship of art. That's to say, you're not out in the street, you're not using a sort of adaptive mode of appreciation of objects but you are in a gallery and you're adopting a very different mode of appreciation, you are aware of your own body displacing volumes of air, you're aware of the volume of the room that you're in, you're aware of the way when you move it appears that the appearances of things change and so on. You are aware of the fact that you are having thoughts and memories. So this method developed in *Photo Path*, was, as I say, a gesture to draw attention to the conditions of perception without actually altering the environment too much. But I soon became dissatisfied with this because it appeared that the spectator wasn't being given enough guidance. A work of formalist painting or sculpture, is, in a sense, a sort of set of prompts where the spectator is urged to look at certain things. The Camden Arts Centre texts furnished these kinds of prompts. The relations between the texts became very formal with all of their recursive, self-referential repetition, and this then became precisely that form which Don Judd had said would be an interesting thing, a mental form which worked at the interface between internal reality, and external reality and drew attention to these mental processes at that interface.

*How much did the fact that* Photo Path *drew attention to its locale have to do with the debates that were going on in sculpture at the time around notions of objecthood and its critique?*

Oh it was completely situated within those debates, it was an 'intervention', as we like to say, in those debates.

*So had you read Michael Fried's critique of minimalism?*

Yes, I knew Fried's work through one of his students, who was teaching art history at Yale when I was there. We were exposed to a lot of Friedian ideas before they were very widely disseminated.

*Was this work a joke, if you like, at the expense of Friedian and Greenbergian notions of sculptural scale?*

It wasn't intended in any way as satirical or humorous. The other thing which had happened to me at that time was that, as I had just left university, and felt my training as an artist was over, I should really think very hard about what I wanted my practice to be. I was no longer able to ignore the growing sense of isolation of the art world from what, before I entered the art world, I'd thought of as the real world. As such there was an implicit, as I think with a lot of conceptualism, anti-market, anti-capitalist dimension to the work, because it was a work that you could not pick up and take away. In fact it wouldn't make sense to pick it up and take it away, you couldn't buy the photograph and put it anywhere else than where it had been laid. This gesture was also an ecological gesture, because, in common with a lot of young artists in that period, I was sick of objects, of junk, of all this welded steel and bronze, it seemed so useless, rusting away, filling up basements of museums. Who needs it? And so the early work was a way of clearing out the clutter, letting the air blow through the roof, and having something that was light and comparatively cheap and that could be scrapped.

*So, if this work was largely indexed to the debate on sculpture and commodification how much of this was in turn linked to an engagement with photography itself?*

Well, that I think grew directly out of that disenchantment with the perceived isolation of art. Because wanting to go beyond that gesture of rejection into something more constructive, more articulated, and something in a sense more engaged with the outside world, then it did seem to me that photography offered a window on the world, not in the traditional sense, but rather a window through which you could punch a hole in the gallery wall and bring into the gallery issues that had previously been considered not proper within the gallery. Now, to say that today is to say nothing, but I think it's hard to imagine how shocking it was to see writing and photographs on gallery walls in the late sixties. I mean it just wasn't done, it wasn't art. So it was important for me to do that which was not done and to do it very directly by not putting my own photographs in there, but by just taking advertising photography and putting that on the gallery wall, blowing it up, chopping it around, putting text with it, and so forth.

*That is quite a step from the* Photo Path *to producing works based on mass cultural imagery. Can we talk a little bit about this change because there's a lot going on here. How much would you say your involvement in the use of photography was the result of your increasing intellectual disappointment with what Modernism excluded as aesthetically viable?*

That question opens up a lot of things. In no particular order: Yes, I was very disappointed intellectually by the art world, I was attracted into it from the working class, which is to say that I had no experience, growing up, of the art world, of the intellectual world, of the literary world, of any of those worlds and so they were all, for me, equal. They were all for me, in my fantasies, more or less the same thing. I didn't know you had to choose. I didn't know you had to choose whether to be an intellectual or an artist, I didn't know there was a difference, you see. I think that's something that you have to learn, and grow up with, so by the time I got into the art world, and I might just as well, I suppose, have wound up somewhere else, I found that for the most part, I was expected to adopt basically the attitude of a connoisseur. Most of the language around me seemed to be the language of connoisseurship. The language in the studios, my teachers, the language of critics, was taken to be very serious and very meaningful but I found it really quite trite. I felt there was a pretentiousness about art and this was confirmed by the way that art was viewed by the vast mass of the population. All this became acutely distressing for me. So I wanted to bring back more contact, quite simply, with the social world. There was hardly any engagement with the everyday social world, of the sort that is familiar from literature, in film, and in pre-Modernist painting, in all of the art that I'd valued as a student. So yes, I did want to find a way of working that was more engaged with the external world, and the photograph did offer that in a very direct way. How did I get to using the ads? Well I got there through language. Let me just say this quickly before I forget about it, because if you look at the 1973 book of mine, *Work and Commentary*, you'll see as you go through it, the word pieces change from one page to the other and you find that by the end of the book the word pieces are referring to ethics and values. From references at the beginning of the book to purely conceptual situations, they begin to take account of memory, and the place of memory in perception, and then by the end of the book they're taking account of value judgements. And the book ends with one of the earliest uses of an advertising photograph by me which is a photograph from a catalogue of a nuclear family, mummy, daddy, one boy, one girl, which, in a sense, you could say is a foundation of ethical formation for anyone. So this was one way of making direct reference to the real life situations, even if there was a danger of it drifting off into that area that Art & Language were so fond of, which was philosophy and art for its own sake.

*Well, this is what I wanted to expand on because despite your disappointment with the Modernist artworld your engagement with photography was obviously situated in the artworld, that is, at the same time as you were producing the* Photo Path *and the work subsequent to that, such as* Work and Commentary, *you were in a sense looking over your shoulder at what Art & Language and other analytic conceptual artists were doing.*

*Photo Path*, was the beginning, if you like, of my gallery career, and that was as a result of a visit from Charles Harrison, who was editor of *Studio International* at the time. He had seen something that I had written. I was teaching at what was then Nottingham College of Art, in conjunction with Nottingham University, and some people I was teaching with asked me if I would write a paragraph or two about the work I was doing which they wanted to put into some sort of reference work that would be a sort of guide to British artists. I wrote something and then forgot about it, I never ever saw the book. Then I got a phone call from Charles Harrison, whom I didn't know, and he came to see me and he talked to me and saw my work and as a result, invited me into the 'When Attitudes Become Form' exhibition. Charles Harrison was fundamentally important in launching conceptual art in England, because until that time, the so-called British conceptual artists were working in isolation; I thought nobody else was doing anything like the sort of work I was doing. I'd just come back from Yale, and was working not in response to any conceptual work I'd seen, but in direct response to those situations I have just described, so I thought I was just doing something that was a bit interesting, a bit novel, and I had this sort of optimistic young man's idea that if I kept working at it somebody would notice me, which was rather naive. But I didn't know anybody else who was working in a way that would subsequently be called conceptualist, whereas Charles, as a magazine editor and a critic, was out there looking. He put the British version of this show together and because of his intervention and *Studio* magazine which, up until then had been pretty much a British art establishment showcase for painters, he suddenly turned that all around and really single- handedly gave conceptual art a platform in England. He was very important. Now what happened subsequently to that is that Charles became ever more closely involved, at both a personal and professional level with members of Art & Language, who were, you know, really quite aggressive in their self-marketing. Now, he didn't join them and drop his activities as a critic, he continued to be a critic, but given he was now actually a member of Art & Language this helped establish a platform for Art & Language. That is, there was always a preference whenever anything got written by Charles, to emphasise the historical importance of Art & Language.

*Can we be a bit more specific? What I would like to talk*

*about now are those ideological conflicts that were internal to the debate in early conceptual art about visuality, image and text, cognition, pleasure and so on. Your work was, for instance, characterised by Art & Language as weakening the philosophical demands of conceptual art's analysis of the propositional content of art through its reliance on mass produced imagery, just as you characterised Art & Language, as producing work which confused the intellectual practice of art with self-reflexivity. Where did you want these early works to be positioned in the debate between analytic conceptualism and other conceptual practices of the time? From reading all the work that was done during that period, your own stuff included, there is an obvious tension between those artists such as Art & Language who were concerned with clearing the ideological encumberances of Modernist notions of the visual from art, and artists like yourself, and perhaps John Stezaker, who were looking to conceptual art in order to re-theorise art's connection to popular culture. Now maybe that's a simplistic distinction, but, it is true that you and John Stezaker, around that period were more concerned with locating art in a space of shared meaning within the culture.*

Yes. I thought that what Art & Language were doing was purely formalist and therefore uninteresting. It seemed quite clear that they were mimicking philosophers, from the form of their publications, the style of their language, but more substantially they were adopting the subject position of the philosopher as it existed then in Britain in relation to the rest of the intellectual world. Philosophers set themselves up as the accountants of the intellectual world and would decide if this or that pronouncement by an historian, or this or that statement by a political economist, was 'valid', according to whether it would meet their criteria of truth value or not. Now, when those questions are asked of history and political economy, they do have a certain weight as questions. When you ask such questions of art, it's totally without consequence. So I thought of Art & Language as simply constructing a playpen that was situated in one corner of the big playroom of art. However, I would have been in agreement with Art & Language that the implicit in art practice should be made explicit, and that the explicit statement should be subject to criticism. But if you're going to bring theory to art then the theory has to be potentially publicly accessible. Now I don't mean by that what many people would think I mean, I don't mean "Anybody ought to be able to understand it", I don't go in for that idiot populism. What I do mean, is that the theory should not be taken seriously in the art world and nowhere else. It should be exportable and it should be subject to testing in the arena of the disciplines that you're engaging with. Art & Language have no currency whatsoever, if that was ever their intention, outside of the artworld; and in fact I don't believe it was their intention, I think they were more like the Surrealists, I think that's how they thought of themselves: as an avant-gardist group making provocations. I think you should see their work mainly as satire, even though I don't think they intended themselves all the time to be satirical. I think often they thought of themselves as being serious philosophers, but their work is not taken seriously in the philosophical world, none of them are teaching philosophy in universities, they haven't managed to export their work, they haven't managed to attract the interest of co-workers working on similar problem of representation. My own feeling was that just as my art should be in direct engagement with the forms of imagery found in the outside world (hence my turn to advertising imagery and to the rhetoric of text image relations) art theory should engage with bodies of theory being developed in allied areas. This led me to semiotics.

*I don't really want to dwell on this, but Art & Language never saw themselves as philosophers doing philosophy of art, they never saw themselves as artists doing art as philosophy. What they saw themselves as were artists doing philosophy in order to test the very boundaries of what it was to do art and to talk about it. And I think the voice of the satirist has a legitimate place in there. You may disagree with Charles Harrison's history, the official history of Art & Language, on many points, but I think you do have to acknowledge that the self-image of Art & Language during that period was not bound up with wanting to be something that they possibly couldn't be. What I really wanted to talk to you about was this very real ideological split around the visual.*

In terms of that basic difference between me and Art & Language, rather than trust either your or my reconstruction or Charles Harrison's reconstruction, I think one should rather go back to the original documents. In my case, everything I might say about my relation to Art & Language and these debates, was said in that period and published in the journal *Art-Language* itself. I don't know whether you are familiar with the piece 'In Reply' which was published in Volume 2, Number 2 of *Art-Language*. It was written in response to an attack from Michael Baldwin, because they were into excommunicating heretics in that period. That document has more validity for me than any subsequent reconstructions would have. I saw them as being influenced by Joseph Kosuth who identified totally with Ad Reinhardt; and thus with this whole question of self-reflexivity, which is nothing other than art for art's sake. Who cares, finally, about the definition of art? What does it matter? I can't see it, so I think ultimately it comes down to this: either you get it or you don't and I just never got it, they were disappearing up their own fondaments, as far as I was concerned. And my argument was precisely that, I said the debate wasn't getting anywhere, you've got to get into some sort of engagement with the social world. Well subsequently they made their own turn to politics, I'm not claiming that I was the one who kicked them into it, but I think the writing was on the wall, it was there for them to see, but it took them a long time to get there.

*You still really haven't answered my question about the debate on the visual.*

I don't know what you mean by that.

*I mean, the attack on the primacy of the visual in analytic conceptual art as an attack on the separation between seeing and thinking.*

I think I hear what you're saying. That art doesn't have to be visual, that art can be defined or exemplified in linguistic terms, and so on, these things are without doubt true. But when I say 'art', I don't mean some Platonic form somewhere, transhistorical, I mean a set of institutions that we've inherited from previous definitions of art. What use are those institutions put to now? For me, there isn't anything outside of those institutions and outside of the practices within those institutions, so for me, definitions of art are not to be arrived at through philosophical reflection. Definitions of art are to be performed in practice within art institutions. So I was performing a definition of art, rather than trying to write one, because I didn't see the purpose in writing one, I couldn't see any value that might come out of it. Written definitions of art don't make sense to me; what matters is how whatever is being accepted as art gets imbricated in social relations to the world. What interested me was in how 'art' might be able to create an alternative space of reflection on the mainstream media practices given the cultural dominance of TV, cinema and advertising. That was my purpose, there was no way I was saying this is what art is. I just wanted to be able to do something in the institution of art which had a real connection with things outside of art, with both an intellectual world outside of art, and with a visual world outside of art.

*You may have had little interest in what might count as art, but nonetheless your relationship to the cognitive and aesthetic resources of art was part of the wider reassessment of the forms of art during this period. In your work, as in other work, there is a resistance to the reduction of art to its historical conditions of spectacularisation.*

That came out of minimalism, everybody shared that same minimalist aesthetic. It was just uncool to do anything that wasn't clean and austere. The style, that's what you are talking about, one shouldn't over intellectualise this.

*But there was an ethics there, don't you think?*

Yes, there was an ethics in not having luxurious consumer goods, so there's a politics either implicit or explicit in it. But that was less to do with the austere style it was more to do with the materials. Bob Morris' sculpture or Donald Judd's sculpture was austere, but boy, did it sell. Judd particularly became very well off. So to choose not to do something that some rich guy could buy and put on his land or in his condo, to do something that would blow away, literally, or to do something that was so cheap that nobody would be seen dead with it in their penthouse apartment, that was a certain sort of ethic, if you like, a political act. I think it's important to keep a sense of the shifting relations between the form of the work and its reception; minimalism didn't always mean one thing.

*OK, well, can we expand this a bit further, or rather go back to some of the things that I was talking about earlier to do with the photographic document. Now clearly your work, John Stezaker's work, and other artists who were using pho-*

*tography during this period, were not at all concerned with referencing the history of photography itself, that is, there was no interest in what we now know as the documentary tradition, and little interest in photographic Modernism which was being disseminated out of New York during the period.*

None whatsoever. Nobody knew about it.

*So what photographic resources were in place in the late sixties? We obviously can point to Ed Ruscha and the work that he was doing from 1965, which once again comes out of a minimalist aesthetic, in its intractable refusal to display the signs of authorship, its seriality and so on. How much was Ed Ruscha a presence for you?*

I'd seen his work, but in that period I remember thinking that he wasn't really anybody one should take seriously. Basically he seemed to be some sort of Californian stand-up comedian. So yes, looking back the British contingent was very small, there was Art & Language, me, John Stezaker who was a bit younger, and Keith Arnatt who was a bit older. One thing I shared with Art & Language was a sense of disapproval for anyone who wasn't totally serious. What was unserious about Ruscha was that the work looked like entertainment. It looked as if there was a spontaneous and desultory shifting from one thing to another without any sense of a development in response to more broadly formulated theoretical issues. So I am closer to Art & Language in taking theory seriously. And this is certainly one of the differences between artists in that period, there were those who took their theory seriously and those who didn't think about it.

*It's always problematic looking for precedents in this way because you force history to conform to the expectations of the present, but nonetheless I think Ed Ruscha via Andy*

*Warhol's early work did create a set of co-ordinates that allowed a younger generation of artists to get to the point where some of the things that you have been talking about were taken seriously. That is, a desire for a photographic practice that went out to meet the surface appearances of the social world, a practice that took on the technologies and ideology of the mass media; and which had been suppressed in its political forms since at least the 1930s.*

Yes, I think this in an interesting issue because I actually went back and discovered a number of precedents, stuff that I thought that I was doing out of my own head, but I found had been done already. I discovered Russian formalism, Heartfield - nobody talked to me about John Heartfield at art school, because it wasn't considered as art. Now you can't imagine a student not knowing about John Heartfield today because there are so many books and articles that weren't available in that period. I discovered John Heartfield when I started having to turn myself into something of a photo historian because I had just taken a job in a photography department. So I can see the historical precedents for my own work, I can also see the historical precedents for lots of other work too, and I think maybe this, in a sense, is one of the points of your show: to make available certain things to a younger generation. I think it's both easier for this generation and more difficult for them; and it's the same thing that makes it easy and difficult. I mean, one thing that's easier for them is they don't feel the terrible weight of history any more, they don't feel this need to develop art along one single teleologically pre-ordained path, because they don't have to deal with any of that Greenbergian Modernism which fed into minimalism and conceptualism. For me those were just like late stages of Modernism, in the way you might talk about late capitalism; the final gasp of Modernism. And Post-Modernism I think released people, released a whole generation from that sense of obligation to the past, that sense of looking over their shoulder all the time. And that's made it a lot easier. But I realise now that in looking over my shoulder during that period, I was looking over my shoulder with blinkers on, and those blinkers had been placed on me by my education as an artist. So I wasn't able to look over my shoulder and see John Heartfield - he just wasn't in my field of vision.

*There is a big difference between the kind of work that was using photography in the early seventies in Britain and American conceptual artists who were using photography. For instance Dan Graham's* Homes for America. *There is a strong sense in this work that at the same time that it is engaging with questions of photographic truth, it is also extending an American vernacular tradition. There is no sense of that in any of the British work, it's not as though yourself and John Stezaker were producing an English vernacular art out of conceptual art. Perhaps you could comment on that.*

I won't speak for John's work because at the time I didn't know it. I got to know John later. Retrospectively I can see that we had something in common. He was trying to integrate elements of film imagery into his work, I was trying to integrate elements of advertising imagery in my work, and so retrospectively it could be easy to see us both as presaging, to a certain extent, the photo activity of the eighties, the 'appropriated image' and so on. But, I've always worked pretty much in isolation, whether from a fear of influence or for some other reason. I was communing very much with these problems that I thought I'd inherited from minimalism, trying very much to work things out for myself. It's a bit like what one does in one's writing, and it's the same in one's art work. You are trying to describe for yourself where you are, you are trying to pull the bits of yourself together. You finish off the work, whether it's a piece of writing or an artwork, in an attempt to pull the bits of yourself together so you can look at them and see where you are - or rather, have just been so you can move on. And that's what was happening in that earlier work. I've got this preoccupation with mental structures, which came out of that critique of minimalism, I'm developing this obsessive interest in the environment of advertising, which becomes increasingly politicised across this period, and I'm re-discovering my working-class origins after a period of denial. I was trying to bring all of this into the single space of the work. So in a sense this work of synthesis is 'expressionist'. I think there's a misconception that there's expressionist work and there's work that is not expressionist, this is a superficial, stylistic distinction. I am much more inclined to say this now because at one time I hated all reference to expressionism and I still don't like expressionist aesthetics, but there's a level at which the banal commonplace is true that all art is 'self-expression'. If there wasn't a self involved in art, nobody would be doing it. But the important thing is that this is not all it is. If that is all it is we are just prancing around like four year old egotistical brats.

*It seems to me that this early work was doing a number of things. One, it was critiquing the avant-garde and in the process, lowering the cognitive distance between art and popular culture, an intellectual distance that Modernism had set up. Stezaker's work, for instance, was first and foremost concerned with negotiating that distance, and as such trying to break it down. And then there's the debate over language in art, the textualisation of the visual which is bound up with the introduction of semiotics into art theory, and then in turn the theorisation of language itself as a social act, as a process which produces the subject ideologically. Could you talk a little bit now about the intellectual resources that were coming into play for you during the early seventies because your reading list was very, very different from say Art &*

*Language's or Keith Arnatt's.*

That short piece I wrote in reply to Art & Language actually mentions Saussure as a more promising theory of language than that offered by anaytical philosophy if one wants to get out of the impasse of art for art's sake, and art theory for the sake of art theory. So that was at the beginning of my interest in semiotics. This interest in fact started when I came back from Yale in '67 and stumbled across this little Jonathan Cape translation, *Elements of Semiology* by Roland Barthes and it changed my life. It came at the right time, I was looking for what the structuralist critics were looking for, a scientific criticism. I wanted a non-anecdotal, non-subjective criticism. We can see now that it was something of a dream, and was never to be realised and led to the most dreadful sort of formalism, but at the time it seemed to me important, and still seems to me important. What was crucial about it for me was that here was a theory which was able to turn its attention, almost indiscriminately, to advertising, to cinema, to literature. This seemed to me to offer a broad base where you could actually connect with, as I said before, other people and other fields and have a discussion in common. So naturally my fantasy was that art would become reintegrated into the broader field of cultural criticism.

*This has happened to a large extent, the criticism of art has now been integrated into the broader spectacle of visual production.*

Yes, well, this is a sore point. What I wanted, when I started putting those advertising images on the wall, was some sort of integration of contents. But of course, it's happened not at all in the way that I wanted. Art and art criticism are being swallowed by the world of advertising and fashion.

*As I have pointed out, the photographic document is an*

*under-theorised presence in conceptual art. It is only in the mid-seventies when photo-theory develops its autonomy as a discipline that the theoretical status of the document becomes an issue. Allan Sekula, for instance, publishes his first major essay on documentary practice in 1975. What was your understanding of this debate during the period?*

The word 'document' is used in the title of your show in relation to conceptualism and what this suggests to me is, for example, Richard Long, Land art. I don't know if you want to call them conceptualists but I suppose a lot of people would, they produce an intervention or event in the landscape, and then, in order to be able to publish the work, and show other people that they have done the work, they have to take a photograph, so it documents the work. In the case of Hamish Fulton, it moves to the point where the photograph is no longer just a documentation of the event but it's a beautiful image in the tradition of 19th century landscape photography. So I'd think of 'document' in relation to conceptual art in that way. That's very clearly different from my use of photography in *Photo Path* and it's clearly very different again from my use of photography since the eighties. When I started taking my own pictures, for a variety of reasons, it was to the documentary genre that I went. Why? Well, the reason for that, first of all, in a sort of Modernist way, was I considered what it was that was specific to photography. And what seemed to me to be peculiar to photography which nothing else did, at least not in the way photography did it, was street photography. Somebody can go into the street with a movie camera and a team, but then you attract attention to yourself and you change the event. But the classic, unobtrusive street photographer intervenes in a very minimal sort of way, and can almost say 'I am a camera'. It's almost like the glance that Baudelaire spoke of in the work of Constantin Guy, the 'painter of everyday life'. So you might say that a street photographer is the painter of modern day life par excellence. I thought that was something that photography did that nothing else did in quite the same way. And that in doing it, it automatically took on a trace of contemporary history, and I thought, even if in a hundred years time, or two hundred years time, nobody has the slightest bit of interest in what Victor Burgin thought he was doing as an artist, there would be somebody who has an historical interest in what this person was wearing, or what that sign said. So I thought, this is a way of getting history into the work.

*That was always Benjamin's defence of photography.*

Yes, and I think it's an everlastingly valid claim for photography, and now for video.

*That's very interesting to hear coming from you, given that in the eighties you, along with a number of other theorists, were committed to a thorough-going critique of the would-be veracity of the photographic document. To hear you defending the naturalistic function of the photograph is to put me on the back foot.*

There isn't a contradiction because the critique that I and others were making was directed at naive theories of the production of photographic *meaning*. You know, the belief that the meaning is given in the same moment that you see what there is. Meaning is not given with brute 'denotations'. We won't disagree over what the denotation of the photograph is, to use that classic semiotic language, we will all agree, yes that's a cat, yes that's a lamp post. What we are liable to disagree about is the meaning. I have a photograph of a boxing match that I show to my undergraduate students, this is the first picture that they ever see in my introduction to semiotics class. It's a newspaper photograph showing two boxers, one is leaping in the air, obviously he's just won, and the other one is being supported by the referee. You obviously can see what it means, it's the end of a boxing match, and this guy's won, and then I say, well no that story's not true. Actually this is an advertising shot, it was never used, but this was set up, these guys were actors and if you look at it, you can see only two sides of the ring because there isn't a third and a fourth side because they were left out so the camera could get access. And after I've finished that story, and the class is totally persuaded, I say, well that's not true either and tell them a different story and then another, each one equally persuasive, and by that time the class is laughing or groaning or whatever, but they know damn well that they can't just look and see the meaning, there's a process of assembling and construction which goes on. So there's no contradiction between my saying this photograph might be historically interesting because it will show what people were wearing in that period and my theoretical position that doesn't in itself tell you what a photograph means or meant then or could mean.

*I think you're being somewhat disingenuous here because in the eighties what was at stake in your writing was a break with the model of realism, so naturalism by definition came up for scrutiny and criticism. It was nigh impossible to defend a sophisticated notion of realism in relation to representation. Realism, and by implication naturalism, although they are not, as you are perfectly aware, historically synonymous were in the eighties non-terms. Let's put it this way, you're absolutely right about the radical instability of the meaning of the image, but there are limits to that radical instability and it's the limits of that instability, if that's not a contradiction, that never got discussed. So the idea that we can apply any kind of reading, or infinite number of readings to an image seems to be completely implausible.*

I absolutely *never* said that.

*Yes, but I think that the debates that took place - and you see this in innumerable pseudo-post structuralist essays on these questions - allowed a huge number of people in academia to talk as if that was the case, because there was a political agenda underwriting the epistemological line. If images are radically unstable then hermeneutics becomes separated from ethics.*

At this point I want to grab my own books off the shelf and start reading passages from them. I think I could have answered all of these questions from *The End of Art Theory* (1986) alone. There is an impassioned speech towards the end of that book where I speak out against the position you criticise (p198). You say that post-structuralist theory was institutionalised in the eighties in the art schools. My impression is that only the shallowest caricature of it was institutionalised. A perversion of it went into the art schools, and it's because of this that theory can now be attacked very easily. There's a fantasy when you're writing, I guess all writers have it, that everyone is going to read what you write and that those who read it will remember it; and what really depresses me about this, demoralises me, is that I find so often that theoretical work has to be done all over again. I'd have to publish *The End of Art Theory* all over again in order to express myself in relation to a lot of what's being produced now. People have forgotten the debates in all their complexity and so people have forgotten the answers that were given in all their complexity and so you have to start all over again. And if theory was institutionalised then I have to say it wasn't done properly. We haven't had a development of the work of the seventies and the early eighties, we've had a collapse of it in the art world. When I wrote *The End of Art Theory*, you can see it was written from a full engagement with art criticism and art journalism, and ten years down the line I think it is significant that I don't pick up an art journal, and I don't expect to be read by any artists. I've just published another book and you know, there are images in it and photographs are discussed, but it never occurs to me for a minute that anybody in the art world is going to read it. And if they did read it, would they understand it? Frankly, I'm very demoralised by the situation. I don't think I'm holding up too high standards. I get a lot of hostility from people who think I'm making it all too hard. But some questions are difficult questions and you can't have easy solutions to them. I feel that in the seventies and eighties, there was a recognition of this, *Block* was around, artists were reading *Screen* and other things were happening at the ICA, and it wasn't a wholly fashion driven culture.

*You sound angry.*

I suppose I'm irritated at being asked to go back and reconsider my answers to those questions. Because my answers to those questions remain the same. I can think of ways in which I might have done different things. However, I don't feel that I was fundamentally wrong theoretically. That sounds sort of arrogant. I'm not saying there is one way, and that was my way, all I'm saying is that I feel that there has been an organic development in my own work, I don't feel any more in or out of art practice now than then; even if my theory is not published in art magazines any more. So whatever my public reception now the work is still about what was concerning me then. My new book is called *In/Different Spaces: place and memory in visual culture*, its all about psychical space. That's all my work was ever about. That's what that work in the 1970s at the Camden Arts Centre was about. If you go back to any of those early interviews, that's what I talk about. So there was something I was interested in which began with minimalism and I've been interested in it ever since, and it' s got more and more complicated as I've taken on questions of the space of politics, defined in the broadest sense to include questions of race, sex, gender and so on. I'm working on the same things I was working on back then. I wish the art world allowed a space for people to have a long term consistent development, and not to be told: "I'm sorry your right time's over". If I appear more often in a university context these days it's simply because the university has allowed me that space to continue working.

John Hilliard

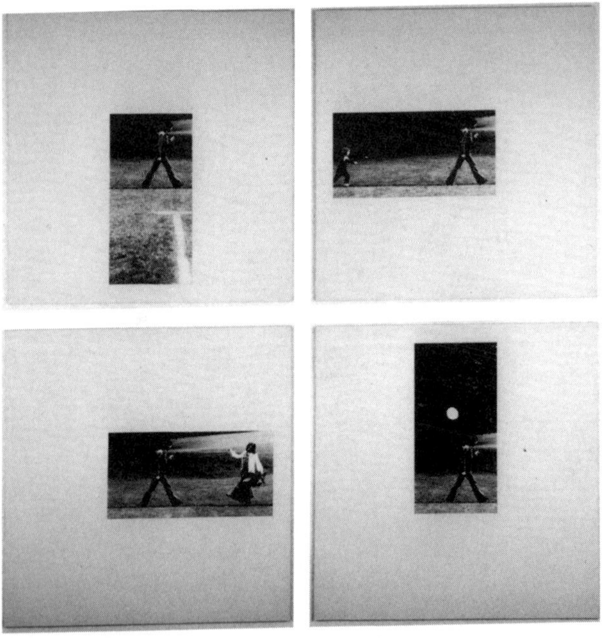

*Across the Park*, 1972

## INTERVIEW WITH JOHN HILLIARD

*Perhaps we can begin by discussing your perceptions of what you felt was at stake using photography in the late 1960's.*

It's not so much a question of what was at stake, but of what it meant to use photography as a medium for working with at all. Despite its long history of association with art, in the post-war period it hadn't really been used by artists as a first order medium - certainly not in any pronounced way. Maybe by the Pop artists to some extent. Initially in the sixties it was a means of documenting something without really thinking that the document might later become the form of the work to be presented. Once that decision had been made it squared very neatly with the prevailing zeitgeist, which favoured ways of working which were relatively discreet. In a curious way photography also squared with the desire, phenomenologically speaking, for a form of realism, so that the documents of photography seemed to be in accord with the geometry of minimalism. If you think of exhibitions like 'The Art of the Real', photography's causal connection to the 'real' appeared to be in sympathy with that agenda. Even its black and whiteness had an austerity that fitted very well with the reductive aesthetic of the period.

*Would you agree with Jeff Wall's line on the use of photography in conceptual art? I'm thinking of the essay that he wrote for the MOCA conceptual art show catalogue in 1995 where he talks about early conceptual photography in terms of the Modernist paradigm. He argues that one of the reasons photography became available, or seemed to be usable to artists, was that it had not been through a process of self-reflexive critique in the way that Modernist painting had. This is because photography's indexical relationship to the real made it impossible to construct an anti-representational theory of the modern, making it appear as if photography was antithetical to the modern. So what attracted conceptual artists to photography were those things that Modernism deemed as extraneous to value and quality in painting: social detail, repetition, allegory. These characteristics then provided the conditions of photography's anti-Modernist self-reflexivity: a defence of the ordinariness of art through the use of photography and the critical detachment of photography from the professionalised, unreflective categories of photojournalism and fine art aestheticism.*

Without wishing to dispute that idea, I think one has to be wary of looking back at the sixties through today's spectacles. When photography was first used by artists associated with, or coming out of conceptual art, it was very much just as a handy, easily available tool. Self consciousness about the photograph and an awareness of its functioning within its own language is something that only followed afterwards, although not all artists using photography took that route.

*It's possible to argue that the response by photographers to the need to examine photography's historical condition finds its expression in the embracing of photography as an amateur practice. The displacement of conventions and of professional codes is pursued in the name of an indifference to the aesthetics of picture-making. Conceptual artists using photography were certainly not interested in fine art photography or post-fifties documentary reportorial photography. They weren't interested in so-called professional forms of training.*

The references, rather than being to genres like amateur photography, were much more towards painting and sculpture. A lot of artists using photography, including myself, made use of some kind of modular structure, which had its immediate precursor in the symmetry and repetitious patterns of minimalism. Insofar as there was some kind of relation to photography as a commonly available medium it was much more as a part of minimalism's perceived egalitarianism: the idea that one should seek to use an artistic method which didn't bring with it the stigma of some esoteric specialism. So photography was appropriate in that sense. The one significant aspect of its connection to amateur photography was its use as a convenience, as something which achieved its results fairly rapidly and easily. I suspect Jeff is talking about these things because he is presently very interested in 20th century photography and the way it connects to Modernism. But it's one thing to take that position at this point in time, its another thing to think back and try to remember how you considered and used photography in the sixties.

*The point at issue here is that conceptualism involved a radical de-skilling or re-skilling of the categories of art and as such established a quite obvious break with Modernism through a break with the retinal. Now if you are using photography as a conceptual artist you are faced with certain problems about the pictorial. That is why I think a professionalised photographic practice was as much a problem for conceptual artists using photography as was the powerful institutionalised legacy of abstract painting and sculpture. That's why in many ways a lot artists using photography, weren't that interested in talking about photography as such.*

I think most artists using photography were rather ignorant about its history, and I would include myself in that. Certain artists, like Victor Burgin for example, made it their business to become acquainted with that history. But in general artists using photography simply thought of themselves as having rather different needs. They were not trying to achieve the same ends as someone doing reportage or fashion photography. They were using photography in a way in which it hadn't been used before; and the subsequent scrutiny of the medium was directed at discovering what was specific to it. For example, I might have become aware of the way newspaper photographs made use of captions in a very questionable way, but that relation between word and image clearly applied across the board, not just to photo journalism but to photographs as and when they were juxtaposed with writing in any context, including art.

*At which point though did you begin to look at the photograph as a defeasible entity, that is as something whose truth-value was highly questionable or could be questioned? How did you get from photographing the early sculptures to the work that you did immediately after that when you were concerned with questions of photographic veracity?*

There were probably two simple steps. The first was to decide to use photography explicitly as a means of representing the site specific installations I was producing at the time, because the nature of those installations was inherently transient. Although all art now necessarily falls under a lens as a way of being recorded and disseminated, it seemed to me that with work which wouldn't have an enduring presence, the role of the camera became particularly pronounced and should be acknowledged. So, if in the first place there was a rather unthinking use of the photograph as document, subsequently there was a very conscious and deliberate use of the photograph as something that stood overtly in place of the object that it represented. That in turn highlighted the difference between the representation and its referent - raising questions about the veracity of the medium and its reliability as a representational tool.

*How much of this was in response to the ethics of conceptualism, that is to the critique of the commodity?*

Photography certainly seemed to be useful in this respect

because of its commonality as a medium and its dissociation from fine art. As something that could be easily distributed, photography had a kind of 'immateriality', that was very appealing. It sounds pathetic now to say this, but there was something a little anarchic about using the photograph as an artwork. The first time I showed photographs was in 1969, and I remember provoking rather surprised reactions to the idea of making an exhibition which was explicitly photographic in nature within the context of art. These reactions were either very adverse or very positive, but there was at least some recognition that this might be an interesting thing to continue with.

*Your work at the time seemed to be very much tied to the analytical, linguistic demands of conceptual art in a way that Gilbert and George, for instance, weren't. Their photographic work from that period was very much a diaristic extension of their performance, and as a consequence, had a literary content that the majority of work being produced did not have.*

If I actually sit down and think about it, I find it difficult to make a list of many artists who do use the medium analytically. Photography as used by artists seems generally to have been relatively uncritical and unself-conscious.

*How familiar were you with Ed Ruscha's work of the time?*

In the late sixties I'd seen Ed Ruscha's books. I remember seeing the Parking Lots reproduced in a publication from Minneapolis.

*His 'Five Girlfriends' from 1955 were reproduced in the 'Konzeption' catalogue in 1969.*

Right. Which I saw, which I have a copy of, but it didn't particularly stick in my mind. I certainly had the idea that artists in the sixties had made use of photography beyond its secondary status in Pop art. There were odd things that I was in some way peripherally aware of. Having said that, I also had my own needs for beginning to use the medium and my needs were much more like those of my immediate contemporaries such as Richard Long, Gilbert and George or Bruce McLean, people either making sculpture that was impermanent or people involved in performance or any other kind of temporary work. Photography for those artists was firstly a means to stabilise an otherwise transient object or event, and that's rather different from using it from the outset as something in itself.

*This only applies to the very early work, doesn't it?*

Yes. But I'm making a comparison with photographic work by other artists already in existence at that time, like the Ed Ruscha pieces you mentioned.

*But a massive shift takes place a couple of years down the line to allow you to start taking photographs of yourself taking photographs. Turning the camera on yourself is a powerful re-orientation.*

It seems to me there was an inevitability to that. If you are functioning within a cultural moment where there is an inherent awareness of the language of the various media being deployed in the arts I think it is almost given that if you start using photography you would very rapidly say "hang on a minute, I can't just use this in a completely unconscious way. I can't only use it as a means to an end. I'm bound to take note of all its specific properties, and subject them to some scrutiny, and to some critical appraisal".

*So this was a learning process for you.*

Absolutely, because I didn't know anything about photography. I hadn't been taught photography and I made very stupid mistakes.

*So in a sense the cultural climate gave validity to those kinds of moves. Is that how you sensed it?*

If photography had not been a potentially legitimate tool for artists generally in the post-war period, then it would not have been appropriated and analysed. What the sixties gave licence to was a kind of adventurousness right across the board, an encouragement to experiment, to try new things, not to be needlessly constricted by the terms of the status quo. Circumstances allowed that it wasn't a problem to think about using photography as a medium.

*But even in the space of a few years, your photographs are very different to your contemporaries. When you think of Ed Ruscha's work, at the same time as he's borrowing the rhetoric of the avant-garde, that is, embracing the amateur in order to distance himself from professional photography and from the heavily professionalised pretensions of painting and sculpture, he is opening up art to a new vernacular content. Now, when you turn the camera on yourself in the early seventies this takes the debate a long way from notions of the vernacular and literary.*

One of the big reference points for artists in Britain in the sixties and seventies was American art. Ed Ruscha is an example of someone with connections to Pop art. The minimalist artists had a very different kind of aesthetic, and a different set of references, and I think the British tendency towards analysis and an interest in the philosophy of language seemed more drawn to these. Minimalism's own interest in the linguistic was more of an influence on me at that point than other areas of American art. But I think this pointing the camera at myself that you mentioned, a kind of reflexivity, is also connected to the tautologies of minimal and conceptual art, and these tautologies are born from a desire to have an artwork which reveals its formal mechanisms to the viewer, and doesn't require some kind of specialist, esoteric information or aesthetic judgment to penetrate it. It doesn't seek an overly subjective relation to its materials. It wants to become clear, available, accessible. The use of tautology is to do with that imperative, and I think my own use of tautology and reflexivity is to do with a similar desire to construct a model which tries to be as clear and as unadorned as possible. Not to have anything there which is needless or excessive.

*How much of this might have related to a kind of incipient Brechtian notion of the laying bare of the formal apparatus as a critical act?*

My contact with Brechtian values was from contemporary American theatre like the La Mama Company, or the Living Theatre, some of whose performances I saw. But self-consciousness in theatre, the diffusing of its mystique, the narrowing of the gap between spectator and performer, ensuring that the spectator was let in on the workings of the mechanics of the performance, was being re-iterated in the cinema of Godard, in music, in writing and in the arts in general at the time.

*There are two ways of addressing this question about laying bare, isn't there? Quite obviously there is the Brechtian, avant-garde response that we've just talked about and the Kantian-Modernist account of the laying bare of the medium that we've also touched on. Both involve an ethics of self-disclosure: that it is the job of art in the modern period to declare to its audience that it is no more than art, that there is a producer behind the work, and that the illusions of traditional forms of picture making, or of theatre, simply reinforce a distance between the art and the spectator. All that was very much in the air in the late sixties and seventies.*

Yes, of course. Conceptual art wasn't just a matter of dematerialisation, it was a matter of demystifcation as well.

*But something else enters the framework in the early to mid-seventies, the relationship between photography, ideology and mass culture. In response to the precedents of Victor Burgin and John Stezaker there comes a point where your work shifts gear again in response to wider cultural pressures.*

I think the explanation for that is quite simple. If an initial consciousness about the medium of photography is directed towards the fundamentals of its production, its chemistry, the mechanics of its instruments and so on, then those are the very things that provide the subject matter. If you then move in a slightly different direction away from production and towards the way photographs are displayed and presented, then the kind of subjects that would be suitable for inclusion are likely to be of a different nature. As soon as I started being interested in cropping and framing, then the range of subjects that I began to select from, changed. And, similarly, when I became interested in the effects of differential focusing within the same field of view, the subjects that were suitable had to be both apt in relation to the job in hand, but also make reference to a kind of imagery that was the subject of those procedures in other contexts. So what this move allowed me to do was admit an interest in related fields like film. My use of changing focus, for example, originated in watching focus pulls on the screen. Once I became interested in the way photographs were used, through the way they were displayed and through the way they conveyed information more generally about the things they depicted, then I became more concerned with the image, with representation, and to some extent with ideology. This is when I really engaged with the image as a vehicle, because my history of making sculpture was very deliberately as a means of working with what I thought of as the real. Having originally set out to represent the non-representational through the photograph, I've ended up by default working with representation itself as a subject - something I had initially quite deliberately set aside.

*I think we ought to talk a little bit more about the legacy of conceptual art itself. How aware were you at the time of questions to do with the dispute between the retinal and the anti-retinal? For instance, so much of Art & Language's practise from 1967 through to 1972, through to the* Indexes, *was concerned with forms of anti-retinal artistic production. Did you feel threatened by that theoretical engagement?*

I don't think it was something that I really thought of in that way. The idea of the retinal and non-retinal is a concept that I associated with a kind of Greenbergian critical position with regard to painting. Like many artists in London I had an interest in American abstract painting. Maybe that's why I tried to categorise my own early work with photography as being materialist and very much concerned with producing something as a presence in the world, even though it was a photograph and not a piece of painted canvas or steel. For me it had a similar status. Its modularity was determined by the existing structures inherent in the medium of photography, but it was also absolutely in accord with the modularity of minimalism and with my own previous work with sculpture. What you are describing as the retinal and what I'm referring to when I talk about my subsequent engagement with the image is something that followed on afterwards. That work, starting around 1972, I wouldn't have imagined doing even one year before.

*The reason I mentioned this is that there was practically no discussion on photography and representation during the 'classical' period of conceptual art from about 1966 to 1972. There's no discourse on the social possibilities of photography until really Victor Burgin and John Stezaker begin to start writing about popular culture in about '73, '74, if you like, in conscious opposition to Art & Language. How did you line up around that?*

I lined up as a curator, but not until 1977. The various things we've been talking about need to be considered as part of a larger situation. Just as the ideas that Brecht had about theatre found their parallels in other art forms, I think the interest in social issues, among the artists you mentioned like Victor Burgin, John Stezaker, Steve Willats and also Art & Language, were very much part of a more general position at the time. It was as if a rather specialised interest in language itself had to be applied to something. Somebody like Vic, who's early work is concerned with number and sequence and linguistics, applied this to photography, and then moved on to articulate a social commentary on sexuality and class. My own work didn't enter into that area. Insofar as I engaged with ideological issues, they were much more generally to do with representation - with gender representation and so on. But I wouldn't have described them as being overtly political, whereas I think a lot of that work clearly was. I actually curated a show in Newcastle with Victor Burgin, John Stezaker, Art & Language, Steve Willats, Conrad Atkinson and Terry Atkinson, but not myself. I didn't see myself in that connection, but I did see that group of British artists as being representative of something very current at the time. It seemed to me to be where the thrust of British conceptual art had moved to.

*Yes, this is something that needs to be discussed. From around 1973 through to '76 there was a huge amount of photographic based conceptual work dealing with the semiology of popular culture. You yourself move into the area of gender representation and engage with ideologies of film. Overall a whole new area of practice opens out. What was your perception of things?*

Well, apart from anything else, presumably the medium became admissible and taken for granted in a way that it couldn't have been in the late sixties. Once you had a generation of artists who had opted to use photography, who successfully exhibited works in that medium, who had been written about, who drew a certain amount of critical approval, then the medium was given credibility within art. For a younger generation, clearly there was some benefit to be had from that, because they could then head straight into redefining and extending it.

*At what point did these questions begin to affect your practice?*

In 1972. Starting with a work like *60 Seconds of Light* in 1970, probably the first piece I made which was deliberately seeking to examine the nuts and bolts of the medium itself, I then spent a couple of years really going through all the physical possibilities that photography seemed to offer. Obviously its not something that you would want to go on and on doing. Initially, the reason for doing it was to discover something for myself and to make a point more generally about the lack of any absolutism within the medium as a representative vehicle. I was trying to make that point outwardly, and inwardly I was making a discovery for myself about the limits of photography and the way it performed. Clearly, as a guiding motive, that has to be finite. I actually seem to remember not really knowing what to do next and I don't think I made any work for about six months. I decided instead to read some philosophy, which I'd never really done before. I read a certain amount at art school, at St Martins, because it was recommended and referred to in the course I was on, but nevertheless I wasn't very well informed about the subject, and I felt there were so many philosophical references within contemporary art at the time that I needed this information if only to address the work of other artists that interested me. I used to get up very early every morning and read till about lunchtime. I found that was a very good time to absorb ideas. Out of that period of reading I was able to determine a way to 'go on' and the way I decided on was not to continue to look into how photographs were produced, but into how they were used, the way they were presented, the way they related to text, the way they would present information quite differently according to a variety of choices that the producer could make.

*Did you have any affinity with what Stezaker and Burgin were doing with found photographic images? Around 1973 there was a renewed expansion of the languages of photography, a sense that not only could the artist-as-photographer produce work solely within the confines of the studio, but also appropriate extant photographs and work from those, either rephotographing them or montaging them.*

For me that wasn't something of interest, and maybe one of the reasons it wasn't interesting was that I always had a prescription for a kind of image that needed to be brought into being, that was unlikely to have a prior existence. If I set certain tasks that an image should perform, then the most efficient way of providing that image would be to construct it myself. Maybe I just found it more interesting in the end, anyway, to originate my own material, rather than to redeploy existing images. John had a very particular interest in collage and still does, and Victor Burgin has also written about its importance in twentieth century art.

*In 1972 you began to employ narration. There is a recognition that images could also tell stories, and that these stories were not only to be constructed according to the amount of information that you might locate in the image but through the use of text as well. This does tie in quite closely with what both Stezaker and Burgin were doing, even if the stories they were hoping to tell were quite different from the stories that you were telling. How do you see this?*

Just to clear up this question about my relationship to other artists using photography, I've always had my own needs for working in the way I do and for the changes I've made in my work. They're not really coming from the direct influence of other people who I think of as being colleagues or contemporaries who work in the same medium. I have an interest in what other people are doing, but that's rather different from it being an essential influence. There might be a degree of simultaneity in deciding to shift one's work in a certain way, but I would simply put that down to the effect of exposure to a shared pool of information at any one point in time. To answer your question about narration: it's something I always have an uneasy relation to because in my own work there is no 'true' narrative, there is no narrative development, there is actually only an implied narrative and the articulation is of a single moment in time. It may offer itself to be construed from different positions. but nevertheless what's being addressed is only a single moment. In that sense, there is not truly a narrative space.

*But you establish a narrative space of inclusion. For instance in* She Observed Her Reflection in the Glass *(1976) by setting a female figure in an interior who's smoking and looking forlornly into the distance, then you establish some narrative relation.*

Narrative suggestion, I would say. Just as importantly, what is introduced is an element of fiction. What characterises all the initial work I did with photography is its 'factuality'. It's not just that the images are unadorned and wanting to reveal themselves to you. Part of what is revealed is the image's causal origin and the way it is now constituted as a photograph. So it contains both its own history and its present reality as a set of available facts. It does seem to me that putting a woman with a cigarette and a rather melancholic gaze in an interior is very different from setting up a darkroom clock or a film-box or myself photographing in order to be photographed. The introduction of staging to allow a kind of fiction, something that would never exist in this particular form if I hadn't coaxed it into being, this is something rather different.

*This is a very different kind of staging to the staging that was more common in a lot of photographic based conceptual work from the period. If you think of some of the work that Bruce Nauman did in the late sixties and early seventies, where he staged various events or banal acts in the studio, which he then photographed himself or he had colleagues photograph, there was no attempt at fictualisation. These were kind of 'least events', the photographer might then record and represent it a first- order way. In this respect the turning to photography in the studio was important motor really in the development of photography within conceptual art. But the kind of work that you were doing by 1976 had moved away from that performative tradition and was looking to questions of sexuality and the conventions of mainstream film. How did you reach the point where questions of gender began to inform your work?*

The gender issue is, for me, an extension of a larger concern about the way photography performs as a representational medium. Obviously one of the ways in which we make use of the photograph as a viewer is highly voyeuristic, it's a way of accessing intimate, private, exotic, violent, situations in a very covert and secure kind of way. It interests me that we have this inclination towards those kinds of images, and it interests me that photography offers itself to be used in this way. This links to the separation I was making between fictionality and factuality. I was trying to equate a distinction between fact and fiction with a distinction between the physicality of the medium and the psychology of it. The representation of gender, for example, or the representation of violence, or the representation of the exotic, seems to me to engage the latent psychology of the medium, the psychology of the percipient and of the person who makes the photograph. The idea of working in a more loaded kind of way is also motivated by a desire to build on from the austere limits of the legacy of minimalism and early conceptual art that restricted work with photography to a visually impoverished zone. I would argue that what I do now and what I did when I first started working with photography in a rather self conscious way, is just as analytically driven and as rigorously constructed. The difference is that it also seeks to give you something pleasurable, it seeks to feed your desire for an image which is highly associative. This might be nostalgic, sentimental, or romantic, all the kinds of qualities that would have been anathema in a period when the rigour and precision of language was treated like a Holy Grail.

*Did you feel that the rigour and the political idealism and the collective enterprise of conceptual art was dead by 1973?*

No, what I thought was that it could go hand in hand with some other imperatives. I don't think it was dead, which is why I'm saying I believe what I do now is just as analytical and rigorous in its structure as any other work I've done with photography but that it allows itself another dimension. The analytical and critical demands of conceptual art have been redirected to a different set of subjects.

*So you don't see yourself as trying to exit conceptual art through embracing popular culture and narrative film?*

I don't see myself as having exited conceptual art in the sense that the analytical demands of conceptual art for me were an appealing facet of that period that are retained in my practice. What I'm doing is simply acknowledging and allowing a space for a set of other interests. My own interest in the visual embraces cinema and extends in photography to advertising, fashion etc. If I go and see a film, I'm not just watching the edits and the way the whole film is assembled from beginning to end, I'm not just looking at the lighting or the camera work. I might be aware of those things but I also have to confess to being absorbed in the narrative and deriving pleasure from that. It's the same with reading. I find it very difficult to read something that I consider to be badly written, but if I read something I consider to be well written, where I have pleasure reading the construction of sentences themselves, I'm even more delighted when that form of writing produces an interesting narrative. I'm striving towards a similar duality. On the one hand one might be engaged by the means of construction of this work, and engaged by its degree of reflexivity, but equally one might be engaged by its other properties. Now those other properties, which are probably more difficult to quantify, may well be described as being somewhat erotic, or exotic, or romantic or whatever, and I'm interested in the mix. I think this is why I was resisting the idea of having abandoned, or moved away from, the programme of conceptual art because I think that kind of self consciousness, the awareness of the functioning of language itself, can be put to good use within the larger narrative context of popular culture.

*So, are you saying that the use of photography within conceptual art allowed you to make connection with these forms?*

Not just that, but also the peculiar nature of photography which is unlike painting, for example. If we think of painting, we think of pictures as exhibited in a gallery, or possibly of home decorating, whereas a medium like photography is interesting because it's got so many different contexts of use, so many different purposes. Someone who specialises in making hospital X rays is very different from someone who is employed to do reportage by a national newspaper, who in turn is very different from a photographer like Ansell Adams, who is very different from Victor Burgin, and so on. We might also include architectural photography and fashion photography. Once you engage with the medium then doors open to all these other areas of use and it's not surprising to me that one might be led towards some of those other applications and refer to them and draw on them as an artist. Dealing with questions of gender I would not be hard pressed to refer to Helmut Newton, which neatly leads us back again to your earlier question about sexuality. My position in the seventies, was quite ambivalent. On the one hand I was in sympathy with a lot of feminist writing, and feminist thinking. On the other hand, I acknowledged my own erotic impulse, where it was being driven by images of women and it seemed to me that that couldn't be denied, and somehow one had to articulate both those positions. One had to say that one was aware of an exploitative use of the camera towards the body, but at the same time one acknowledged the visual pleasure to be derived from erotic imagery. I was seeking to express both views, and probably still am. Interestingly I talked about this, albeit much later than the period that you are talking about, when I made an exhibition at the ICA in London in 1984. In the catalogue for that exhibition there's an exchange of letters between myself and

Michael Newman and in answering one of his letters about the issue of the representation of women, I actually say something which criticises a feminist position when it seems to overlap with the prudish moralising of somebody like Mary Whitehouse. Michael suggested that it would be prudent to edit out that particular part of my letter, and indeed that's what he did. Subsequently there has been a reaction against an over- dogmatic, over-moralising position on sexuality and censorship among feminists themselves, and recently there has been an outpouring of womens' erotic literature. I feel somewhat heartened by that move. But it's a difficult territory to inhabit, and I'm all too well aware that it draws a lot of criticism.

*Would you say that you were embracing the pleasures of a voyeur then?*

In part, yes. I can't see voyeurism as easily separable from photography. But it's a critical embrace.

*Do you think this is what artists using photography during this period of conceptual art eventually learnt to deal with?*

Well it's impossible to speak for everybody. I certainly think there are other artists using photography who include that awareness in their practice. That's obviously true of some of Victor Burgin's and Jeff Wall's work.

*It's interesting that you should pick out those two figures because both Burgin and Jeff Wall produced self-images in the early, mid 1970's, you think of the Jeff Wall piece that he did in the studio.*

You might then go on and say, if voyeurism is inherent within the use of photography so is narcissism. The use of self portraiture or the use of the portrait of oneself as made by somebody else is something very common within photography. It's a usage to which the medium is frequently put, and artists certainly have some history of incorporating themselves in their own photographic work. In fact of course, neither myself nor Victor Burgin, nor Jeff Wall, even though all three of us have at one time or another incorporated ourselves within our own images, have done so with any regularity. With Jeff I immediately think of just two works. With Vic I think of one work in particular.

*The photograph of himself in the mirror in the toilet.*

In the women's toilets, yes, and with Jeff Wall there is a double self portrait where he is standing behind himself, sitting in a chair, and there's *Picture For Women*, in which he is also included. There might be something else, but they are the two pieces that spring to mind. In those cases and certainly in my case, it's been a question of logical necessity that there should be an incorporation of the artist in the work. I think that is very different from the position of someone who is more indulgently narcissistic in their art, or from Cindy Sherman's use of herself where there's a fundamental requirement that she should be the constant feature in all her pictures.

*What do you actually think in general terms of the period we have been talking about 1966-1976? How do you feel about it in retrospect? How much of this conversation is you attempting to deal with things that you have barely thought about for a long time? You have talked about the fact that in your current work, in certain respects its no different from the work you were doing during that period, but is this strictly true?*

I'm not going around self-consciously thinking that what I do now is based upon what I did in the sixties and seventies.

I'm not referring back to particular works or a particular position. I'm thinking rather more presently than that, but at the same time, I know very well that my current stance is highly formed by that period. I was in my early twenties in the late sixties when I felt I knew for the first time what I was trying to do as an artist. In 1966 I remember perfectly clearly becoming aware of what I thought I was up to and what I wanted to do. It was a very particular awareness. All the things that had a bearing on me in that period of my life have a long echo and they are very persistent. But of course there are important distinctions.

*The biggest difference is that in the late sixties and early seventies, photography was institutionally weak, now its central to the new museum. Video, photography, and the new digital technologies are very much part of what I would describe as a kind of dominant, critical Post-Modernist paradigm. For instance, when you read, what Burgin and Stezaker had to say on photography and on the institutionalisation of the traditional hierarchy of media in the early seventies, now it actually seems almost quaint. How do you perceive those changes?*

I felt that the decision to work with photography needed to be explained and asserted. It's not that I was trying to convince anybody else to do this, but I felt it was a very particular and important thing to be doing, and it was a position that needed to be articulated. That's still the case, although the way I would now present it and explain it would be different because my own interests and my own working methods have changed. But I can't imagine that initial proclamations in favour of using the medium could have been described as being quaint. Doubtless all of us wrote in a way in which we wouldn't do now, but I'm sure what was written was clear and considered.

*Yes but, the market consolidation of photography has made all those earlier debates on the radical and supposedly progressive identity of photography redundant, and in the process made the debates seem quaint or mundane. I know Victor Burgin would be the last to talk these days about the radicality of photography in and of itself. However 25 years ago there was a great deal of art-world idealism attached to its social uses.*

The fact is it would be impossible to assert that position today, because its not just that a younger generation of artists came along fairly rapidly in the seventies to take up the debate about photography, and to begin to explore different ways of using the medium, but now in the nineties it is such a commonplace among the younger generation of British artists, particularly those using a form of autobiography. So to assert the radicality of the medium wouldn't really make a lot of sense. In any case it does seem to me that within that context the medium is not being used in a critical way. Its being very much taken for granted, taken as it is, in a way that is reminiscent of its initial use in the sixties as something casual, informal, except in this case it's become more of a style, something which doesn't beg to be questioned. I think that's also part of a contemporary ethos, a sort of take it or leave it position, a wilful casualness in the way the medium is used. Obviously for myself it would be impossible to do that, its too late, there's too much water under the bridge.

Alexis Hunter

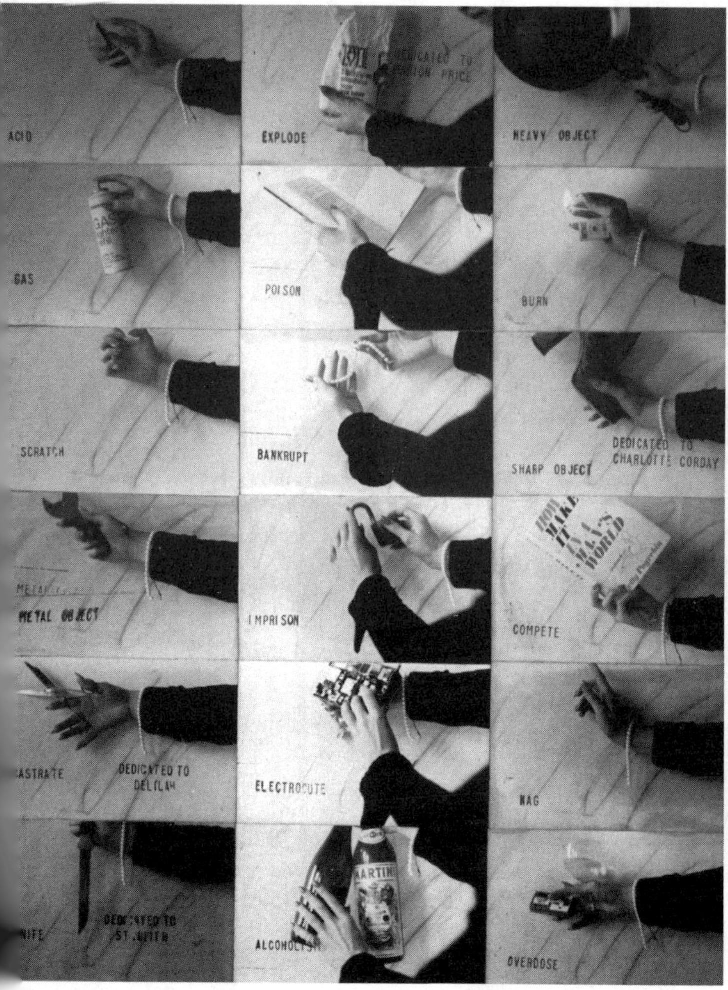


*Sexual Warfare*, 1975

## INTERVIEW WITH ALEXIS HUNTER

*The early self-images* (Voyeurism/Indecisive Action, *1973) present a serial disclosure/dissemblance of the feminine. Did you see yourself as imposing your subjectivity on what appeared to be the gender-neutral objectivity of conceptual art's use of seriality?*

Conceptual art of the early 1970s was not gender-neutral. It was obvious it was a man who was taking the photographs, as he often authored the photograph as a 'reflection' or a 'shadow'. It was also clear during this period that radical work exhibited in an establishment space, like a public gallery, was made by a male artist: the use of seriality showed 'his' interest in showing 'us' the processes of perception, even if the seriality was not about his sexuality or gender. *Voyeurism/Indecisive Action* was one of the sequences taken by a male photographer - as in *Identity Crisis* - and shows even by covering her head, denying her gaze, the subject exposes her body. It therefore contributes to the voyeurism of the viewer despite the fact she is the instigator of the work. Working in commercial animation as a technician I knew seriality could be used subliminally to work on the unconscious.

*In these terms did you see feminism 'filling in' the missing theory of subjectivity in conceptual?*

For feminist artists the 'personal is political' was one of the most important slogans in the 1970s. Being subjective as women in our work was the bravest and most radical thing we could do at the time. This subjectivity became the most hated aspect of our work: myself using my own hands not models', Mary Kelly using her own son's diapers, Susan Hiller photographing her own pregnant belly, Tina Keane making performances based on her relationship to her daughter. There were more links to performance art by men at the time, for instance by Stuart Brisley and Marc Chaimowicz, which were less objective because of the way they used their corporeality. In exposing their vulnerability *as men* these artists were a counterpoint to our more ruthless subjectivity. Even though we were selected to show with conceptual artists this gap between subjectivity and objectivity was obvious, opening up a distinction between 'socio-political' art and conceptual art.

*By the mid-seventies as analytic conceptualism implodes and many artists return to some form of picture-making, the debate on photography, semiotics and mass culture takes on a vanguard role. Cinema, advertising and TV provide the dominant cultural framework; analysis of the image is attached to a post-Situationist critique of commodification and reification. Along with Victor Burgin, John Hilliard and John Stezaker, your work situates the photographic images in this space. What distinguishes your work, though, beyond saying the obvious, that it marks out a politics of sexual difference, is that you actually produce a photography which is pleasurable and emotive in popular cultural terms. In your cinematic-type* Approaches to Fear *series, the burning shoe sequence for example, the effect is* dread*ful and threatening in a way that was considered deeply suspect at the time. This is because in its symbolic de-positioning of the feminine it mobilised the embodied pleasures of popular culture. As such did you feel that you were including another kind of spectator in the work, not just a female spectator, but a non-specialist one?*

One aspect of my popularism was to make images that appealed to the part of the brain that snaps to attention on seeing a fetish - the mother's shoe and fur for instance - and danger - fire, sharp objects, cracks, blood. This part of the brain is not gender-defined, as it processes survival instincts rather than reproductive instincts. The important thing was to get people to look at the work in the first place, those who would be bored by black and white photographs with dense text. It was important to hook them in with violent high-coloured images, as artists did in religious pictures and B-movies. The female viewer could then identify with the hand in the narrative and reach the resolution in the title. I did not believe in preaching to the converted and used all the devices to capture the viewer's attention, even ambiguity and humour.

*To extend this line of questioning, did you see yourself as making alliance with those artists who had been through conceptualism and wanted to work in ways that operated in a wider cultural space?*

John Hilliard's early pieces showing how people mis-read photographs and how editing can completely mis-represent reality made me feel that photography could be used as a device showing alternative meanings, rather than be seen as a 'mirror' of reality. My interest was not in disseminating popular culture for an intellectual audience but using the devices within it to explain feminist theory to a non-art audience. So really my work went in the opposite direction to those artists.

*One of the major lines of continuity between your photography and early conceptual art is of course its staged character. The studio photograph in Bruce Nauman's early work for instance treats the inconsequential or ordinary gesture or activity as the primary unconscious stuff of artistic production. In these terms reportage is not so much denied by the staged nature of the work as attached to the controlled activities of the studio. I am interested in whether you felt your early photographs were operating in a similar kind of way, that is in terms of the idea of the studio as a 'safe' place to structure your activities?*

The photographic image represented a private, intimate space in the memory. Working in the studio made the working process more like a still-life painter setting up, moving objects around within a defined area. *The Approaches to Fear* series were of a photographed performance. I made films on Super 8 as studies for movement timing, because the pace of movement was very important, in order to show the *state of the mind* governing the action of the hands.

*In contrast to this you also took your camera outdoors on 'location', so to speak. These photographs of pub interiors, the street, waste ground, mark out a documentary-type ambition to produce an archive of your immediate surroundings. A number of conceptual artists also used photography for its connection to the textures of everyday life, without wanting their images confused with photojournalism, or do its work. What kind of function did you see your-extra-studio photographs as having?*

My first experiments with serial photography used outside locations and explored the fourth dimension, the different stages of sudden death, and abstract social encounters. When I decided to make work specifically for a female audience, it became more studio-bound and interior, personal and 'artificial'. The first *Approaches to Fear* were reportage: the insect stings, cat scratches, bloody wounds were all real. It was only later I 'made things up'. I think that's why people found them so shocking. They didn't expect a women to use her work as a kind of catharsis. But I didn't *make* things happen: it was ordinary-life in the end. I used natural sunlight for lighting. *Approaches to Fear* used a reportage technique combined with a studio technique.

*Conceptual art in its general forms of presentation was*

*above all a graphic art. Most artists looked to magazines, books and pamphlets as the most efficient means of distribution. You never really pursued this avenue, despite the content of your work. Why was this?*

A very interesting question. My work was considered very populist and dangerous: I was not asked to publish the work in *Screen* magazine or any of the magazines that would have been appropriate. In fact the first magazine cover that used an image was *Artscribe* when James Faure Walker was the editor. *Artscribe* then was almost wholly concerned with formalist painting. My one attempt to infiltrate the womens' glossies stopped short when instead of publishing the work they published a degraded photograph of my face. The most important medium for feminism was the national press. It was the *principles* and the theories of feminism we were trying to get across, not just a puff about our work. It was possibly naive not to concentrate on getting my work printed rather than having controversial exhibitions. I did not make that connection between publishing and art school teaching. There was an academic way of working which was 'politically correct'. The concept and the concept's relationship to the medium used was worked out then processed in a very linear way. My working method has always been far more intuitive so difficult to write about academically. The titles came after the work was made, not before. My interest was in the aesthetics of accident and misrepresentation as an artist and not as an academic. The visual should be used *as* theory not *about* theory.

*In the final analysis what do think was useable in conceptual art for women artists?*

It was the way conceptual art emphasised and utilised the perception of the viewer which was so useful to feminist artists. It was a way of connecting directly to other women without any of the prejudices they might have about aesthetic language. And this is why artists chose distanced, popular mediums such as film, photography and performance. Conceptual art enabled us to find a gap in perception in which to situate our work within popular culture.

David Lamelas

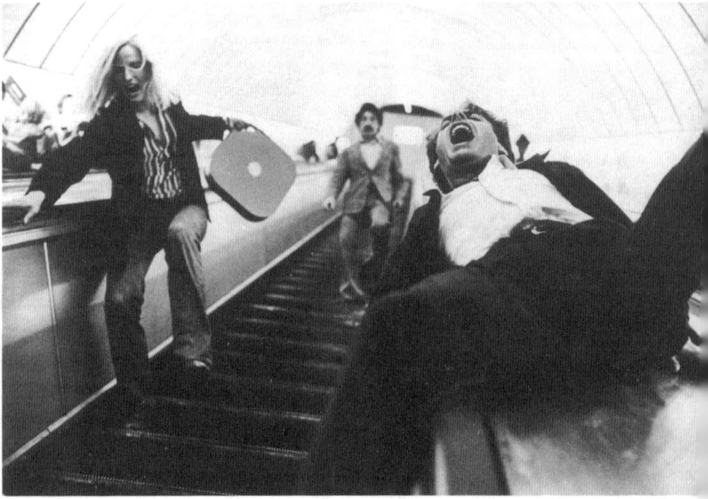

*The Violent Tapes*, 1975

## INTERVIEW WITH DAVID LAMELAS

*You came to England in the late sixties from Argentina, where you were born, and left at the point when conceptual art was in decline. What did you feel you gained from working in England during this period?*

When I moved to London with the British Council scholarship to Saint Martin's School of Art - a few months earlier I had made my piece at the 1968 Venice Biennale, *Newsroom about the Vietnam war* - I had already made my own process of 'dematerialisation'of art; and at St.Martin's I very soon isolated myself from the sculpture department and retreated to the library. This was a much cleaner environment for my research, free of plaster dust. The great thing was that the new generation of British artists was emerging with concerns similar to mine, leaving sculpture behind in favour of a less object-oriented work, and moving to the use of other media: in my case, film and photography. I immediately connected with this new group of artists and we had many meetings on these topics, centred around the house of Barry Flanagan, one of my instructors at St. Martin's; and the house of John Latham. We met every Thursday night for a few months. This was particularly useful to me for understanding my new situation, their work and concerns, and also helped to establish the direction of my work in the new London art community. London was extremely fruitful for my work. I adapted to the new culture, wanting to learn the English language. So that helped me to think of my work as a 'deconstruction', and then a 'construction', like a language. First you deconstruct, word by word, and then you put the words together and create a whole new meaning.

*Conceptual art's collective identity was very much built on the idea of it as an international phenomenon, that is, something that resisted the art market's economic interests in nationalising art. Were you particularly conscious of your own national identity in your contribution to the London art community of the time?*

So-called 'conceptual art' was indeed an international phenomenon. Use of this term was a way of grouping together various artists with similar concerns, from all over the world. I was not particularly conscious of my own national identity. Because of my youth I was not set in my ways and I tried to become as English as possible. The discovery of the current youth culture - David Bowie, Brian Eno, the Roundhouse, Portobello Road, etc. - made me feel just like another young Londoner.

*Conceptual art soon divided itself ideologically between those who saw the analytic work on the propositional status of art as primary (Joseph Kosuth and Art & Language) and those who saw the period more loosely as an opportunity to nominate different contents and experiences for art as part of the wider questioning of the category of 'art'. Photography obviously played a large part in the latter. Did you feel more sympathy with the latter than the former?*

The latter of course, though I find rather simplistic the separation between those who saw the anaylitic work on the propositions of art as primary and those who saw the period as part of the wider questioning of the category 'art'. In my case, so-called 'conceptual art' was a way of looking at art in all its dimensions and analytically expanding this analysis to the world outside the art world.

*The critique of Modernism in analytic conceptualism is based on what is perceived as the false antithesis between the literary and the visual (inherited from the Enlightenment's quest for a strong, secular notion of art's autonomy), and therefore of art's relationship to time and space. For Modernism what distinguished literature from painting was its temporality. The value of painting lay in its instantaneous impression on the senses, all else - all literary and allegorical content that is - was held to be extraneous and distracting. Conceptual art's textuality and emphasis on the extended apprehension of the art-work through time was clearly a disruption of this. Did you see your own work on the 'time' of photographic representation as engaging in this debate?*

Time-representation was at the core of my interests, so I was certainly engaging in these debates. My work had always functioned in relationship to time. As early as 1966 my installation at the Di Tella Institute in Buenos Aires *Connection of Three Spaces* was placed in three separate spaces. That means that the complete work was achieved by the mental accumulation of the three separate segments. This relationship to time was also found in my work *Situation of Time,* an installation with 17 television sets switched to a blank channel for the eight hours duration of the gallery hours, and in the Venice Biennale installation about the Vietnam war. The latter piece existed daily during visiting hours, for the duration of the Biennale.

*To develop this line of questioning. Was your use of photography at the time directed against the Modernist artistic subject and spectator?*

I have always been committed to studying the relationship between visual perception and thought, so I use photography not like a Modernist photographer but in a wider use of the medium to represent my thoughts about art, reading, listening, memory, entertainment, information, etc. I wanted a conceptual connection between the image and the spectator, to analyse the syntax of the image.

*The early work (*Brussels, *1969,* Dusseldorf, *1969) opens the 'time' of the perception of the photograph to a minimalist seriality. A number of other photographers such as Douglas Huebler and Robert Barry (after Ed Ruscha and Andy Warhol) were doing this. What is noticeable about your work is not just the fact that it promotes a critique of authorship but that it is reporting on the appearance of the city. I say this because with the use of the photographic document in early conceptual art there is a turn once again in art to the urban vernacular. There is a kind of nomination of the social relations implied by certain buildings and architectural settings as sociologically interesting. Did this concern you?*

My choice of the photographic medium was a purely intellectual one. First came the idea, and then a list of media to represent it best. Then after much deliberation the medium was chosen. The question of social relations did concern me at the time. Each location chosen because of its urban function. For example, the film and photo installation *Gente di Milano* representing an architectural landmark in Milan focused on the immediate surroundings of the gallery where the work was to be shown. I saw it as a site-specific project. In the same way, I would choose a person to be photographed in my work by connecting them to the cultural, political or sociological reference to the city they live in. For example, the French writer Marguerite Duras was seen as representative of Parisian intellectuality.

*The early photographs could be best described as a laying-bare of the canonic contents and aesthetic hierachies of art-photography (for instance the 'decisive moment'). But in 1974-75 there is a conspicuous change of emphasis. You start to use cinematic mis en scene and narrative in your photographs, as if you were to reverse the very terms of your enquiry. The 'time' of perception of the art-work is now conventionally a matter of diegetic flow from one frame to the next, as in* The Violent Tapes *(1975). Could you talk about these developments.*

The process of photo-manipulation in popular culture became an interest of mine in the early 70s. London was a rich source of popular media at the time, so I started paying attention to film advertising and film stills. I remember going around the West End theatres for entire afternoons from cinema lobby to cinema lobby studying the movie stills presented to attract the public. A whole language, a syntax of meaning, a transposition from a motion picture to one single still would, hopefully, represent the concept of the whole movie. My piece called *Film Script,* a 10-minute film plus three slide projectors showing 210 slides, is an analysis of how this process of manipulation is achieved. In another, *Rock Star (Character Appropriation),* I disguised myself as a rock star, analysing the thin line between photography, fact and fiction. So in this particular case a staged photograph pretended to be a journalist's picture and so was a cross-over between the different types of photography: studio photography - fiction - journalism - documentary.

*Entitling the sequence* The Violent Tapes *and depicting what is seen to be a life-threatening chase, you appear to enact a Faustian pact with the symbolic violence of mass culture itself. Would this be true?*

*The Violent Tapes* of 1975 is a result of this evolving process. For several months I studied film books in London bookshops, analysing movie stills one by one. The difference between documentary violence and fictional violence was the first idea of this piece. I developed a literary film synopsis that I translated later as a typical movie chase of the time. Violence has been purposely glamourised in this series of photos to depict the way that the entertainment industry communicates violence, beautiful people, interesting surroundings and camera angles, entangled in a series of visual signs to erode the 'real' violence. The doom of death and censorship is impending off-frame in this series of black and white photographs.

*In your film* The Desert People *(1974) you set up an impossible narrative. A group of people are interviewed about their experiences visiting a tribe of North America native Indians, yet at the end of the film the car in which they are travelling to the reservation crashes over a precipice and they are all killed (presumably).* The Violent Tapes *is a fictive chase involving the pursuit of a non-existent film tape. The earlier film* To Pour Milk into a Glass *(1973) shows an event - milk being poured into a glass - being repeated as a process of destruction. The early photographs record what are ostensibly non-events, events without any would-be artistic significance. Whether you are employing the reflexive strategies of 'structuralist' critique or deconstructing film narrative as reported truth, there seems to be a sense in which the the event in perception hasn't 'happened' or is radically unstable. The event seems to be produced through its mediation. Is this an accurate description?*

Yes. In other words the 'event' takes place elsewhere, in the viewer's mind through a process of reflection on what happens within and outside the frame. The event is irrelevant, usually reduced to the concept itself, to a level of abstraction, seemingly a non-existent study. I tend to provide clues as to the possible event, for the visual construction of the concept or idea of the piece, through an accumulation of visual signs; in fact, the event is constructed by the viewer through this almost mathematical multiplication of symbols, and it is about the process of memory and reflection. One example is my piece *To Pour Milk into a Glass*, a 16 mm film and eight photographs, produced in London in 1972. In this work I make a direct reference between the content of the frame -

the container of information - and what is photographed, a glass - the container of liquid. There are here eight different variations of pouring milk around and inside the container, until the last frame where the glass is shattered. The milk is then poured over the glass fragments, uncontained but *contained* within the frame of the film and photographs.

*What kind of political and cultural transformation did you feel your work was contributing to in the late sixties and early seventies?*

Hopefully, my work was contributing to a process of change in art, taking it beyond the conventional art forms and art systems and giving it a new function in society. My work's aims were always to disrupt the established order of the previous avant-garde, including that of my own work.

John Stezaker

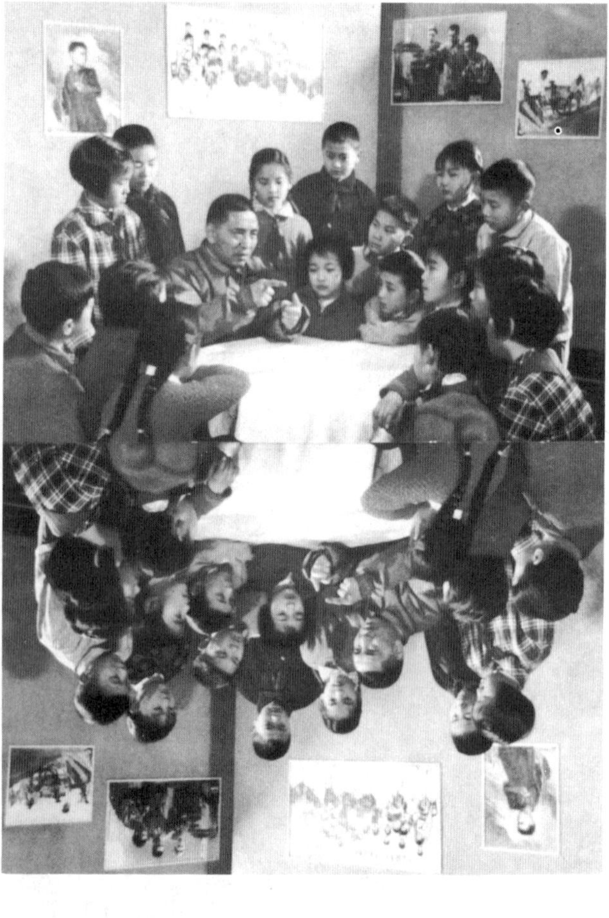

*I (Bourgeois Individualism)*, 1975

## INTERVIEW WITH JOHN STEZAKER

*In your writing from the early seventies you critiqued the a priori identity of the artwork. The artwork, was you argued, logically and ideologically prior to any pre-given essence and unity of art. In what way was this identifiable with the programme of analytical conceptual art?*

Did I identify with the programme? Well I don't know quite what the programme was, but I assumed that most of it came out of thinking about Duchamp. I was quite interested in making connection at that time between, what one might call, the conceptual framework of Duchampian art and a certain area of philosophical thinking. From my point of view, I'm not sure exactly how I connected with conceptualism. I know what I felt was problematic about it, yet I felt conceptualism was also a liberation from particular habits and conventions. In particular it bought in the found object, found image and that to me was of great importance. What I found was problematic about conceptualism was the self-referential sense in which it was complicit with an idea of aesthetic autonomy, and that's what I was critiquing. The idea of aesthetic autonomy was pushed to the point of philosophical absurdity by me. For example the works I did for the 'New Art Show' at the Hayward Gallery in 1972 were deliberately self referential to the point of paradox. So they were conceived a little bit like the idea of a germ, infiltrating by seeming to go along with the analytical mode whilst actually representing the paradoxes that underlay them. That wasn't enough eventually, it just turned into a critique upon critique. In fact the self-enclosure of art seemed to reach its extreme with conceptual art, but to me what conceptual art represented above all else was a realisation that the Modernist programme had reached a dead end.

*What was your response to Joseph Kosuth's 'Art after*

*Philosophy' when he first published it in 1969?*

Well, I suppose it completely embodied everything that I felt was wrong with analytic conceptual art, in the sense that he was using dubious philosophical sources to establish the idea of the aesthetic autonomy of the art work. His work actually embodied a point of connection between a self-referential Modernism and a self-cancelling kind of conceptualism, reaching the same zero point that Roland Barthes talked about with regard to Modernist literature in *Writing Degree Zero* - the playing out of end-games I think Barthes calls them, the Hamlet-complex of literary form. I felt we had reached a point of artistic suicide through conceptualism. It was obviously a cul-de-sac. Yet it had these liberating qualities that allowed a completely different way of working, in particular the idea of finding things. This was the key thing for me, because it gave a justification to the practice of collecting images. In this sense it allowed me space to use strategies that came from outside the field of art, for instance Situationism, which was again very liberating. Other artists such as Vic Burgin was confronting a similar kind of cul-de-sac in a similar kind of way and finding a similar route out at first.

*What did you make of Kosuth's reading of Duchamp's, because 'Art After Philosophy' was predicated upon Duchamp's 'ready-made' as the originary point of modern practice?*

It's a long time since I read the Kosuth piece, but the appropriation of Duchamp was rather unfortunate at that time. The problem with conceptualism is that it took Duchamp's to be some sort of analytical philosopher in a way in which he clearly wasn't. And I don't think he much approved, from what I gather, of the activities of conceptual art or at least the image that they promoted of him. To me he is a much more pathological figure; and one whose involvement in a whole variety of things, for instance sexuality, I identify with very strongly. I don't think he was a conceptual game player in the way that he has been represented as being. My feeling about his activities were that, yes he was in a sense the best aspect of conceptualism in that his work was a meditation on what it is to produce an artifact in a world of artifacts, or an image in a world of images. The ready-made for Duchamp was a point of interruption in the flow of images. This was a bit like a Situationist intervention. And I think he is closer to Situationism in many ways than to conceptual art. I think he was a much more political figure than he even allowed himself to believe. I like the way he describes his ready-mades, as arrests, sometimes more pessimistically as delays. I think he felt that somehow the media-machine was a central mythologising force within the culture and the artists duty was in some ways to create a series of stoppages, arrests of that perpetual flow.

*What was at stake for early conceptual art in the late sixties and seventies was the renewed intellectual status of the artist and this clearly preoccupies you in your early writing on intentionality, for example. How did you see the intellectual function of the artist at the time?*

This is very difficult, because of course I'm now having to try and project myself back and think how I thought at that time. I know how I'd answer the question now. At the time I probably felt along with everyone else who was involved that this was a way of recovering something of the intellectual status of the artist. Art had reached a kind of rather abysmal intellectual status in the sixties and I suppose the image of the artist as the kind of impassioned and emotional anti-intellectual is something we all know about in art schools from this period. I was brought up at that time with a desire to destroy one's elders, as one would expect. I don't know whether that's a sufficient answer, but yes, at the time I felt this was important, but now I'm not so sure.

*But how did you want to differentiate yourself for instance, from Art & Language's project at that particular time?*

As I said before, they seemed to represent for me a kind of cul-de-sac, and there didn't seem any way out of this position. It seemed as though the Modernist enterprise in so many different areas, whether it was politics or art, was reaching a point of crisis. I think that the '68 Paris riots were one such response, which gave birth to a whole variety of different ideals in politics and in art. Certainly I felt that there had to be a way out of the crisis and that the way out for me was in some ways to relocate where one was coming from as an artist. At the time English Abstract Expressionist art dominated and separated the realm of art from the realm of popular culture. This was very obviously a reaction against the previous generation of Pop artists, and minimalism was much the same; conceptualism just seemed to complete that separation.

*But at the same time, along with Art & Language you were involved in the construction of what you saw as a different kind of spectator. That is your early work followed Wittgenstein's critique of the idea of the production of meaning as an image coming before one's mind rather than as a process of rule following.*

You mean the late Wittgenstein. Yes, I was certainly very influenced by Wittgenstein. This was partially the reason I was engaged in the kind of textual practices I was in the late sixties and early seventies. In other words the use of text came out of reading Wittgenstein; and I suppose that idea of meaning as use was a liberating idea. It did help art escape some of its constraints, especially media constraints, and enabled art to insert itself into the world in ways that hadn't previously been allowed for.

*Photography has played a large part in your work since 1969, and as with Joseph Kosuth, in the early work you use photography to explore relations of identity and non-identity between photography and its objects, for example your photographic wall pieces. In one a piece a camera in a fixed position takes a photograph of a white wall, the photograph is placed on the wall and then another photograph is taken. This is repeated until the field of view of the camera is filled. Now this work would seem to use photography to ask what constituted an 'art event' and the conditions of photographic truth. Would this be a fair estimation of what you were trying to do in your early work?*

It's very difficult to think back that far, what I was doing in those works, it's 30 years, a long, long time ago, but I think it was something to do with the feeling that the world existed in a kind of doubling. All the work of that time involved a sort of doubling, there was the world of the everyday and there was the world of the represented, the media world, and there's a sense of the whole of our experiential worlds becoming bifocated between image and reality. And in some ways I wanted to create short circuits and points of contact between their disparities. That example you gave is a classic example of the various infinite regresses I attempted to set into motion, which in one way or another seemed to me to reveal something about a kind of giddiness in the relationship between the real and the represented, a sense of a void emerging within it.

*This goes back to this question of the conceptual art's ideal spectator. Did the demands placed on the spectator to think through the processes intellectually involved in looking at a work like that, carry the day for you?*

At the time I was reading a lot of Borges and I was very interested in the idea of infinity. I suppose I felt the culture we were entering into in the post war period, a culture of an infinity of images, a labyrinthian culture - was better revealed by that point at which the everyday world yields to its illusion, its representation, than through some Piranesian kind of evocation of the sublime. The work was still certainly quite tactile and bodily. Whether it demanded that much of the spectator I'm not sure. Perhaps the slightly later work where I was beginning to manipulate certain intellectual paradoxes, where I came closest to the form of analytic conceptualism. I tried to impose the paradoxes that emerge out of Göedel upon language itself. I was certainly demanding a great deal from the spectators in that way - I admit that. A lot of it seems very esoteric. It was just a way of coming to terms myself with what I felt was the essential idea of the work that I had been doing previously, trying to refine it down. It was a reductive process, one which I could only say I escaped through the use of paradox really. I felt there was a sort of transcendent element in that use of paradox.

*So what kind of status did the image have for you in the late sixties and early seventies?*

When I started at the Slade in 1967 I was, you might say, a kind of rather late Pop artist. I was using collages as a way of generating images to create paintings, but I became increasingly dissatisfied with the idea of just the process of enlarging images up into paintings, it seemed somehow wrong. So photography for a while then became a kind of object of interest but the work rather than actually doing what I had originally intended, was broken by this interlude of conceptualism in which I spent most of the time interrogating the new medium that I was approaching: black and white photography. I was using photography in a very simple way, just because that was virtually all I had available to me within the limits of a very simple camera apparatus.

*For most conceptual artists using photography at the time the idea of using photography badly was attractive, in order that the photographic image could be seen to be distancing itself from professional art photography and the documentary tradition.*

That's true, yes.

*Were you conscious of those forms of distancing?*

Yes, and when I think about the images I was producing at that time they are involved with mirroring devices, devices which were to do with a kind of estrangement of the photographic image in a fairly classic formless way. I remember John Hilliard's work at that time was in much the same sort of vein. A lot of us at that time, were beginning to look at photography in a metaphysical sense, what it is as an object, how it related to the world around us. I think for example of Vic Burgin's *Photo Path* which is one of the most beautiful realisations of that very simple idea. I think there was something very Cubistic about that first approach to photography by artists in the late sixties. We almost seemed to go back to some of the concerns that Picasso was involved in at the very beginning of the century, the idea of incising space through illusion, representation, or looking at that very simple interconnection between image and reality and the point at which they can become confused. I was actually even more impressed by Juan Gris's work in this respect. He made this a special point of meditation in his work, that falling away of the world into the otherness of the image. We clung very closely to that surface, like the Cubists did. The way this led into semiology is very interesting too, because Gris's work is a kind of semiology, a mixing of different kinds of representation, seeing the way that they abut with one another. This was a way of probing the seamlessness of the represented world, of the world as already represented, trying to find fissures within that.

*The represented world of early Modernism, you mention Gris but also Braque and Picasso, was grounded to a large extent in domestic interiors. The basic semantic units of those early works were tables, walls, doors, and clearly in your early work there's still a strong conventional attachment to those simple bits of everyday reality. I don't know whether you acknowledged this at the time.*

No, I wasn't thinking about Cubism then, I started really seriously looking at Cubism much, much later. About 1978 I really started getting very interested in Cubism, well Cubist collage in particular. What Cubism was saying by arranging found tickets, bits and pieces of newspaper and all the rest of it onto a flat surface and then using drawing and paint and other ways of incising that space, was "the world is in our face, it's absolutely frontal and the creation of depth has got to occur against that surface". Henceforth we cannot imagine a world as an empty canvas on which we impose our vision. The empty canvas is full of images, full of things, bits and pieces of the everyday world, and we have to struggle to create space within that depth, but that depth is no longer something we can imagine as a horizontal projection as perhaps any painter before Cézanne might, now it is a kind of vertical dimension, it is that gulf between the real and the represented, between us and the world, that's where depth is felt. I don't think Cubism was about flatness, it was about achieving depth. I go along with what Merleau-Ponty said about Cézanne on that. That is, depth isn't an automatic property of the laws of perspective, it's something that has to be fought for because depth has to be achieved in a surface, and one has to feel the gulf between the surface of real and a space that opens up within that. I'd call that the vertical, depth in a literal sense.

*In 1973,'74 or thereabouts, a fundamental change takes place in your work, you begin to open up a distance from analytic conceptualism through a thorough going critique of the avant-garde; and your central argument is that the self-reflexivity of conceptual art and the avant-garde generally fears and rejects the shared meanings of the social world. So called freedom from conventionality and dominant ideology transforms itself into a rejection of a common and popular culture. Your interest in photography now becomes a concern with social ideology of the image and mass communication. Now this of course is part of a wider shift in the culture, could you talk about this change in your work.*

Yes, the early seventies was a period of political extremes and of political discovery for my generation. We were journeying between Maoism and Situationism and a variety of extreme positions. Situationism in the end left the biggest imprint on my thinking though I had no connections with the actual political movement and in fact I only read *Societé du Spectacle* in 1970 which is a couple of years after it was published. But Maoism had an equally important impact on a number of people including myself at that time. The promise of an absolute abolition of capitalism, of capital, was a very utopian idea, it all seemed quite possible then, and of course we only got a very partial picture of, to say the very least, of what was going at that time, and I still feel deeply ashamed at any kind of interest in it but it's an interesting paradox. Conceptual art had given one the possibility to begin to use strategies that didn't belong to the tradition of art, so combined with Situationism there was a very potent sense that something else could be done, or could begin to work in a different way. At the time I thought of myself working as a kind of cultural strategist intervening. I did a show in Paris and showed the whole of my work on the outside of the gallery using recognisably Situationist techniques. At the time the key element was the combination between the image and caption which was a form that nobody seemed to have used in anything outside advertising or propaganda and this seemed a very interesting device to be used. A number of artists during this period started working with images and text combined. However, I don't know whether through some kind of perversity I was never quite happy with any of the stuff that I did along those lines until the captions themselves started to become reflections on themselves in a rather peculiar way and it became very introverted again, almost Wittgensteinian. The captions started to break up into ambiguities, and that wasn't something that I planned, it was just the way the work seemed to go and led eventually to dropping captions altogether. There seemed to be no way of using them. I was very taken with Walter Benjamin's idea at the time that photographers were only partially responsible for their images because they just supplied images which could be captioned in any way they liked, so they could be read in any way they liked, so to appropriate one's own captions was to actually take charge of that seemed a kind of radical thing to do. But equally my feeling was also that the caption did something else, which was that it annihilated the image or annulled it at least, as a sort of instrument of cognition. By reducing the image to one reading in one was actually depleting it and one was going along with the general flow of communications, rather than representing a genuine Situationist intervention, it was actually just more of the same channelled communication and counter communication, so the stage after that was a rejection of captions. And that's where I really count my work as beginning, I see everything we have been talking about up to now as really juvenile, or at least a sort of working through a lot of things before I reached the starting point of what I've been doing since.

*So would you say that you felt at this point a confidence in using photography in a way that hitherto you hadn't felt?*

Well, by this time I wasn't using my own photographs any more, I was using others, found images. Though having said that, I can't remember a time when I haven't been collecting images. It's just that the status of that process of collecting has just gone through various phases in my life, at one point they were simply stuff that I collected in preparation for paintings, at other times it was just another activity that seemed to go on in parallel with the photo work that I was doing. By the mid-seventies the actual process of collecting started to take on a significance which I could acknowledge in the main body of my work. I saw myself as looking across a field of images and trying to find connections, mostly through the use of captions, sometimes though by diagrammatic activities like forms of wall display in order to suggest a didactic reading. Although you'd find if you did try and read it in any linear way, you'd find yourself rebounded around the work. In this sense I couldn't completely relinquish that formalist sense of self-containment. And I think for good reason. It was this probably that took me away from captions in the end, made captions actually impossible to use, because I wanted to dwell on the image and language was yet another way of evading the image. However pictorial the imagery I employed, it was reduced, dissimulated in a sense within the process of presentation.

*This dwelling on the image certainly distinguished your work at the time from Victor Burgin's.*

Yes, perhaps.

*You were also keen to distance yourself from a politicised semiotic practice. I take it that you were sceptical of Burgin's incipient deconstructionism when you said that you weren't interested in any kind of counter-cultural "authentic speech". Could you talk a bit more about this dwelling on the image?*

The removal of captions, the absorption into the image itself, and an acknowledgement of the essential ambiguity of the image, was very important to me. Vic was very much more interested in the idea of a semiological reading. I felt, however interesting that was, the semiological reading was always under the gaze of disenchantment, it was always dissimulative. The suggestions and nuances of an image would be teased out, pinned down, reduced to a series of connotations and denotations, and all the rest of it, and what was left, was nothing. I was much more interested in the opposite vantage point, I wanted to simulate as opposed to dissimulate, I wanted to enchant rather than disenchant. That sounds like a more recent speech, but in a way it was partly because I became interested in Jung about that time. I was actually much more interested in the idea that in consumer culture there was a kind of reservoir of the collective unconscious at work. I referred to it in texts at the time as the collectivised unconscious as a sort of parody of that. But in a way I was interested in how the archetypal manifested itself through the stereotypes of the image culture that we live in and that was quite different. It made the image irreducible in a strange way. And this is where this absorption in the image came from. I remember I began collecting things in which I began to see the manifestation of an archetype. One thing I remember very clearly at the time was collecting images of packets or packaging of various kinds. It was a series of images that crossed the whole range of advertising and it occurred to me, what makes one want to compress that connection between the technological and the natural worlds is a sort of archetypal desire, a desire for this fusion and break down. So at that point I just lost any sense of a mainstream idea of what I was trying to do and for the first time truly abandoned myself to being guided and taken surprise by the images that I encountered myself, that was the real breakthrough into collage. What I call collage anyway, it doesn't describe what I do, it's the only word I can happily use. Picasso hardly said anything in his entire life on the subject of what he was doing, but one of the most interesting things he did say, which always sticks in my mind, and says a great deal about that moment for me, was that he doesn't look for images, he finds them. That was really the key moment for me, when I relinquished control of the image myself by dropping captions, I was allowing myself to be guided by images. Obviously Picasso did search for images, he went around junk yards and scrap heaps and book shops finding the ready made objects and bits and pieces that inspired him in his work and which he used in it, so he did search, obviously. What he meant was that the searching is more likely to lead you to not find anything, because you don't really know what you want in the first place, so you have to abandon yourself to a kind of searching which doesn't predispose you to a very specific conclusion or image. The finding is the key element because that's the point in which you've abandoned yourself from the search, you've taken yourself outside the linearity of a particular channel. So I became very interested in the periphery of image culture, the sideways, byways of image culture, in which in a way images could become guides as opposed to being guided by me. And the sorts of collections of images I started at that time, I'm talking now about I suppose 1974-75, are still some of the main areas of images I'm still collecting today.

*There's a crucial point in there, isn't there? In order for this abandonment to take place you actually had to theoretically transform your relationship to the culture; and there's something I want to say on this score. What does appear to distinguish your photography, or your use of the found image in this period, is an overwhelming sense of wanting to be immersed in popular culture, its desires, distractions, ideological structures, its coercions and pleasures. Were you then beginning to think about the possibility of producing a different kind of photographic archive?*

Yes this is very true. At that time, the other thing that really had a big impact on me was a rediscovery of Surrealism, which was happening at that time, and an interest in the unconscious. I felt that the full renunciation of the strategic conceptual basis of my previous work involved a renunciation of the idea of a controlling consciousness. I wanted to find a way of immersing myself in the work, in which I could in some ways escape consciousness. I was also very interested in the idea of the consumer as unconscious, or the forms of unconsciousness within which one consumes images. I thought there was an interesting possible connection there between this idea of the aesthetic unconscious and a consumer unconsciousness or passivity, and I was interested in trying to align the two. At the time I used to talk about things taking on the vantage point of the consumer rather than the producer of images, and had the idea that eventually my various collections of images would be published as books without words, perhaps even without titles. I haven't actually done that, they've become sort of fodder for collages over the years, but many of the books from that period do still survive as independent collections and they are rather mysterious things. For example the collection of Big Bens, sunsets and skies, or the beginnings of the first collection of the nudist images, photo-romans, Maoist images. I felt these represented something unseen as a kind a cultural connection that perhaps we don't fully understand, the ghostly presence of an archetype - that's if one sees the culture of images as unconscious. Not some collective unconscious in the Jungian sense, not some explicable and dissimulative unconscious as in Freud, but an unconscious that's out there in a world, in the actual images that are in circulation. I felt that I was looking not just at my own psyche but also at a collectivised psyche. And this I believed was unrepresented, and therefore important because so much of our culture seems to be unconsciously acting out awful apocalyptic scenarios, the most obvious being the threat of the nuclear bomb. How does a fully conscious rational scientific culture arrive at the actual complete extermination of life on the only planet in the universe known to support it? It's certainly not the product of rational linear thinking, it's something else that's at work beneath that culture. It may be seen to be arrived at through vigilant insomniac irrationality, but it certainly represents a kind of dream, or a fear, that lurks within the culture we inhabit. It's trying to touch really on those kind of collective desires and fears. It is an irrational thing isn't it to have a culture of images, I mean what is the point of producing imagery, they serve very little social function, they're surplus. What is hidden in that surplus, that excess, is what interested me, because its clear that it is the tension between the world of that excess and the world of everyday reality governed by its rationalist forces, the gulf between them, that creates the literally disastrous culture that we live in.

*So did you see yourself as an archivist of the pathological?*

I might have seen myself as that a little later, but not at that time, no. I think they became archives of the pathological a little later, in the late seventies and early eighties, although I wouldn't have used the word pathology even then. But certainly aberration. I was interested in what happens in some of the 'microcosmic' areas of our images culture, images which through a kind of ambiguity of function, reveal something about the nature of images themselves. A good example are the nudist images which are streaked with all kinds of ambiguities. They purport to be something to do with a particular ideology of sun worship or an almost Adamite return to the Garden of Eden. And yet equally they are soft porn that comes through the post in brown envelopes. These images are streaked with aberrance, something that actually reveals something of the imposture of the photographic image itself. And it is this sense of the peculiarity of representation itself that I was really trying to reach for. It seemed that these were kind of fissures within the invulnerability and the indifference of the everyday image. Much later I read *Camera Lucida* and realised I was pursuing was what Barthes would call the *punctum*, that point of punctuation of the image at which the image both touches one and yet at the same time leaves one at an irrevocable distance. Again, I'm talking about this idea of the gulf between the everyday world and the world of images, and this gulf seems to have widened culturally.

*Did you feel any affinity at the time with those conceptual artists using photography who were working notionally with the archive as well, such as Ed Ruscha?*

Oh yes, totally. Ed Ruscha was a particular hero of mine at that time because of his book collections, they were really an inspiration for me, such as *23 Palm Trees*, or *Every House in a Block*, I loved all West Coast conceptual art because it was much more openly strategic in a media sense. Yes he was very important in terms of the idea of the archive. Also I suppose, Joseph Cornell, to go back a generation or two, who has always remained an example to me of somebody who has genuinely immersed himself in the shifting world of image culture and lived thoroughly within it and tried in a way to create his own nest, his own intimate spaces within this anonymous detritus. Also from Cornell, and maybe Ruscha too, I took an understanding of the significance of obsolescence, as the back-drift within that tide of image-turnover, that sense of the image as having been separated from its purported function and drained of its uses. In this it becomes a sort of corpse or skeleton of the image, and as such can have a revelatory aspect in relationship to the nature of imagery itself. Cornell more than anyone, was really the big example for me of someone who so thoroughly lived within that relation that he couldn't extricate himself from it. His endless ledger books, which were aimed at some great cosmic statement were perpetually incomplete, a constant series of digressions and diversions. And this is the problem, once you enter that culture and you really work with found images in that way, there's no real way back to a sort of conceptual vantage point because you are actually being controlled by what is there before you, what you find, by other people's images. I see it as a kind of agricultural phase after photography. Photography is the hunter-gatherer phase, the collagist is the person who goes around second-hand book shops and reaps the harvest of what's already been produced, but you are of course at the mercy of that.

*You said that you wanted to put yourself in the position as a consumer of commercial popular images. Now there's a sense in doing that that you wanted to close the gap down between professional art spectator and a non-professional or non-specialist art spectatorship. Was this something that was crucial to you, because it certainly is something that's become crucial to this generation of artists?*

Yes, I think I did have quite specific political ambitions in the early days, but we're talking about the period after that and I would say that it is also a renunciation or a movement away from the idea of any form of social function in art. Again, functionality was the thing that I was most trying to resist. But at the same time I do think that if one could think of it, not so much as a sort of ideological alignment, but more as a sense of trying to touch on things that are communal on a deeper level, then I would say yes, my desire has always been to close that gap. But having said that I don't think that work which aims to close that gap does so very effectively usually. I think paradoxically the more private one is in terms of ones obsessions, the more one touches on some kind of social cultural collectivity. I think I cut my ties with any idea of kind of instrumental connection with others at that time.

*Do you think that was the major weakness of conceptual art?*

Yes, essentially. Or one of them. I think it was the crucial weakness of a lot of the political work that emerged out of conceptual art and has resurfaced recently as well. The problem with the strategy is that it only makes any sense in terms of its ends, and its precisely this instrumentality in communications that I felt had to be broken. One had to go beyond use-value. But I would say now that perhaps what I was trying to do at the time was break with the idea of the collective in a much more radical sense. All political forms of communication are about saying "we", "we are this", "we do this", "we want this", "we demand this". I would say that I was more interested in alterity, otherness than with this sense of conjoining differences. All these forms of conjunction had become deeply suspicious. Maoism which as I have said, I had a temporary flirtation with, was also manifestly coercive and I had to get outside that form of coercion. That is, I had to break the idea of bringing people together through a particular idea. Rather, I saw art as a form of confrontation with one's own separation from others, that's why funnily enough our separation from others is what we had in common with them.

*Is that one of the reasons that you were so interested in producing artists' books and other kinds of publications because that could engender a strong intimacy with the image?*

Yes, precisely. However, my problem was like Cornell I could never complete any of them. I have many books in progress, some of them for twenty years, so they have never come to publication for that reason, it certainly wasn't because I wanted to spread the word or anything.

*So given what we've said so far do you think one of the strongest legacies of the moment of conceptualism is it's displacement of art from the dominant role of exhibition?*

Yes, I think so. I would never have believed I'd be still talking about conceptualism. Yet it has become almost the dominant mode. You only have to go round art galleries to see that you're exceptional if you're not working in one way or another in a conceptual mode. What is actually refreshing about a lot of the newer conceptual art is that it has gone for a much more West Coast idea of media intervention: the idea that the arts can work in any medium, in any sort of way, that the art work is not necessarily something that one is looking at the outside of. All these in one way or another are a legacy of conceptualism. I think the problem with a lot of contemporary conceptual art is exactly the same problem as early conceptual art, in that it is unfortunately exhausted by its own ends. It operates by strategy alone, and the strategy either works or it doesn't, hence we have so many one-shot artists who have one good idea and that's it, there is no further movement because you've got to have another good idea. The fundamental limitation of these strategies is that you are not allowing yourself to being taken by surprise. The outcome is perfectly predictable. Having said that, I do admire some of the work. For example Richard Wilson's sump oil installation. I can't think of anything more stunning as an experience, but unfortunately where do you go from there? And that's much the same problem as conceptual art, and in the end within the nineties. What is being produced is a very real limitation on the role of the artist. One is actually in much the same position as the advertising executive coming up with a good idea, the merger is almost complete now, and therefore art just becomes another of the image-strategies of the media culture that we live in. Rather than being a confrontation with the peculiarity of the culture - art becomes implicated in cultural turnover. How many generations have gone into the void already? Some of the earliest figures that have been associated with so-called young British art are already half forgotten figures, two years later. It's extraordinary, the movement; I don't think I'm just being conservative and old fashioned when I say that this is a very, very severe limitation in terms of the role that it gives to artists. And perhaps the merger with the strategies of media culture have become so indistinct now that they're interchangeable which is a very frightening thought. I think we may now be falling victim to that position. But having said that I'm not exactly sure what my work is doing on a cultural level but it certainly avoided the problems of strategic 'intervention'. On the contrary it's motivated by a desire to engage difference, confront the alterity of the image, the otherness of it, in some way, its existence as a fragment. I avoid the seamlessness of the ordinary communications apparatus because I see so much art being condemned to it at this moment. I hope I am not beginning to sound depressingly conservative and reactionary.

Paul-Jac



# Six compagnons à Scotland Yard

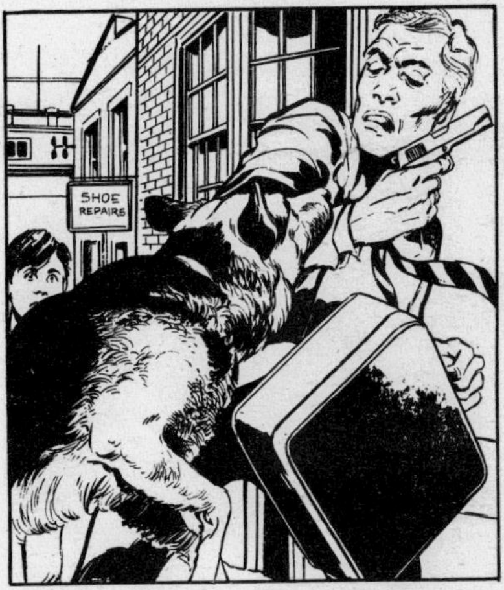


*Illustrations de Robert Bressy*

Hachette

Hachette, 79, boulevard Saint-Germain, Paris VI^e

*A Denis MONDON et François SARANO grâce à qui les Compagnons sont allés en Angleterre.*

*P.-J.B.*

Chapitre 1

# Un accident

C'était un jour de juin, pour ainsi dire le premier beau jour de l'année, tant le printemps s'était montré avare de soleil.

A la sortie de l'école, Gnafron leva le nez en l'air en disant :

« Ce grand ciel bleu me donne une envie folle de voir des avions..., pas seulement là-haut, mais de près. Si nous allions faire un tour à l'aéroport ? Le soir, entre sept et neuf heures, des avions décollent ou atterrissent à chaque instant. »

Bistèque, le fils d'un commis boucher de la Croix-Rousse, hocha la tête.

« D'accord, mais à quelle heure dînerons-nous ?

— Emportons un casse-croûte ; nous mangerons sur l'herbe en regardant les avions et nous nous rafraîchirons à la buvette de l'aéroport.

— Formidable ! » clama le Tondu en jetant en l'air le béret qui cachait son crâne chauve depuis qu'une singulière maladie avait fait tomber ses cheveux jusqu'au dernier.

Corget, un authentique «gone[1]» de la Croix-Rousse, et la Guille, le fantaisiste de la bande, approuvèrent eux aussi. Quant à moi, Tidou, j'étais, bien sûr, ravi. Depuis les vacances de Pâques nous n'avions fait aucune sortie ensemble. Jeudis et dimanches, vent et pluie s'étaient relayés pour nous bloquer à la maison.

«Et Mady? s'inquiéta le Tondu. Elle aimerait sûrement pique-niquer avec nous. Je me charge de la prévenir. Allez préparer les casse-croûte. Rendez-vous à six heures, devant la "caverne".»

La bande se dispersa comme une volée de moineaux. Je rejoignis en courant ma rue de la Petite-Lune. J'expliquai notre projet à maman, précisant bien que nous n'avions aucun devoir pour le lendemain.

«D'accord, fit maman. A votre âge, on a besoin de se dépenser. Je te demande seulement de ne pas rentrer trop tard.

— Promis, maman. D'ailleurs, avec Kafi, nous ne risquons rien.»

Kafi était mon chien, un magnifique chien-loup, dressé comme un chien policier. Lui aussi faisait partie de la bande. En entendant son nom, il se dressa sur les pattes de derrière, posa celles de devant sur mes épaules et pointa sa truffe noire contre mon nez avec l'air de dire : «Tu es sympa de m'emmener, Tidou. Je m'ennuie tellement entre quatre murs!»

Dès six heures moins le quart, lesté de deux

1. Nom familier donné à tous les enfants à Lyon.

œufs durs, d'une tranche de jambon large comme les deux mains et d'un énorme morceau de pain, je descendis avec mon chien vers notre fameuse « caverne », un atelier de tisserand abandonné, au bas d'une « côte » qui porte le nom curieux et terrifiant de Rampe des Pirates.

Gnafron et la Guille s'y trouvaient déjà. Corget et Bistèque arrivèrent un instant après moi... puis le Tondu et Mady, saluée par de grands rires.

Mady, la seule fille de la bande, n'avait rien d'une pimbêche ni d'un garçon manqué. Toute simple, très franche, elle ne manquait pas d'idées ingénieuses et ses fameuses « intuitions », comme disait le Tondu, nous avaient souvent tirés d'affaire dans nos aventures. Pour mon compte, je lui étais particulièrement reconnaissant d'avoir sauvé mon chien, enlevé par des malfaiteurs[1].

« J'avais peur que maman ne me laisse pas sortir le soir, fit-elle. Il faudra que je sois rentrée pour dix heures. Partons vite ! »

Nos vélos étaient prêts. Toujours impatient, le petit Gnafron sauta sur le sien le premier et, jambes écartées, pieds loin des pédales pour imiter les ailes d'un avion, se laissa emporter à toute vitesse le long des pentes de la Croix-Rousse, ce vieux quartier lyonnais perché sur la colline et peuplé de tisserands.

C'était l'heure difficile, celle de la sortie des ateliers et des bureaux. Au centre-ville, la

---

1. Voir : *Les Six compagnons de la Croix-Rousse.*

circulation était hallucinante. Je surveillais sans cesse mon chien qui, conscient du danger, trottait derrière mon vélo, le nez contre le gardeboue.

Une fois sorti de la ville, rien de plus simple pour atteindre l'aéroport. Ah! quel plaisir de retrouver la campagne, de vrais arbres, de la vraie herbe!

En trois quarts d'heure, nous fûmes à pied d'œuvre. Abandonnant les vélos, la bande s'installa sur le gazon tandis que Kafi, ivre de liberté, se mettait à tourner éperdument sur lui-même pour attraper sa queue.

C'était le meilleur moment de la journée pour le trafic aérien. Caravelles, Bœings, D.C. 8 atterrissaient ou décollaient sans arrêt.

« Moi, soupira Gnafron, je donnerais cher pour faire un voyage à bord d'un de ces engins.

— J'en connais un autre, approuva Bistèque, mais ce n'est pas pour demain, à moins qu'on m'offre le voyage... Et toi, Mady, tu aimerais t'envoler pour un pays inconnu?

— L'avion n'est pas plus dangereux que l'auto... mais, comme tu dis, pour moi aussi ce n'est pas pour demain.

— Bah! fit la Guille, l'air malicieux, moi, un voyage dans les airs ne m'effraierait pas. Je craindrais plutôt les repas, à bord. On ne sert, paraît-il, que du caviar.

— Du caviar? reprit Bistèque.

— Des œufs de poisson, en conserve.

— Tu en as mangé?

— Jamais. Mais ça ne vaut peut-être pas une bonne tranche de saucisson. »

Au mot «saucisson», nos estomacs tressaillirent. Une subite fringale s'empara de nous. En un clin d'œil, les victuailles s'éparpillèrent dans l'herbe pour la plus grande joie de Kafi qui, lassé de courir après sa queue, reniflait le contenu des sacs.

C'était drôlement bon de pique-niquer en plein air face au large horizon. Quel appétit! Nous serions volontiers restés là toute la nuit à regarder les avions qui, à présent, évoluaient tous feux de bord allumés.

Le temps passait si vite! Soudain, consultant sa montre, Mady s'écria :

«Déjà neuf heures et quart! Nous avons juste le temps de rentrer.»

Nos affaires ramassées et attachées sur nos vélos, il faisait nuit quand la caravane se remit en route... mais pas pour longtemps. Nous roulions en file indienne depuis quelques minutes quand mon chien, qui trottait à ma droite, s'arrêta net. Pour ne pas tomber, je lâchai la ficelle passée à son collier.

«Kafi!... Reviens!»

Il avait disparu; je criai à mes camarades :

«Stop! Kafi vient de s'échapper!»

Les freins de nos vieilles machines grincèrent. J'appelai mon chien de toutes mes forces. Soudain, sans que j'aie pu savoir d'où il venait, il fut près de moi, me tirant par la manche pour m'obliger à descendre le talus de la route, à cet endroit surélevé.

«Que veux-tu me faire comprendre, Kafi?»

Je connaissais mon chien. Il ne m'aurait pas

alerté pour un rat ou un lapin de garenne. Je le suivis.

« Attends, me dit le Tondu, je vais t'éclairer. »

A la main, il fit tourner très vite la roue avant de son vélo pour entraîner la petite dynamo et dirigea la lumière du phare vers le bas du talus. Mady poussa un cri :

« Oh ! une auto !... Un accident ! »

D'un bond, toute l'équipe fut en bas. Une voiture était dans le champ, sur ses quatre roues, mais avant d'arriver là, elle avait dû faire plusieurs tonneaux comme l'indiquaient son toit cabossé et une portière à demi arrachée. A deux mètres du véhicule, un homme était étendu dans l'herbe. Impressionnée, Mady recula. Je me penchai sur l'inconnu tandis que le Tondu continuait de faire tourner la roue de son vélo pour nous éclairer. Le malheureux chauffeur, blessé à l'avant-bras, perdait son sang en abondance. Il avait dû se couper, en tombant, à l'arête d'une tôle.

« Il s'est sectionné une artère, constata Gorget en voyant le sang gicler. L'accident vient seulement de se produire. »

Je relevai la manche de l'inconnu et appuyai de toutes mes forces mon doigt sur la plaie pour enrayer l'hémorragie. Corget sortit son mouchoir, le tordit comme un câble, le noua fortement autour du bras, au-dessus de la blessure, et demanda à Gnafron de lui chercher un morceau de bois pour le passer dans le nœud et serrer davantage le garrot.

« Remontons sur la route, dit Bistèque, nous

arrêterons la première voiture qui passera en direction de Lyon. »

Hélas ! trois automobilistes passèrent sans répondre à notre appel. Ils nous prenaient pour de jeunes auto-stoppeurs.

« Tant pis, fit Mady, employons les grands moyens. Faisons la chaîne en travers de la route. La prochaine voiture sera bien obligée de s'arrêter. »

Nous nous étions à peine déployés sur la chaussée que deux phares nous aveuglèrent. La voiture fonçait vers nous, sans ralentir.

« Tenez bon ! » cria Mady.

Le véhicule n'était plus qu'à une cinquantaine de mètres quand le chauffeur, voyant que le barrage ne céderait pas, freina de toutes ses forces. La voiture zigzagua dans un crissement de pneus, avant de s'immobiliser. Bondissant de son siège, furieux, le chauffeur s'apprêtait à nous injurier quand Mady lui cria :

« Venez vite ! Un blessé ! Il perd tout son sang.

— Où ?

— Dans ce champ. »

Le chauffeur dégringola le talus et découvrit le visage exsangue du malheureux.

« Ça alors !... Il est mort ?

— Non, reprit Corget, mais il faut faire vite. Remontez en voiture et prévenez l'hôpital de Grange-Blanche, à deux kilomètres d'ici, sur la droite. »

L'homme regagna sa voiture, démarra à toute vitesse et disparut dans la nuit. Dix minutes plus tard, une ambulance stoppait à notre hauteur. Deux hommes dévalèrent le talus, l'un très jeune, sans doute un interne de service à l'hôpital. Ils s'approchèrent du blessé. Apercevant le sang qui tachait l'herbe et le garrot placé par Gorget, le jeune médecin déclara :

« Parfait. C'était ce qu'il fallait faire. »

Et à l'infirmier qui l'accompagnait :

« Vite, la civière!... Vous, les garçons, aidez-moi... Doucement, soulevez le blessé en même temps que moi. Il risque une hémorragie interne. Vous avez eu raison de ne pas le déplacer. »

Le blessé se laissa déposer sur le brancard, sans réaction. La lampe électrique de l'infirmier éclaira ses traits. C'était un homme de quarante à cinquante ans, blond, vêtu d'un complet sombre. Dès qu'il fut chargé dans l'ambulance, le jeune interne se tourna vers nous.

« La police est prévenue.,. mais pour nous, pas le temps d'attendre. Une transfusion est nécessaire. Restez là, vous expliquerez ce que vous avez vu. »

L'infirmier sauta à son volant et, à toute allure, l'ambulance prit la direction de Lyon. Moins de cinq minutes plus tard, deux motards se présentaient.

« Où sont les blessés?

— Il n'y avait qu'une personne à bord. Une ambulance vient de l'emporter. Vous avez dû la croiser. »

Les policiers eurent un mouvement d'humeur, comme si on leur coupait l'herbe sous le pied.

« Vous avez assisté à l'accident?

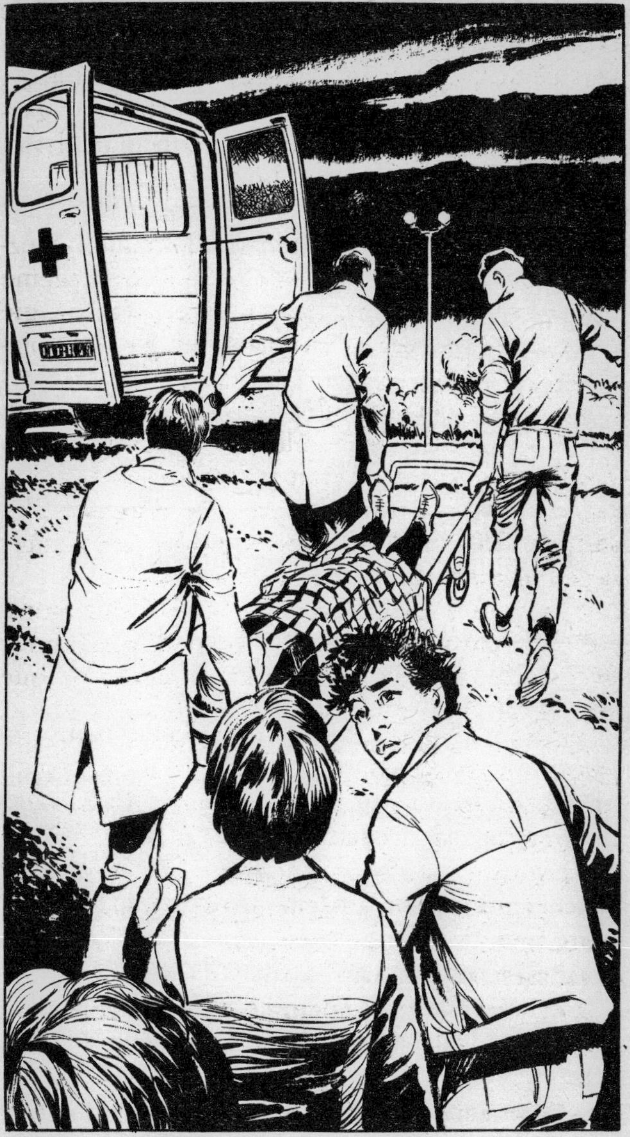

— Non... mais il venait juste de se produire. L'homme, qui perdait beaucoup de sang, vivait encore.

— Quelle heure était-il?

— A quelques minutes près, neuf heures cinquante», fit Mady.

Un policier nota l'heure sur un carnet puis tous deux tournèrent autour de la voiture dont ils relevèrent le numéro. C'était une auto de marque française, immatriculée dans le département du Rhône.

«Toujours la même chose, grommela l'autre policier, on fait un bon dîner bien arrosé, on se met en retard, on appuie à fond sur le champignon pour rattraper le temps perdu... et vlan! c'est la culbute.»

Du véhicule, les deux hommes retirèrent une valise de cuir jaune.

«Il n'y avait que ça dans la voiture?

— Nous n'avons touché à rien, dit Corget. Le médecin et l'infirmier non plus.

— Bon. Nous examinerons cette valise à l'hôpital, en passant prendre l'identité du blessé. Pour le reste, rien ne presse. La voiture ne gêne pas la circulation. Vous pouvez rentrer chez vous.»

Ils remontèrent sur leurs grosses machines en bougonnant, comme s'ils avaient été dérangés pour rien, et disparurent dans la nuit.

«Evidemment, fit la Guille, ils en voient tellement, des accidents, ça ne leur fait plus aucun effet.

— Possible, soupira Mady, mais ils ont tort

de dire que cet homme était ivre. Qu'en savent-ils ?»

Bouleversés, nous allions reprendre nos vélos quand Kafi vint se frotter à mes jambes. Quelque chose brillait entre ses crocs.

«Qu'as-tu trouvé, Kafi ? Donne à ton maître !»

C'était une montre d'homme, en acier inoxydable, dont le bracelet de cuir était rompu.

«La montre du blessé ! fit le Tondu, sans hésitation. Elle a dû tomber au moment de l'accident.»

Je fis signe à Kafi de m'indiquer l'endroit où il l'avait découverte. Mon chien comprit ce que je lui demandais. Il m'entraîna de nouveau vers le champ, en contrebas. A une vingtaine de mètres de la voiture, au pied du talus, il se mit à renifler le sol.

«Si loin de l'auto ? Tu dois te tromper, Kafi.»

Mais mon chien insista jusqu'à ce que je dépose la montre à l'endroit qu'il désignait avec sa truffe.

«Bizarre, fit la Guille. Je veux bien admettre que la voiture roulait très vite. Tout de même, la montre projetée si loin ! C'est impossible.

— Avant de s'évanouir, répondit Bistèque, l'homme a peut-être fait quelques pas pour demander du secours.»

Je redemandai au Tondu d'éclairer le bas du talus, avec le phare de son vélo. Aucune trace de sang entre la voiture et l'endroit où Kafi venait de trouver la montre.

«Après tout, fit Gnafron, cette montre a peut-être été perdue par quelqu'un d'autre.

— Je ne pense pas, fit Corget, les aiguilles sont arrêtées sur 9 h 40, l'heure de l'accident. Le bracelet s'est rompu au moment du choc. »

Et, tourné vers moi :

« Mets-la dans ta poche, Tidou. Nous la déposerons, en passant, à l'hôpital.

— Non, reprit Mady, rien ne presse. Nous la rapporterons demain ou après-demain. Un beau prétexte pour demander des nouvelles de notre blessé... Dépêchons-nous de rentrer. Il est déjà dix heures et demie. »

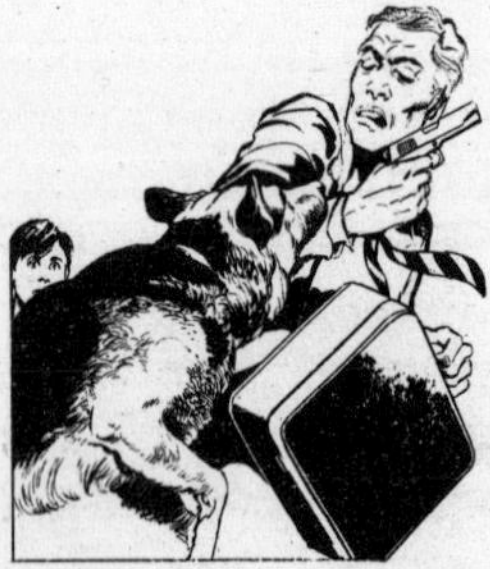

Chapitre 2

# Le mystère de la montre

Cet accident nous avait laissé une pénible et curieuse impression. Nous avions hâte de savoir si notre blessé était sauvé. Le lendemain matin, en allant en classe, je fis un crochet par la rue des Alouettes pour acheter le journal. Comme par hasard j'y rencontrai la Guille et Gnafron qui avaient eu la même idée que moi... et en remontant sur le boulevard de la Croix-Rousse, tous ensemble, nous retrouvâmes Corget, le Tondu et Bistèque, un journal à la main eux aussi.

Cependant, aucune feuille ne mentionnait l'accident.

« C'était à prévoir, fit Corget, les accidents de voitures sont devenus trop nombreux. Les journaux ne peuvent pas les indiquer tous.

— Pourtant, remarqua Gnafron, celui-là était grave. Je pense plutôt qu'il s'est produit trop tard, dans la soirée. L'article ne paraîtra qu'à l'édition du soir. »

Pour être sincères, nous ne nous intéressions pas seulement au sort de l'automobiliste. La veille, en rentrant à la Croix-Rousse, après avoir reconduit Mady chez elle, nous avions longuement parlé de la montre trouvée dans le champ car, après coup, Bistèque et Gnafron affirmaient avoir vu une autre montre briller au bras du blessé, pendant que nous garrottions la plaie.

Or, on n'a pas coutume de porter une montre-bracelet à chaque bras! Cependant, cette montre se trouvait bien dans la voiture accidentée puisqu'elle s'était arrêtée à l'heure même de la dégringolade le long du talus. D'ailleurs elle ne portait aucune trace d'un séjour prolongé dans l'herbe humide. Pas la moindre moisissure sur le cuir.

De là à conclure que le conducteur n'était pas seul à bord au moment de l'accident, il n'y avait pas loin. Qu'était devenu son compagnon?

Avant d'entrer en classe, nous discutâmes encore de cette « affaire de la montre ». Notre imagination voyait déjà un mystère dans cet accident en apparence banal.

« Bah! fit Gnafron, ne nous cassons pas la tête. Attendons les journaux du soir. »

En fin d'après-midi, dès la sortie de classe, toute la bande se précipita donc chez le marchand de journaux de la rue des Alouettes. L'édition du soir des deux grands quotidiens lyonnais venait d'arriver. Sur le premier, rien;

mais à la troisième page du second, un titre nous sauta aux yeux :

SAUVE PAR DES ENFANTS ET LEUR CHIEN.

Hier soir, vers vingt-deux heures, un grave accident s'est produit près de l'aéroport de Bron. Ejecté de son auto, un conducteur, grièvement blessé, a été découvert par le chien d'un groupe d'enfants qui revenaient de visiter l'aéroport. Transporté à l'hôpital de la Grange-Blanche tout proche, l'automobiliste, à qui les enfants avaient eu la présence d'esprit de garrotter la blessure, peut être considéré comme sauvé. Il s'agit d'un Anglais qui avait loué une voiture sans chauffeur à sa descente d'avion. On suppose que, peu habitué à conduire à droite, il a perdu le contrôle de son véhicule. Nos félicitations aux jeunes garçons qui lui ont sauvé la vie.

« Sauvé ! répéta Corget... Vite, filons annoncer la nouvelle à Mady. »

Mady rentrait de l'école quand nous la rejoignîmes, rue des Hautes-Buttes. Comme nous, elle se sentit soulagée.

« Dès demain jeudi, dit-elle, nous irons voir le blessé et nous lui rendrons sa montre, si c'est vraiment la sienne. »

Le lendemain, donc, après le déjeuner, la bande se retrouva devant la caverne de la Rampe des Pirates, avec Mady, mais sans Kafi qu'on n'accepterait certainement pas à l'hôpital. Une demi-heure plus tard, nous descendions de vélo devant les longs bâtiments de Grange-Blanche où nous étions déjà venus voir un vieil ami aveugle[1]. Une employée en blouse blanche,

1. Voir : *Les Six compagnons et le piano à queue.*

installée derrière le guichet d'une salle d'attente, demanda ce que nous désirions.

« Vous voulez voir quelqu'un ?

— L'automobiliste qui s'est blessé, avant-hier soir, près d'ici.

— Tant d'accidents se produisent, chaque jour... Son nom ?

— Nous ne le savons pas, fit Gnafron, mais regardez cet article découpé dans le journal. C'est un Anglais... il a probablement un nom anglais. »

L'employée hocha la tête et ouvrit le registre.

« Vous dites qu'il aurait été amené ici avant-hier ?

— Vers dix heures du soir.

— Harry Simson. Ce doit être lui. Je me rappelle, en effet, à présent.

— Pourrions-nous le voir ?

— Certainement pas. Il se trouve au service des traumatisés graves.

— C'est nous qui l'avons sauvé, précisa Mady. Nous aimerions avoir de ses nouvelles. Nous avons eu si peur pour lui, l'autre soir. »

Mady avait le don d'attendrir les gens. L'employée jusqu'alors réservée lui sourit et se leva.

« Attendez, je vais me renseigner ! »

Elle disparut dans un bureau voisin et revint en disant :

« Patientez quelques instants. Quelqu'un va venir. »

Plusieurs minutes s'écoulèrent. Nous commencions à trouver le temps long quand une jeune fille apparut, au bout d'un couloir. Très blonde, mince de silhouette, elle n'avait pas plus de vingt ans. Elle jeta un coup d'œil circulaire dans la salle, se dirigea vers nous, sans hésiter, et se présenta :

« Margaret Simson ! »

Puis, avec un accent anglais très prononcé, elle ajouta :

« Excusez-moi ! Je ne parle pas très correctement le français. Je suis la fille de l'automobiliste que vous avez sauvé. Le docteur m'a tout raconté. Je suis très heureuse de pouvoir vous remercier. Je regrettais de n'avoir pas votre adresse pour vous écrire. »

Spontanément, elle nous tendit les mains, tandis que ses yeux s'embuaient de larmes.

« Voulez-vous m'expliquer comment vous avez découvert mon père ? Donnez-moi des détails sur l'accident. »

Son accent, ses hésitations à trouver le mot propre, nous auraient, en toute autre circonstance, paru comiques. Nous étions trop émus pour les trouver drôles, tant cette jeune fille s'exprimait avec gentillesse et affection.

Elle nous invita à nous asseoir près d'elle, au fond de la salle d'attente. Alors, Mady expliqua comment, au retour d'une promenade, notre chien avait probablement entendu des plaintes au bas du talus, nous avait alertés et comment nous avions soigné le blessé avant l'arrivée de l'ambulance.

« *Poor daddy*[1] *!* soupira la jeune fille bouleversée. Je ne comprends pas comment cet accident

1. « Pauvre papa ! ».

s'est produit. Mon père est très prudent. Il ne conduit jamais vite... surtout sur le continent où on roule à droite. »

Et elle ajouta :

« Je suis arrivée seulement ce matin de Londres. Mon père a repris connaissance, mais il n'a pas encore recouvré la mémoire. Le docteur pense qu'il a reçu un coup violent à la tête, en tombant.

— Est-ce que nous pourrions le voir? demanda le Tondu.

— Je regrette, c'est trop tôt. Il est très faible, à cause du sang perdu... mais vous reviendrez, n'est-ce pas, avec votre chien qui lui a sauvé la vie... Il sera heureux de faire votre connaissance. »

Il y eut un silence. Je parlai alors de la montre, lui demandant si son père avait perdu la sienne dans l'accident. La question la surprit.

« Sa montre? Il l'a toujours au poignet, ou plutôt elle est posée sur la table de nuit de sa chambre.

— Nous en avons trouvé une, près de la voiture accidentée, nous pensions qu'elle lui appartenait. Nous la rapportions. »

Je la sortis de ma poche pour la lui faire voir. Elle secoua la tête.

« Non, cette montre n'appartient pas à mon père. Je ne l'ai jamais vue chez nous.

— Pourtant, regarde! Ses aiguilles sont arrêtées sur 9 h 40, l'heure de l'accident. Ton père était-il seul à bord?

— Je le suppose. En tout cas, il est parti seul de Londres. Il venait en France pour une importante affaire. On lui avait dit que les taxis étaient peu nombreux à Lyon. Il avait retenu une voiture sans chauffeur à l'aéroport. Cette montre appartient sans doute à la personne qui avait loué la voiture avant lui, et qui l'a oubliée. »

Et prenant une expression inquiète :

« Excusez-moi, le docteur m'a demandé de ne pas laisser longtemps mon père seul. Je retourne auprès de lui... mais vous reviendrez, n'est-ce pas? Oui, revenez dimanche. Il sera presque rétabli et profitera mieux de votre visite... N'oubliez surtout pas votre chien! »

Ne sachant comment montrer sa reconnaissance, elle serra encore nos mains et disparut dans le couloir.

« Vous voyez, fit la Guille, comme nous sortions de l'hôpital, Gnafron et moi avions eu le coup d'œil juste. Son père portait une montre au poignet. Sa fille a raison. Cette montre a été oubliée par le précédent conducteur de l'auto.

— Alors, qu'est-ce qu'on en fait? s'inquiéta Bistèque.

— Portons-la au bureau des objets trouvés du commissariat, dit Gnafron, mais rien ne presse. Elle n'a sûrement aucune valeur et, par-dessus le marché, elle est cassée. »

Nous remontions sur nos vélos pour regagner la Croix-Rousse quand la Guille proposa :

« Nous avons le temps, il n'est que trois heures. Retournons voir l'endroit de l'accident, puisque c'est tout près. Nous trouverons peut-être d'autres indices intéressants. »

En quelques tours de pédales, nous fûmes sur

les lieux du drame. La voiture avait été enlevée. Rien d'anormal autour de son emplacement. Des traces de sang étaient encore visibles ainsi que les empreintes laissées par les dépanneurs. Aucun objet, tombé de la voiture, n'était resté dans l'herbe. Cependant, au pied du talus, parallèlement à la route, Bistèque releva des marques de pas sur une assez longue distance, des marques espacées faites par quelqu'un qui marchait à grandes enjambées en s'éloignant de l'endroit où la voiture avait basculé. En les examinant de plus près, nous les suivîmes plus loin encore, jusqu'à ce qu'elles se perdent sur le talus, en direction de la route.

« Bah! fit le Tondu, ce sont les traces d'un maraudeur surpris en train de voler un accessoire de l'auto, et qui s'est sauvé en longeant le talus avant de remonter sur la route. »

Cependant, l'idée que le père de la jeune fille n'était pas seul à bord me poursuivait. Je pensais toujours à la montre. Son cadran ne portait aucune indication, mais peut-être qu'à l'intérieur?... Avec la pointe de mon couteau, je réussis à ouvrir le boîtier. Sur sa face intérieure était gravée cette inscription :

*BLINDWOOD & COMPANY*
WATCHMAKERS
LONDON

« Une montre anglaise! s'écria le petit Gnafron. Je reconnais le mot *watch*, il signifie "montre" en anglais, et elle vient de Londres. »

Cette découverte nous laissa perplexes. En

France on achète parfois des montres suisses, très rarement des montres anglaises. Celle-ci n'appartenait donc pas à quelqu'un qui l'avait oubliée dans l'auto. A coup sûr, il y avait un autre Anglais à bord, au moment de l'accident... et il s'était enfui sans porter secours à son compagnon.

« Pourtant, fit le Tondu, Margaret l'a affirmé, son père est venu seul en France.

— Il lui a peut-être caché la vérité... ou cet autre Anglais attendait Harry Simson à l'aéroport. »

Embarrassés, nous nous demandâmes si nous devions retourner à l'hôpital faire part à la jeune fille de cette curieuse découverte.

« Non, déclara Mady, Harry Simson a peut-être un secret qu'il ne tient pas à révéler à sa fille. De toute façon, il n'a pas encore recouvré la mémoire. Gardons cette montre jusqu'à dimanche. »

Mady avait raison. Mieux valait attendre pour éclaircir ce mystère.

Chapitre 3

# Margaret et David

Les trois jours qui nous séparaient de notre visite à l'hôpital parurent interminables, tellement nous avions hâte de percer le mystère de cette montre anglaise.

Enfin, le dimanche fut là. Comme la première fois, le rendez-vous était fixé à une heure et demie, devant notre caverne, mais, bien avant, on se retrouvait tous au complet au bas de la Rampe des Pirates, tant nous étions impatients.

« Comment ? Tu emmènes Kafi ! s'étonna Mady en me voyant avec mon chien. Tu as oublié que, à Grange-Blanche, les chiens ne sont pas admis ? »

Non, je n'avais pas oublié, mais la jeune fille serait certainement heureuse de voir la brave bête qui avait sauvé son père.

Je savais que les Anglais ont un faible pour les animaux.

Vélos gonflés, la bande se mit en route. Il faisait chaud. Beaucoup de Lyonnais avaient profité de ce week-end ensoleillé pour fuir leur ville. Peu d'autos dans les rues, peu de monde dans les trolleybus.

« Ne parlons pas tout de suite de la montre, me recommanda Corget, avant d'entrer à l'hôpital. Attendons d'avoir vu Harry Simson. »

La même employée en blouse blanche accueillait les visiteurs dans la salle d'attente. Nous lui étions devenus sympathiques. De loin, elle nous fit signe qu'elle s'occupait de nous. Après être passée dans le bureau voisin, elle revint en disant que « notre » malade était prévenu.

Cinq minutes plus tard, la jeune Anglaise apparut, les traits reposés, plus détendue, en vérité très jolie.

« Je vous attendais, dit-elle. C'est gentil d'être revenus. Mon père va mieux. Ce matin il a pu se lever quelques instants. Cependant, je suis toujours inquiète à cause de sa mémoire. Il a perdu tout souvenir de ce qui s'est passé au moment de l'accident et même de son voyage en avion. »

Puis, jetant un coup d'œil autour de nous comme si elle cherchait quelqu'un :

« Et votre chien ?... Vous l'avez amené ? »

Je lui expliquai qu'il n'avait pas l'autorisation d'entrer et que je l'avais attaché dans la cour à un lampadaire.

Elle nous accompagna dehors et se montra impressionnée par la taille de mon chien.

« Oh ! un si gros animal !... Est-il féroce ?... Est-ce que je peux le toucher ?... Et comment s'appelle-t-il ?

— Kafi!»

Le nom lui parut si drôle qu'elle étouffa un petit rire.

«*Coffee!* Que c'est amusant! Ce chien n'est pourtant pas noir?

— Je sais, fit Mady. *Coffee* signifie "café" en anglais mais lui, c'est *Kafi.* »

Elle le caressa longuement en prononçant *Keufi*, et mon chien, qui reconnaissait quand même son nom, se montra très aimable avec elle.

« Dommage que mon père ne puisse le voir, fit-elle, il aime tellement les chiens... A présent, venez le voir dans sa chambre.»

Sans Kafi, de nouveau attaché au lampadaire (ce qui ne lui plaisait guère), nous suivîmes la jeune Anglaise jusqu'au pavillon où le blessé avait été transféré. Cependant, avant d'entrer, elle expliqua :

«J'ai raconté à mon père ce que vous aviez fait pour lui. Il n'a pas paru comprendre. Il va mieux mais sa mémoire n'est toujours pas revenue. Pauvre daddy!»

Elle poussa doucement la porte. Assis sur son lit, la tête entourée d'un pansement, le blessé ne paraissait pas souffrir.

Son visage, l'autre soir livide, avait retrouvé des couleurs.

Il nous sourit, mais d'un sourire absent, de simple courtoisie.

Devant nous, la jeune fille nous répéta ce qu'elle lui avait déjà expliqué, espérant que notre présence l'aiderait à rassembler ses souvenirs.

«*Yes! Yes!*» approuvait l'Anglais.

Mais on voyait bien qu'au fond de lui-même, il se demandait ce que nous faisions là.

«Pauvre daddy! répéta la jeune fille en lui posant affectueusement la main sur l'épaule. Bientôt, à Londres, quand tu retrouveras ta maison, la mémoire te reviendra. Le docteur l'a dit.»

Puis, se tournant vers nous :

«Oui, le docteur pense qu'il retrouvera ses souvenirs quand il reverra son cadre familier. Aussi, nous repartons dès demain. J'ai retenu deux places dans l'avion pour Londres.»

Puisque notre blessé ne se souvenait de rien, il était inutile de prolonger la visite. Margaret nous accompagna dans le couloir mais, sitôt la porte de la chambre refermée, son visage prit une soudaine expression de gravité.

«A présent, fit-elle, je veux vous demander quelque chose. Je ne suis pas seulement inquiète pour la santé de mon père. J'avais hâte de vous revoir pour vous parler d'une serviette de documents qu'il avait emportée de Londres et qui demeure introuvable. Etait-elle encore dans la voiture au moment de l'accident?

— Non, fit Corget, elle n'était pas dans la voiture. Nous étions présents quand les policiers l'ont fouillée. Ils n'ont retiré qu'une valise jaune.

— Alors, qu'est-elle devenue?»

Nous nous regardâmes tous les six. Je sortis la fameuse montre de ma poche.

«Quel rapport avec la serviette? fit Margaret. Je me souviens de cette montre. Je t'ai dit qu'elle n'appartenait pas à mon père. Ce n'est pas lui qui a perdu cette montre.

— D'accord, mais jeudi nous ne savions pas encore d'où cette montre venait. Regarde!»

J'ouvris le boîtier et lui montrai l'inscription, à l'intérieur.

«Oh! une montre anglaise!

— Oui, reprit Mady, nous avons fait cette découverte l'autre jour, après t'avoir quittée. En France, les montres anglaises ne sont pas courantes. Nous avons pensé qu'au moment de l'accident un autre Anglais se trouvait dans la voiture, et nous ne comprenons pas pourquoi il n'a pas porté secours à ton père... Nous avons d'ailleurs relevé des traces de pas le long du talus.»

Les traits de la jeune fille se tendirent.

«*My goodness*! Que voulez-vous dire?

— Que l'accident ne serait peut-être pas un banal accident. Si l'inconnu qui accompagnait ton père s'est enfui, c'est qu'il avait de bonnes raisons de ne pas rester là. Il se sauvait peut-être avec la serviette. Es-tu bien sûre que ton père était seul, en quittant Londres?

— Absolument sûre. Je l'ai accompagné à l'aéroport.

— Personne ne l'attendait à Lyon?

— Mon père ne connaît personne dans cette ville.»

De plus en plus angoissée, la jeune fille réfléchit et voulut voir l'endroit où s'était produit l'accident.

«Est-ce loin d'ici?

— A vingt minutes de marche, on va t'y conduire. »

La jeune Anglaise rentra dans la chambre prévenir son père qu'elle s'absentait et sortit avec nous. Heureux de recouvrer sa liberté, Kafi lui fit encore mille grâces.

« Tu vois, fit Corget, en arrivant sur les lieux, il ne reste plus aucune trace dans l'herbe. L'accident ne s'explique guère. La route est droite et large. Ton père était-il sujet à des malaises ?

— Il a une santé robuste et c'est un excellent conducteur.

— Pardon, Margaret, fit le petit Gnafron, mais, selon nous, ton père a pu être assommé par cet inconnu, ce qui expliquerait le coup sur la tête, et l'accident. Ce que contenait la serviette était donc si important ?... De l'argent ? »

La jeune fille secoua la tête.

« Non, pas de l'argent. Mon père est un inventeur. Tout jeune il travaillait dans le tissage. Il a inventé plusieurs sortes de... navettes, c'est bien le mot français, n'est-ce pas ? Depuis longtemps, il rêvait de réaliser un "système" pour broder la soie, afin de remplacer le tissage à la main. Il y travaillait depuis des années. Enfin tous les plans étaient prêts. Lyon est la capitale de la soierie en Europe. Il pensait présenter ses plans à des industriels de votre ville. Cher daddy ! Il a toujours été pauvre, mais il espérait faire fortune... pas pour lui ; il se moque de l'argent, mais pour moi. Tous les plans étaient dans sa serviette...

— Quelqu'un, en Angleterre, était-il au courant de ses travaux ?

— Il travaillait seul, chez nous. Maman est morte il y a cinq ans. C'est moi qui m'occupe de lui. Il est un peu distrait, comme tous les chercheurs. J'ai suivi son travail depuis des années, il était parfaitement au point.

— Qu'est-ce que tu vas faire? Prévenir la police?

— Nous n'avons aucune preuve, et mon père ne se souvient de rien. Jamais on ne croira à autre chose qu'à un accident. D'ailleurs, ce qui compte à présent, pour moi, c'est la santé de mon père. Je ne peux pas rester ici à m'occuper de cette affaire... Peut-être plus tard, quand il sera guéri et qu'il pourra dire ce qui s'est passé... »

Elle soupira et ajouta :

« Ah! si j'avais su, je l'aurais accompagné; mais, je vous l'ai dit, nous ne sommes pas riches. Pour moi aussi cet accident est une catastrophe. Je n'oserai plus revoir David.

— David? » reprit Mady.

La jeune fille se troubla et rougit, consciente d'en avoir trop dit.

Mais il était bien tard, et peut-être éprouvait-elle le besoin de se confier.

« C'est vrai, poursuivit-elle, vous êtes si gentils avec moi, je peux vous parler comme à des amis... David est mon fiancé. Nous habitons presque le même quartier de Londres, lui dans une des plus belles avenues de la capitale, moi dans une petite rue. Nous devions nous marier dès que mon père aurait vendu son "système". Mais si les plans sont perdus...»

Elle eut un soupir. Alors, Mady demanda :

«Pourquoi cela vous empêcherait-il de vous marier?

— C'est délicat à expliquer. Nous ne sommes pas riches. Les questions d'argent nous ont toujours préoccupés. Si je me marie, daddy n'aura plus personne pour s'occuper de lui. Il n'aura pas les moyens de prendre une gouvernante capable de lui servir aussi de secrétaire. Bien sûr, la famille de David pourrait l'aider, mais jamais mon père n'accepterait.

— Que fait le père de ton fiancé?

— Il est fabricant de *bowlers hats.* Je crois qu'en France on dit des chapeaux melons.

— C'est cela, fit Mady, des chapeaux melons; mais on n'en porte plus que pour se déguiser.

— En Angleterre, pays qui a inventé la mini-jupe, ils sont encore courants dans certains milieux. William Heddle, le père de David, est fournisseur de la cour de Sa Majesté. Pour lui, c'est presque un titre de noblesse. C'est pourquoi, aussi, j'aimerais que mon père devienne célèbre par son invention. Nos deux familles seraient en quelque sorte à égalité. Ainsi, j'ai promis à David de l'épouser seulement quand daddy aurait vendu son brevet. Hélas! à présent, c'est fini.»

Elle soupira de nouveau et regarda sa montre.

«Il faut que je rentre. J'ai laissé mon père trop longtemps.»

En revenant vers l'hôpital, chassant ses

soucis, elle nous posa toutes sortes de questions, sur mon chien qu'elle admirait, sur nos familles, sur notre travail de classe. Puis elle parla de Londres qu'elle aimait beaucoup parce qu'en dépit de ses traditions la capitale anglaise était devenue très moderne. Elle raffolait de ses parcs et même de son brouillard qui, disait-elle, rendait les paysages féeriques.

«Oh! si je pouvais vous inviter là-bas, pour vous remercier de ce que vous avez fait. Vous êtes tellement gentils!»

Elle était si émue, au moment de nous quitter devant l'hôpital, que ses mains tremblaient en serrant les nôtres. Elle embrassa affectueusement Mady et caressa Kafi qui l'avait tout de suite adoptée.

«Je suis triste de vous quitter, mais je vous écrirai. Vous ne ferez pas attention à mon mauvais français. Donnez-moi vos adresses!»

Mady dicta la sienne, rue des Hautes-Buttes, où la jeune fille lui écrirait pour nous tous.

«Et la tienne? dit Gorget. On ne sait jamais... Si les plans ne sont que perdus, nous parviendrons peut-être à les retrouver.»

La jeune fille sourit un peu tristement, sortit de son sac à main une carte de visite où elle griffonna quelques mots avant de la remettre à Mady.

Puis, pour abréger les adieux, elle donna une dernière tape à Kafi et courut rejoindre son père.

Alors, quand Margaret eut disparu, nous nous penchâmes sur l'épaule de Mady pour jeter un coup d'œil sur la carte.

MARGARET SIMSON
77 Hanover Street
London W.I.

«Quelle fille sympa, cette Margaret, soupira Mady. Oh! j'aimerais tant, à présent, faire aussi quelque chose pour elle!»

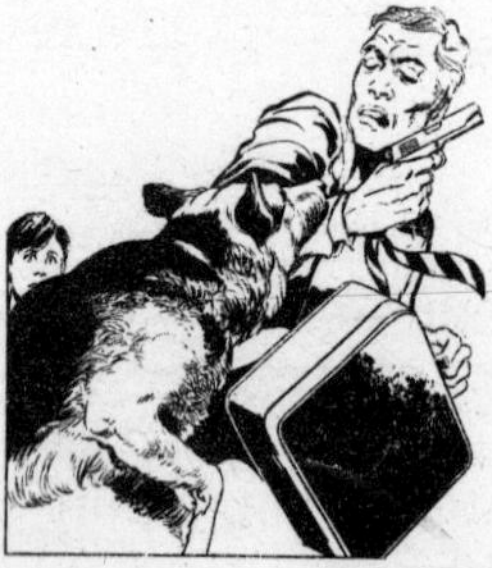

Chapitre 4

# La lettre de Londres

Dès son retour en Angleterre, Margaret nous avait adressé une carte pour nous remercier une fois de plus, mais elle disait aussi sa déception de constater que son père ne recouvrait toujours pas la mémoire.

Depuis, plus rien ; ce qui laissait supposer que l'état de Harry Simson ne s'était pas amélioré.

« Pauvre Margaret, avait fait Mady au reçu de cette carte. Elle doit être désespérée : son père malade et son mariage compromis ! Ah ! si nous pouvions mettre la main sur les plans du fameux "système", comme elle disait... Mais de quelle façon ? »

Car notre visite au commissariat, pour déposer la montre anglaise, ne nous avait guère laissé d'espoir. Nous nous y étions présentés un soir. Après une longue attente, nous avions enfin été entendus par un inspecteur mais cette entrevue nous avait plutôt découragés.

« Comment voulez-vous que la police s'occupe de cette affaire ? avait expliqué l'inspecteur.

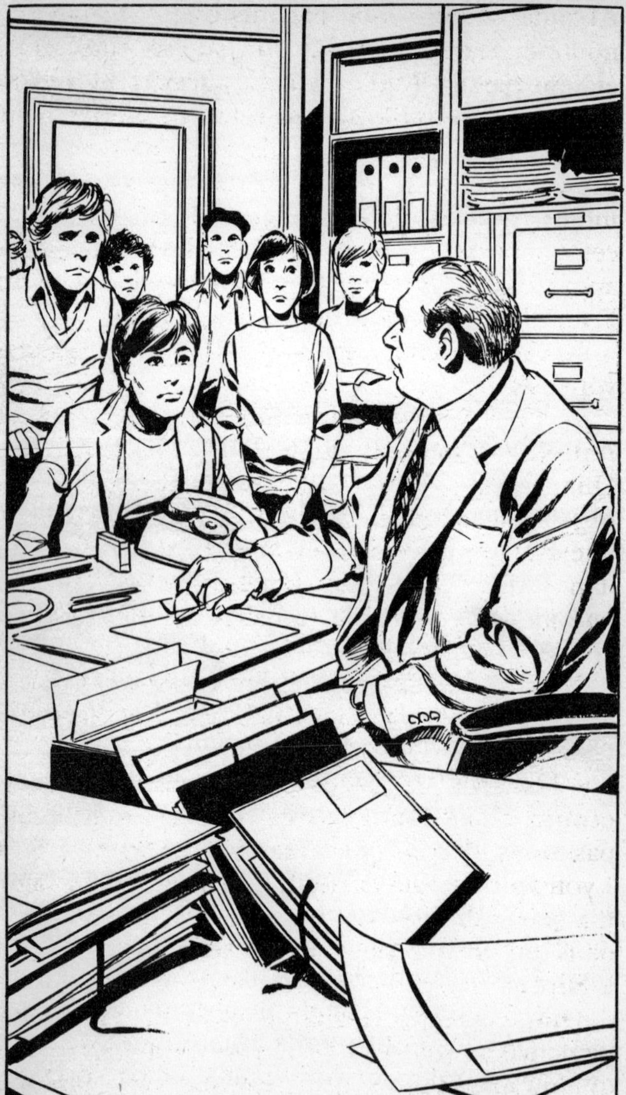

Aucune plainte n'a été déposée, ni par ce nommé Harry Simson, ni par sa fille. S'ils étaient persuadés d'un vol, ils auraient au moins écrit. Il est possible qu'une serviette renfermant d'importants papiers ait disparu, mais rien ne prouve qu'elle n'ait pas été perdue et, encore moins, qu'elle ait été volée à Lyon. Quant à cette montre de fabrication anglaise, elle a pu appartenir à un touriste britannique ou à un Français ayant séjourné en Angleterre.

— Alors, avait demandé Corget, qu'allez-vous faire ?

— Pour le moment, rien ne nous permet de reprendre l'enquête qui a conclu à un accident. Quant à la montre, déposez-la au bureau des objets trouvés... ou plutôt non, gardez-la quelque temps et donnez-moi votre adresse. Ici, dans le bric-à-brac des objets trouvés, elle risquerait de se perdre avec celles qui n'ont jamais été réclamées. »

Nous étions sortis déçus du commissariat et le petit Gnafron avait fait, en haussant les épaules :

« Toujours la même chose. On ne nous écoute jamais. Mais que cet inspecteur ne croie pas nous décourager. Harry Simson venait à Lyon voir des industriels en soieries. Son voleur n'a pas subtilisé les plans pour les enfermer dans un tiroir. Vous voyez ce qui nous reste à faire ? »

Oui, notre seule chance était de visiter les principales soieries de Lyon pour savoir si quelqu'un était venu présenter les fameux plans. Les recherches seraient difficiles, mais en comptant Mady, nous étions sept... et, en fin d'année scolaire, le travail à la maison ne nous accaparait guère. Tous les soirs, après les cours, nous pouvions descendre en ville, et même pousser des pointes en banlieue. Ainsi en fut-il décidé. Hélas! comme au commissariat, le fait que nous n'étions encore que des gamins nous attira des déconvenues. Quand nous nous présentions dans les bureaux d'une usine, l'accueil ne variait guère : «Impossible, absolument impossible de vous recevoir.» Et si, par hasard ou par ruse, nous arrivions à «accrocher» un chef de service, c'était pour nous entendre répondre que nous lisions trop de romans policiers.

Cependant, notre ténacité allait finir par être récompensée. Un jeudi, tandis que les autres Compagnons exploraient les ateliers de banlieue, Gnafron et moi revenions à la charge, à la Manufacture de Soieries du Sud-Est, une vieille et importante firme lyonnaise, quand un ingénieur, intrigué par notre entêtement, consentit à nous ouvrir son bureau. Et, à ma grande surprise, j'eus à peine parlé de métier à broder la soie qu'il tendit l'oreille.

«Des plans pour un nouveau métier?... Effectivement, nous avons eu, récemment, des propositions à ce sujet.»

Mon sang ne fit qu'un tour. Je demandai vivement :

«Quand?

— La semaine dernière.

— Un Anglais?

— Quelqu'un qui parlait correctement notre

langue, mais avec un fort accent britannique, en effet.»

Et, très intrigué :

«Mais où voulez-vous en venir, mes enfants ?

— A coup sûr, il s'agit de plans volés à un autre Anglais que nous connaissons.

— Volés?...»

Haletant, je racontai toute l'affaire, depuis la découverte du blessé jusqu'à notre visite au commissariat, et je montrai la fameuse montre qui ne quittait pas ma poche. Cette fois, l'ingénieur ne songea plus du tout à nous renvoyer et nous désigna deux sièges.

«Ces plans, demanda Gnafron, est-ce que vous les avez achetés ?»

L'ingénieur sourit.

«Mon garçon, on ne se lance pas dans une telle aventure sans réflexion... mais, je le reconnais, les plans de ce métier étaient originaux et extrêmement séduisants. Deux collègues les ont vus. Le directeur lui-même s'y est intéressé. Malheureusement, ils n'étaient pas complets. Deux planches importantes manquaient. Quand l'inconnu est revenu, comme convenu, deux jours plus tard, je les lui ai réclamées. A présent, je m'en souviens, il a paru troublé. Il a déclaré avoir oublié ces planches et a promis de nous les faire parvenir sous huitaine.

Nous ne l'avons pas encore revu.

Mais si ce que vous venez de me raconter est vrai, nous ne le reverrons probablement jamais... à moins qu'il ait réussi à se procurer les feuilles manquantes.

— Comment était cet homme ?

— Plutôt grand, d'un blond un peu roux, avec un visage anguleux et une curieuse démarche.

— A-t-il donné une adresse, en Angleterre, ou à Lyon ?

— Aucune. Ce qui nous a un peu surpris, je le reconnais.

— Vous dites que sa visite remonte à la semaine dernière ?

— A vendredi. Il faudrait prévenir la police.

— Nous sommes déjà allés au commissariat, pour rapporter cette montre. L'inspecteur n'a pas cru ce que nous lui expliquions.

— Cette fois, c'est grave. L'invention représente une grosse somme, certainement des centaines de millions d'anciens francs. La police doit être avertie.

— C'est ce que nous avons essayé de faire, en vain ! fit le petit Gnafron. Est-ce que vous pourriez intervenir vous-même ?

— D'accord, je m'en charge ; mais on vous demandera peut-être des renseignements. Donnez-moi votre adresse ! »

Puis, après réflexion :

« Non. Tout compte fait, il est préférable d'attendre. Nous sommes la seule maison, à Lyon, susceptible de s'intéresser à cette invention, en tout cas celle qui en offrirait le meilleur prix. Par conséquent, l'homme reviendra, s'il réussit à se procurer le complément des plans. A ce moment-là, je vous préviendrai, en même temps que la police. De toute façon, je vous remercie d'être venus, et je m'excuse de vous avoir éconduits lors de votre première visite. »

Aimablement, l'ingénieur nous reconduisit à la porte de l'usine et nous courûmes vers la Croix-Rousse battre le rappel des autres Compagnons. Une heure plus tard, réunis dans la caverne, à l'exception de Mady, qui passait l'après-midi chez sa grand-mère, nous commentions avec passion la surprenante découverte que nous venions de faire.

« Cette fois, conclut Corget, nous tenons presque la preuve que Harry Simson a été dévalisé. Une chance que, dans sa distraction, il ait oublié une partie des plans.

— Oui, approuva la Guille, mais en ce moment le voleur n'est probablement plus à Lyon. Il a dû retraverser la Manche pour essayer de se procurer les dernières feuilles. Il faut immédiatement prévenir Margaret... s'il n'est pas trop tard.

— Toi, Tidou, fit Gnafron, tu es le plus fort en anglais : rédige le télégramme. »

Sur un bout de papier, je m'essayai à aligner quelques mots. Un télégramme pour l'Angleterre devait coûter cher. Il fallait condenser le texte au minimum. Mais comment, en deux ou trois lignes, faire clairement comprendre à la jeune fille le danger qui la menaçait, surtout avec un vocabulaire aussi pauvre que le mien. Je renonçai.

« Alors, une lettre, déclara Gnafron, une lettre en français que nous expédierons par avion. Margaret l'aura demain matin. »

Le télégramme déchiré, je rédigeai une lettre détaillée, en évitant les mots difficiles que la jeune fille ne comprendrait peut-être pas. Puis nous courûmes au plus proche bureau de poste où un employé assura que notre missive serait à Londres le lendemain matin, de bonne heure.

Soulagés, nous remontions lentement la Rampe des Pirates, quand la silhouette de Mady apparut, devant la caverne. Elle paraissait nous attendre. Avait-elle appris du nouveau?

«Où étiez-vous? demanda-t-elle, en courant à notre rencontre. Je vous cherchais. Maman vient de me dire que vous êtes passés chez moi tout à l'heure et que vous aviez plutôt de drôles de mines.

— Il y avait de quoi», fit le Tondu.

Mise aussitôt au courant de notre découverte, elle resta confondue.

«Nous venons d'expédier une lettre à Londres, expliqua Gnafron. C'est tout ce que nous pouvions faire. Tu ne nous vois tout de même pas partir en Angleterre avec armes et bagages pour débrouiller cette affaire?»

Loin de protester, Mady nous regarda au contraire d'un air bizarre mi-amusé, mi-malicieux.

«Et pourquoi pas?

— En Angleterre tous les sept... et avec Kafi par-dessus le marché? Tu es folle!

— Justement, pas si folle. Regardez ce que je viens de trouver chez moi en rentrant.»

Elle tira de sa poche une enveloppe affranchie avec un timbre anglais.

— Devinez?

— Une lettre de Margaret?

— Non, de son fiancé. Lisez! Vous allez tomber des nues.»

Elle déplia une feuille de luxueux papier sur lequel se penchèrent six paires d'yeux.

*Londres, 22 juin.*

*Chers amis,*

*Permettez-moi de vous appeler ainsi, bien que je ne vous connaisse pas. J'ai beaucoup entendu parler de vous par Margaret. Je sais également qu'elle vous a parlé de moi. Nous n'oublierons jamais, tous les deux, que vous avez sauvé son père.*

*Depuis son retour à Londres, ma fiancée est toujours préoccupée par la santé de son cher daddy. A plusieurs reprises, elle a manifesté le regret de n'avoir rien fait pour vous remercier. Je sais qu'elle aurait aimé vous inviter en Angleterre. Alors, je prends cette initiative à mon compte... et en cachette.*

*Mes parents vous accueilleront avec empressement. Surtout, ne refusez pas. Vous me chagrineriez. Bien entendu, je me charge de tous les frais et de l'organisation du voyage par avion. Vous recevrez les billets en temps voulu. Insistez auprès de vos parents pour qu'ils vous laissent partir. Dès aujourd'hui, occupez-vous des papiers et autorisations nécessaires.*

*Je compte donc sur votre venue en vous demandant de ne rien dire à Margaret. Votre arrivée sera pour elle une surprise.*

DAVID HEDDLE

*39 Regent Street*
*London W.I/*

P.S. — *N'oubliez pas de faire vacciner votre chien. Sans cette précaution, il serait mis en quarantaine en arrivant en Grande-Bretagne... Et excusez mon français peut-être incorrect. Depuis mon année d'études dans votre beau pays, j'ai un peu oublié la langue.*

La lettre terminée, nous nous regardâmes, abasourdis.

« Tous à Londres avec Kafi ? s'écria le Tondu. C'est une plaisanterie ! »

Non, apparemment, c'était sérieux, même très sérieux. Il était clair que le fiancé de Miss Simson tenait à notre venue. En tout cas, la somme que représentait ce voyage pour toute la bande ne paraissait pas l'effrayer.

« Bien sûr, fit la Guille, s'il est riche, pareille dépense ne compte pas plus, pour lui, que pour nous le prix de billets d'autobus de Lyon à Villefranche... Tout de même, ce n'est pas une raison pour abuser de sa générosité.

— Evidemment, approuva le Tondu. Cependant, imaginez qu'une fois là-bas, nous puissions l'aider à mettre la main sur l'agresseur de Harry Simson ?

— Comment ? répliqua Bistèque. Nous ne connaissons pas dix mots d'anglais. Je nous vois mal menant une enquête en plein Londres.

— Pardon, tu oublies Kafi, coupa Gnafron. Nous savons de quoi il est capable. Souvenez-vous de notre aventure, à Pierroux, quand il a identifié la trafiquante de drogue en flairant son écharpe perdue dans la montagne[1].

— Evidemment, approuva Mady à son tour,

Kafi est extraordinaire. Il serait capable de retrouver le voleur rien qu'à l'odeur laissée sur le bracelet de la montre... et nous ferions tellement plaisir à David. D'après sa lettre, il est aussi sympathique que Margaret. »

La discussion s'anima. Quelle réponse donner à cette lettre ? Hésitations et scrupules s'envolèrent vite. Au bout d'une demi-heure, toute la bande tombait d'accord. Mais le plus difficile restait à faire. Comment convaincre nos parents de nous laisser partir pour Londres ?

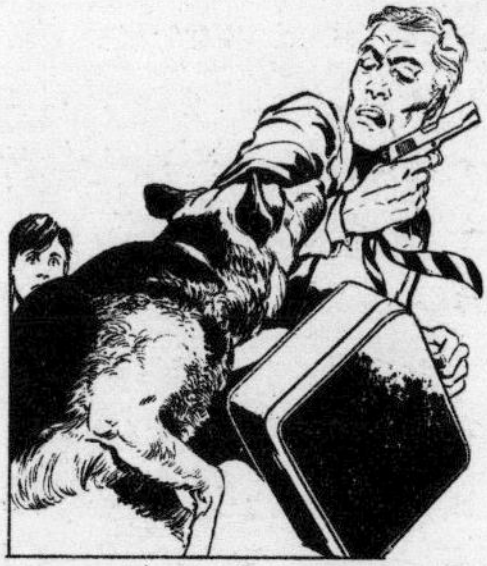

1. Voir : *Les Six compagnons et l'avion clandestin.*

Chapitre 5

# Miss Simson ne répond pas

Les jeux sont faits. Dans quelques instants, nous nous envolons pour l'Angleterre. Décider nos parents à nous laisser partir pour un pays étranger n'a pas été chose facile. Enfin, ils ont accepté!

De son côté, David a tout organisé. Nous devons prendre, à l'aéroport de Lyon-Bron, la Caravelle d'Air-France qui, depuis quelques semaines, assure une liaison matinale avec l'Angleterre. L'avion ne décollera qu'à 8 h 20, mais nous sommes déjà là depuis plus d'une heure, avec nos pères et mères, sans parler des frères et sœurs (21 personnes en tout) qui ont tenu à nous accompagner comme si nous partions pour un voyage interplanétaire.

Pensez donc! Ni mes parents ni ceux de mes camarades, à part le père de Bistèque qui a fait son service militaire dans l'armée de l'air, ne sont jamais montés en avion.

Et ce sont des conseils, des recommandations sans fin. Mais, dans le hall de l'aérogare, un haut-parleur annonce en français et en anglais :

«Messieurs les voyageurs à destination de Londres sont priés de se présenter au contrôle, pour le départ.»

Messieurs les voyageurs... c'est nous! Je sens battre mon cœur très fort. Mal remis des vaccinations de toutes sortes qu'il a subies, Kafi me regarde, inquiet, se demandant s'il ne va pas encore être piqué. Non, il s'agit seulement de la présentation des titres de transport, des cartes d'identité, des bagages. Enfin, après d'ultimes embrassades, nous quittons nos parents, pour suivre une hôtesse de l'air en uniforme qui nous conduit vers l'aire d'embarquement.

Quelques instants plus tard, nous grimpons la passerelle au flanc d'une imposante Caravelle tandis que Kafi, lui, est conduit vers la soute réservée aux animaux.

Nous avons eu si peur, jusqu'au dernier moment, qu'un incident ne vienne tout gâcher, qu'en s'asseyant dans son fauteuil, Mady résume en soupirant d'aise ce que nous éprouvons tous.

«Enfin! ça y est, nous partons!»

Et le petit Gnafron ajoute, émerveillé :

«Dire que dans moins de deux heures nous serons à Londres! Pourvu que je n'aie pas le mal de l'air. J'ai l'impression que, tout à l'heure, mon estomac va chavirer. Pourtant, ce matin, par précaution, je n'ai pas déjeuné.

— Ce en quoi tu as eu tort, assure la Guille.

— Et si David n'est pas à l'aéroport, s'inquiète déjà Mady, que ferons-nous?

— Ah! ne te tracasse pas, dit la Guille. Il a promis de nous y attendre. Tout ira bien.»

Mais le sifflement puissant des réacteurs annonce le départ. Lentement, l'avion pivote et se dirige vers l'extrémité de la piste d'envol. Une dernière fois, nous apercevons les mouchoirs agités par nos parents, groupés sur la plus haute terrasse de l'aérogare. En français et en anglais, l'hôtesse de l'air recommande le bouclage des ceintures de sécurité... et tout à coup, de chaque côté de l'appareil, à travers les hublots, le paysage se met à défiler à une allure folle. Assise à côté de moi, Mady laisse échapper un petit cri :

«Ça y est, Tidou! On a décollé.»

Nous n'avons rien senti au moment du décollage. Très rapidement, nous nous élevons. Au-dessous de nous, j'aperçois un instant le confluent du Rhône et de la Saône, au sud de Lyon.

Déjà, la grande ville et sa banlieue s'estompent. A peine sommes-nous remis de nos émotions que l'hôtesse de l'air, toujours aimable, passe dans l'allée en offrant des bonbons et des petits gâteaux. Nous nous découvrons une faim subite et faisons provision de friandises.

Quelle vitesse prodigieuse! L'hôtesse a tout juste fini sa tournée qu'elle annonce le survol de Dijon, à une altitude de sept mille mètres, alors que la température extérieure est de moins quatre degrés.

« Formidable ! murmure le Tondu. Je me sens relaxe comme jamais. Pourvu qu'on nous offre encore des petits gâteaux. J'ai la fringale. »

Cependant, peu à peu, la réalité nous revient à l'esprit. Nous allons débarquer en Angleterre et nos notions d'anglais sont encore très imparfaites. Bien sûr, nous avons commencé l'étude de cette langue à l'école et, depuis la lettre de David Heddle, nous avons mis les bouchées doubles en nous jetant sur livres et dictionnaires... mais la prononciation ! Saurons-nous reconnaître, dans la bouche d'Anglais authentiques, les mots si consciencieusement enregistrés dans notre mémoire ?

Pour mon compte, un autre problème me préoccupe. Ce voyage, offert par le fiancé de Miss Simson, je veux que nous le méritions... et, pour le mériter, il faut que nous l'aidions à récupérer les fameux plans que Harry Simson n'a malheureusement pas établis en double et que son état ne lui permettra peut-être jamais de reconstituer. Or, depuis l'accident, nous n'avons plus appris grand-chose, sinon que l'agresseur de Harry Simson n'est pas revenu à la Manufacture du Sud-Est et qu'il n'a pas réussi à se procurer les feuilles manquantes mises en sécurité par Margaret.

Ainsi, à des milliers de mètres au-dessus de la terre, nous pensons toujours à cette mystérieuse affaire. Cependant, nous n'avons guère le temps d'en discuter.

En effet, l'hôtesse de l'air annonce déjà le survol des côtes de la Manche, à la verticale du Tréport. Les têtes se penchent aux hublots.

Bordée d'une longue frange jaune, la mer se détache en sombre.

«Mon Dieu! s'exclame Mady. Si nous tombions à l'eau!»

Sa peur est de courte durée. Presque aussitôt, en effet, apparaît devant nous une autre bande claire : la côte anglaise! Déjà, le sol se rapproche, très vert, semé de petites taches qui doivent être des maisons. A l'intérieur de la carlingue, on commence à s'agiter. L'hôtesse donne l'ordre de boucler les ceintures. Pendant quelques minutes, nous tournons en rond dans le ciel tandis que le sol se rapproche de plus en plus.

Soudain, les roues de l'appareil effleurent la piste. Nous sommes arrivés. Une porte s'ouvre. Une bouffée d'air, plus frais qu'à Lyon, nous saisit. Pour la première fois de ma vie, je foule un sol étranger. Nos valises et Kafi récupérés, nous suivons les autres voyageurs vers les postes de contrôle et de douane où, bien entendu, tout est écrit en anglais. En tenue impeccable, douaniers et policiers nous attendent.

*«Please! Passports!... Identity cards!... Open the luggage!... Have you got anything to declare?»*

Bien sûr, ces phrases, nous les avons rabâchées cent fois, mais, dites par des Anglais, nous les reconnaissons à peine. Heureusement, nos papiers sont en règle. Cependant, je suis soudain très inquiet en voyant l'officier de police froncer les sourcils devant les certificats de vaccination de Kafi. Il m'explique, en désignant mon chien, quelque chose que je ne comprends pas. Il essaie alors de parler français. Kafi ne peut être autorisé à débarquer en Grande-Bretagne parce que certaine vaccination ne remonte qu'à six jours et que le règlement prévoit un délai d'une semaine. Kafi devra donc rester vingt-quatre heures à l'aéroport. Cependant, nos mines dépitées émeuvent le policier qui en réfère à un supérieur. Il s'ensuit une longue discussion. Finalement, ayant vérifié d'après son poil luisant, son regard vif, sa truffe fraîche, que mon chien est en parfaite santé, les deux hommes se mettent d'accord pour une petite entorse au règlement.

*« All right !... You can go with your dog ! »*

Ce qui signifie que je peux emmener mon chien.

Mais l'incident nous a fait perdre un quart d'heure. Les autres passagers se sont déjà dispersés quand nous débouchons dans le hall de l'aéroport, le *London Airport.* Pas de David Heddle. A-t-il cru que nous avons manqué l'avion ? Bien sûr, il ne nous est pas possible de le reconnaître parmi tous ces Anglais, mais lui nous identifierait sans peine, avec Kafi.

Rassemblés au milieu du hall, nous attendons. Tout à coup un grand jeune homme, coiffé d'un chapeau melon, se précipite vers nous, à bout de souffle.

« Les Compagnons de la Croix-Rousse, je suppose ! Excusez-moi. Je suis en retard. Au centre de Londres, j'ai été pris dans un embouteillage. »

Puis, s'inclinant vers Mady :

« Mady, je pense ! Et, avec toi, tes camarades ? »

Instinctivement, la bande s'aligne comme pour une revue et Mady nous désigne les uns après les autres, en articulant nos noms que David répète avec application, transformant Corget en « Courgette ».

Ce grand garçon blond qui mesure bien un mètre quatre-vingts est aussi sympathique que Margaret. Sa simplicité courtoise, la franchise de sa poignée de main nous ont conquis.

« Vous devez me trouver ridicule, avec ce chapeau, fait-il en voyant Mady jeter un regard vers son couvre-chef. Cette coiffure n'est plus du tout à la mode dans notre pays en train de devenir très moderne, mais il faut bien que le dernier fabricant de chapeaux melons de Londres donne l'exemple. D'ailleurs, vous en verrez d'autres, dans la capitale. Heureusement pour notre commerce... »

Puis, s'emparant de la valise de Mady, il nous entraîne vers la sortie de l'aérogare. Sur le parking nous attend une curieuse voiture, du genre camionnette, à carrosserie de bois, comme nous en verrons d'ailleurs d'autres, et sur laquelle on peut lire cette inscription :

WILLIAM HEDDLE ET FILS
*Chapeliers*
Fournisseurs de la cour de Sa Majesté

« Excusez, fait David Heddle, vous étiez trop nombreux pour tenir dans ma voiture habituelle. J'ai pris la camionnette qui nous sert à la livraison des chapeaux. »

Nous nous y entassons, avec nos bagages,

tandis que Mady prend place à l'avant, avec Kafi.

«Quel beau chien! ne cesse de s'extasier David, si intelligent, paraît-il. Est-il vraiment dressé comme un chien policier?»

Et la voiture démarre, sur le côté gauche de la chaussée, ce qui nous effraie presque.

«Ah! que Margaret va être heureuse! s'exclame David. Vous savez, je ne l'ai pas encore prévenue de votre arrivée. Elle sait simplement que je passerai chez elle vers onze heures, pour une surprise. Elle doit m'attendre avec une impatience folle.»

Puis, d'un ton plus grave :

«Nous sommes toujours inquiets pour son père. En définitive, j'ai décidé Margaret à le faire entrer dans une clinique pour y suivre un traitement spécial. Il a quitté sa maison avant-hier. Depuis la lettre où vous mettiez Margaret en garde, le voleur n'a pas cherché à s'approprier les autres feuilles des plans. Elles sont en sûreté chez moi. Cependant, Margaret n'est pas tranquille. Elle pense qu'il n'a pas dit son dernier mot. Ah! si nous pouvions rentrer en possession des plans désormais inutilisables pour lui, mais si précieux pour Harry Simson!»

Et, sur le ton de la confidence :

«Vous le savez peut-être, Margaret a repoussé la date de notre mariage jusqu'à la guérison de son père, ce qui est normal, mais aussi jusqu'à ce que cette malheureuse affaire soit réglée. Bien sûr, comme on dit en France, mes parents sont un peu “vieux jeu”, mais ils apprécient les qualités de Margaret et ils espèrent que tout s'arrangera. »

Tout en parlant, David Heddle conduit rapidement. Cependant, malgré sa hâte, il n'hésite pas à faire un petit détour pour nous donner un aperçu de Londres. Bientôt, nous franchissons la Tamise, plus large que notre Rhône, et pénétrons au cœur de la capitale anglaise.

« Vous allez apercevoir Buckingham Palace, indique notre conducteur, autrement dit le château de la reine. »

Il ralentit devant un long bâtiment protégé par d'imposantes grilles où d'extraordinaires sentinelles montent la garde. Plus loin, c'est Trafalgar Square et sa colonne surmontée d'une statue, plus loin encore, Piccadilly Circus... qui n'est pas un cirque comme nous l'avions cru, mais un important carrefour.

« Notre magasin est à deux pas d'ici, dans Regent Street, explique David, mais nous allons directement chez Margaret. »

En moins de cinq minutes, nous sommes à Hanover Street. La camionnette s'arrête devant le numéro 77, un immeuble ancien, tout en brique.

« L'appartement de Harry Simson est au troisième étage, dit le jeune Anglais, malheureusement, il n'y a pas d'ascenseur. »

Nous descendons de la camionnette avec Kafi, heureux de se dégourdir les pattes, et nous suivons notre guide qui monte deux marches à la fois. Sur le palier du troisième étage une petite plaque indique le nom de l'inventeur.

« Alignez-vous derrière moi, que Margaret vous découvre tous en même temps, avec votre chien, recommande David. Elle n'en reviendra pas de sa surprise. »

Il appuie sur le bouton de la sonnerie. Aucun bruit de pas dans l'appartement. Il sonne une deuxième fois, une troisième. Pas de réponse. Alors, à travers la porte, il appelle :

« Margaret !... C'est moi, David ! »

Etonné, il consulte sa montre : 11 h 25.

« Etrange ! Elle savait que je viendrais vers onze heures. Elle m'a dit qu'elle ferait une petite visite à son père mais serait sûrement rentrée avant onze heures, surtout si je lui réservais une surprise.

— Elle a peut-être trouvé son père plus fatigué, fait Mady ; elle est restée à son chevet.

— C'est ce que je crains. Attendez-moi, je fais un saut à la clinique. C'est à cinq minutes d'ici, en voiture. »

Il dégringole l'escalier, trois marches à la fois et disparaît.

« Pas de chance, soupire le Tondu, si son père est très malade, la surprise tombe mal. »

Patiemment, nous attendons, sur le palier. Moins d'un quart d'heure plus tard, nous reconnaissons les pas précipités de David Heddle, dans l'escalier.

« Margaret n'est pas allée à la clinique ce matin. Son père ne l'a pas vue. Elle a peut-être fait une course urgente en ville.

— En tout cas, elle n'est pas rentrée, dit Gorget, nous n'avons pas bougé d'ici. Pendant votre absence, nous avons entendu sonner le téléphone, dans l'appartement. Elle n'a pas répondu à l'appel. Preuve qu'elle n'est pas chez elle.

— Ou qu'elle a passé une mauvaise nuit et s'est endormie très tard, reprend Gnafron. Elle a pris un somnifère et n'entend rien. »

Une nouvelle fois, David Heddle consulte sa montre.

« Midi! Elle est peut-être malade, en effet. Si elle était sortie ce matin, elle serait rentrée préparer son repas. »

Et, après réflexion :

« Un instant! Je descends chercher une clef chez le gardien. Il a certainement en double celle de l'appartement. »

Le temps de redévaler l'escalier, de remonter en courant, il reparaît, à bout de souffle, une clef à la main. Il ouvre doucement la porte, avec appréhension. Rien d'anormal dans le vestibule, ni dans le living-room. En revanche, le lit de la jeune fille est à moitié défait, les couvertures rejetées, comme si elle s'était levée précipitamment en pleine nuit. D'ailleurs, la lampe de chevet est restée allumée. Remarquant les vêtements de Margaret sur le dossier d'un fauteuil, Mady en conclut qu'elle est sortie en robe de chambre... mais pour aller où ?

« Je ne comprends pas, répète David en inspectant de nouveau l'appartement, aucun désordre dans les pièces. »

Mais, tout à coup, Kafi dresse la tête, les oreilles pointées vers le plafond, comme s'il entendait quelque chose :

« Qui habite au-dessus? demande vivement le Tondu.

— Personne. Le quatrième est un grenier, aménagé en atelier par Harry Simson.

— Pourtant, mon chien ne se trompe pas. Il y a quelqu'un là-haut. »

Nous nous ruons dans l'escalier pour monter vers les combles. Soudain, devant une porte entrebâillée, Mady pousse un cri et recule :

« Margaret ! »

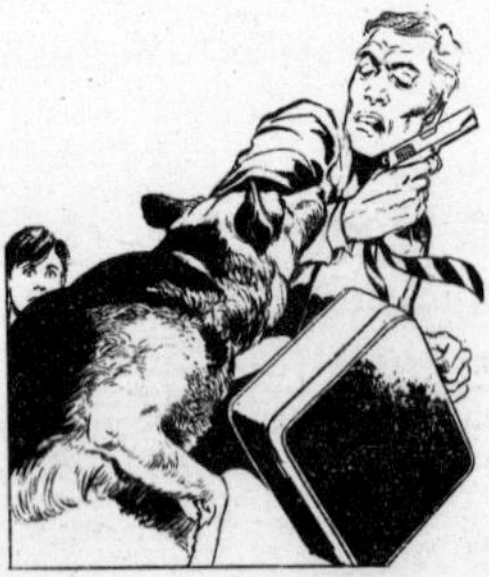

Chapitre 6

# Le récit de Margaret

David Heddle se précipite. Margaret est attachée, assise, à un pied de table, un bandeau devant les yeux, un bâillon sur la bouche. La tête penchée sur l'épaule, elle paraît inconsciente.

« Aidez-moi ! crie David affolé. Détachez les cordes ! »

Tandis que lui-même arrache bandeau et bâillon, nous dénouons les liens. Presque évanouie, la jeune fille ne réagit pas. L'Anglais la soulève dans ses bras pour la descendre dans la chambre où il la dépose sur le lit. Il s'empresse de lui passer de l'eau fraîche sur le visage et tapote ses joues pour l'aider à reprendre ses esprits. Puis il lui soulève la tête et l'oblige à avaler quelques gouttes de whisky.

Ranimée par l'alcool, Margaret ouvre les yeux, promène sur les visages qui l'entourent un regard plein de stupeur.

« *Good Lord !* Où suis-je ?... A Lyon ?

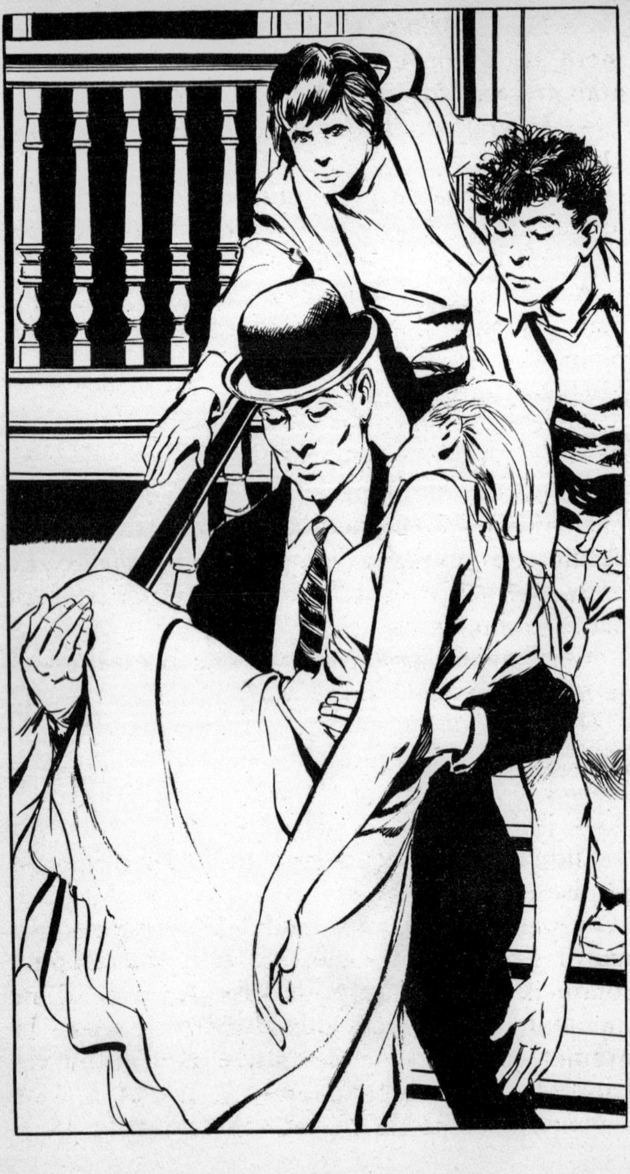

— Non, *darling*, chez toi, dans ton appartement de Hanover Street. Ce sont tes jeunes amis français qui sont venus à Londres.

— Je ne comprends pas! Explique-moi, David!

— C'était la surprise que je te réservais. Je les ai invités à passer quelques jours ici. Ils viennent d'arriver, en avion. »

A ce mot « surprise », elle sourit faiblement mais, presque aussitôt, son visage se referme, plein d'angoisse.

« Que s'est-il passé ?

— Nous venons de te trouver dans l'atelier de ton père, ligotée, bâillonnée. Essaye de te rappeler. »

Une lueur d'effroi passe dans ses yeux. David l'oblige à reprendre quelques gouttes de whisky pour la réconforter. Elle se dresse sur son lit, les mains tremblantes.

« Attaquée, murmure-t-elle, j'ai été attaquée! Je m'en souviens à présent.

— Quand?

— Cette nuit.

— Par qui?

— Je ne sais pas. »

Elle respire profondément puis, par bribes de phrases, elle explique :

« Oui, cette nuit. Il était deux heures du matin quand je me suis éveillée. Je n'avais plus sommeil. J'ai allumé pour lire. Au bout d'un moment, j'ai entendu de petits bruits dans le grenier. J'ai cru que des souris profitaient de l'absence de mon père pour batifoler. Mais, tout à coup, quelque chose est tombé sur le plancher, quelque chose de trop lourd pour avoir été renversé par ces bestioles. Je me suis dressée sur mon lit, l'oreille tendue, et j'ai cru percevoir des pas dans l'atelier, des pas qui faisaient craquer le plancher.

— Pourquoi, *darling*, tu ne m'as pas alerté par téléphone ?

— J'ai eu peur de réveiller aussi tes parents avec la sonnerie... et je me suis dit que tu me prendrais pour une bien petite fille si je m'étais trompée. Alors, je me suis levée. Sur la pointe des pieds, je suis montée jusqu'au grenier, à tâtons. La porte était entrebâillée. J'ai tendu le bras pour appuyer sur le bouton de la lumière. Au même moment, une main a saisi mon poignet, une autre s'est appliquée sur ma bouche pour m'empêcher de crier. En quelques instants, je me suis trouvée ligotée, bâillonnée, aveuglée par un bandeau. »

Elle s'arrête, respire longuement et reprend :

« Je n'ai pas su qui m'avait terrassée, mais ce ne pouvait être qu'un homme. Jamais une femme n'aurait eu cette force. Sitôt débarrassé de moi, il s'est remis à explorer l'atelier avec une lampe électrique. Je voyais, par instants, une vague lueur à travers mon bandeau. Il est resté plus d'une heure à tout bouleverser, sans se soucier du bruit puisque, au-dessous, personne ne pouvait plus l'entendre. Puis il est reparti, en me laissant attachée au pied de la table.

— Qui pouvait être cet homme ?

— Je n'en ai aucune idée. Mais j'ai tout de

suite pensé qu'il cherchait les plans, les feuilles du "système" qui manquaient.

— Tu n'as pas pu identifier sa voix?

— Il n'a pas prononcé un seul mot.»

Lâchant la main de Margaret, David se dirige vers le téléphone.

«Je vais appeler la police.

— Non, David, je t'en supplie.

— Pourquoi?

— Si la police intervient, elle ira aussi à la clinique interroger mon père. Je ne veux pas que daddy soit dérangé en ce moment. Le docteur me l'a recommandé... et puis, la police ne s'intéressera pas à cette affaire. Rien n'a probablement disparu puisque les deux précieuses feuilles sont chez toi.

— Mais, Margaret, l'agression!...

— Justement, David, je ne tiens pas à ce que les journaux parlent de moi. Puisqu'en définitive je n'ai aucun mal, ne pensons plus à tout cela.»

Et d'un air contrit :

«Je suis navrée, David, de ce qui m'arrive juste au moment où tu me réservais une surprise si agréable. Tu as su lire au fond de mes pensées. Rien ne pouvait me faire plus de plaisir que la venue de mes amis français. Mais que je suis désolée de les recevoir comme ça.»

Elle nous sourit, serre nos mains avec émotion et caresse longuement Kafi qui, assis à son chevet, la tête levée, la regarde.

«Comment te sens-tu, *darling*? s'inquiète David.

— A part mes chevilles et mes poignets douloureux, je suis tout à fait bien, à présent.

— Est-ce que tu pourras te lever dans un moment? Pour t'en faire aussi la surprise, je ne t'avais pas prévenue; vous êtes tous invités à dîner chez mes parents.

— Rassure-toi, David, je serai prête. Voulez-vous remonter dans l'atelier voir si rien n'a réellement disparu? J'en profiterai pour m'habiller. »

La laissant à sa toilette, nous remontons au quatrième. Tout à l'heure, nous n'avons songé qu'à délivrer la jeune fille. A présent, le désordre nous saute aux yeux. Tout a été bouleversé : placards ouverts, tiroirs fracturés, appareils renversés.

Des plans de toutes sortes, représentant le patient travail de l'inventeur, sont dispersés partout sur le plancher. Cependant, David, qui est venu plusieurs fois dans ce grenier, ne constate aucune disparition, pas même celle d'un appareil de haute précision d'une certaine valeur, paraît-il.

« Evidemment, soupire-t-il, l'inconnu ne s'intéressait qu'aux plans... Mais qui est-il?

— Sais-tu, demande Corget, si le père de Margaret montait parfois travailler ici, la nuit?

— Souvent. Il disait, en plaisantant, que les meilleures heures pour le travail sont celles qu'on passe habituellement au lit.

— Alors, l'homme le savait sans doute absent depuis l'avant-veille.

— C'est certain, approuve Gnafron, puisque, après avoir ligoté sa fille, il ne s'est plus gêné pour faire du bruit. Il savait que M. Simson n'était pas dans sa chambre. Il devait bien le connaître.

— Et il connaissait aussi bien sa fille, ajoute Mady.

— Comment le sais-tu? s'étonne David.

— L'homme cherchait les plans et ne les trouvait pas. Pourquoi n'a-t-il pas demandé à Margaret, sous la menace, où ils étaient? La réponse est simple. Il craignait d'être trahi par sa voix. Il s'agit donc d'un homme qu'elle voit souvent, peut-être tous les jours..., qui sait, quelqu'un qui vit dans cette maison.

— Dans cette maison!» répète David avec effroi.

Nous nous interrogeons. Soudain, je pense à la fameuse montre anglaise qui a fait le voyage au fond de ma poche. Si le bracelet de cuir est resté imprégné d'une odeur, Kafi doit retrouver, dans le grenier, la trace de son propriétaire.

En me voyant lui tendre la montre, mon chien comprend tout de suite ce que je vais lui demander. Il flaire le bracelet, passablement crasseux, et bat de la queue. Je l'invite alors à se promener dans le grenier pour chercher une piste. Il fait, une première fois, rapidement, le tour des lieux, puis revient à chaque meuble, à chaque placard, mais sans s'attarder, signe qu'il ne découvre rien. Finalement, il se tourne vers moi avec l'air attristé qu'il prend chaque fois qu'il manque à son devoir.

Nous nous regardons, déçus, mais Mady déclare :

« Vous êtes surpris que Kafi n'ait pas reconnu l'odeur de l'homme à la montre, pas moi. Cela prouve qu'ils sont deux dans cette affaire : l'un à Lyon, qui a subtilisé la serviette de M. Simson, et l'autre à Londres, chargé de récupérer les feuilles manquantes.

— Formidable! s'écrie le Tondu. Une fois encore, Mady, tu viens de faire une découverte sensationnelle. »

Puis, prenant aussitôt un air consterné :

« Mais... mais alors, si le propriétaire de la montre est resté en France, Kafi ne retrouvera jamais sa piste à Londres! »

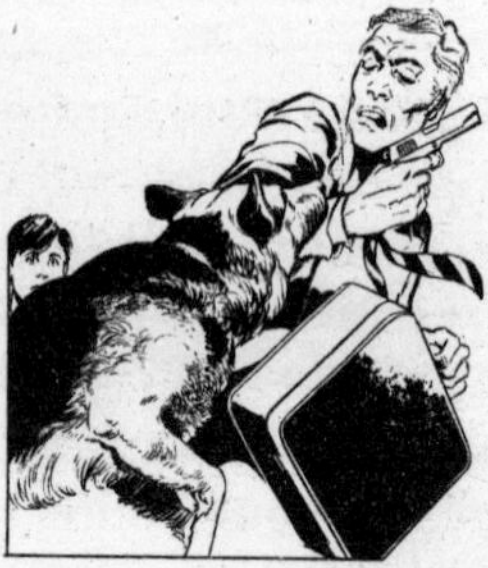

Chapitre 7

# La montre de James Blackmoor

Allongés sur des matelas, dans le grenier-atelier de Harry Simson, nous dormions d'un sommeil lourd. Ou plutôt, mes camarades dormaient, car mon chien, qui rêvait tout haut, venait de m'éveiller en poussant de petits grondements.

Ma montre indiquait trois heures. Incapable de retrouver mon sommeil, je me mis à revivre, par la pensée, les événements de la veille, notre départ de Lyon, le voyage en avion, la découverte de Margaret dans ce grenier, le repas chez William Heddle dans une luxueuse salle à manger où le service, fait par un maître d'hôtel stylé, nous avait fortement impressionnés.

Certes, William Heddle et sa femme nous avaient accueillis avec beaucoup d'empressement et de simplicité mais, comme disait leur fils, ils étaient très « vieille Angleterre » et nous ne regrettions pas de nous être installés dans ce grenier transformé en dortoir, alors que Mme Heddle avait préparé trois chambres dans son vaste appartement de Regent Street.

Margaret était à l'origine de ce bouleversement de programme. Elle avait manifesté une telle crainte de passer désormais ses nuits seule, chez elle, que nous avions proposé sans hésiter cette solution : nous six, les garçons, nous nous installerions dans le grenier, avec Kafi, tandis que Mady occuperait la chambre libre de l'inventeur.

Bien entendu, Mme Heddle avait protesté, presque offensée, ne comprenant pas pourquoi Margaret se montrait soudain si peureuse. Son fils avait donné une vague raison et, finalement, elle s'était résignée à faire transporter des matelas à Hanover Street, en précisant cependant :

«J'admets que, pour faire plaisir à la fiancée de mon fils, vous vous installiez là-bas, mais vous reviendrez chaque jour prendre le lunch ici, n'est-ce pas ?»

Tout en évoquant ces souvenirs de la veille, je pensais de nouveau à l'agresseur de Margaret, à celui de son père. La supposition faite par Mady, qu'il ne s'agissait pas du même personnage, me contrariait. J'avais trop follement espéré, en venant à Londres avec Kafi, qu'il n'était pas impossible de retrouver les fameux plans disparus. Que faisions-nous en Angleterre si le voleur était toujours à Lyon ? Un seul espoir subsistait, celui de voir l'agresseur de Margaret se manifester de nouveau. Hélas ! il ne se risquerait sûrement plus dans le grenier. Alors, comment l'identifier? Nous ne savions rien de lui, sinon qu'il devait connaître Harry Simson ou sa fille, les deux sans doute. De toute façon, les plans volés étaient probablement restés en France, entre les mains de «l'autre», et Harry Simson, qui n'avait pas pris la précaution de les établir en double exemplaire, ne serait peut-être jamais capable de les reconstituer.

Toutes ces pensées tournaient très vite dans ma tête. Elles finirent par me donner le vertige. Après avoir caressé Kafi, je me rendormis.

... Quand je m'éveillai, il faisait grand jour. Perchés sur une caisse, Gnafron et la Guille contemplaient la ville par une lucarne tandis que Corget et Bistèque s'habillaient.

«Eh bien, Tidou, tu te crois venu à Londres pour faire la grasse matinée? Margaret et Mady nous attendent pour le petit déjeuner.»

Le temps d'une rapide toilette au lavabo installé au fond du grenier et nous descendîmes au troisième. Les traits reposés, Margaret nous accueillit avec le sourire.

«Grâce à vous tous, j'ai passé une nuit excellente. Jamais je ne me suis sentie aussi tranquille. Je n'ai même pas fait un mauvais rêve.

— Et vous allez voir, fit Mady, le breakfast du tonnerre qui vous attend, un vrai petit déjeuner à l'anglaise. Vous voulez le menu : porridge, *bacon-eggs*, autrement dit œufs au lard, beurre, marmelade... et thé, bien entendu. Un petit déjeuner formidable, comme tu dirais, le Tondu.»

Formidable, peut-être, mais pas tellement à

notre goût. A part les œufs au lard, délicieux, je n'appréciai guère, et mes camarades non plus, ce que Margaret appelait porridge, qui nous parut être une fade bouillie. Heureusement, Kafi se révéla d'emblée un amateur enthousiaste de porridge et se chargea, en cachette, de liquider le contenu de nos assiettes.

Le breakfast terminé, Margaret proposa de nous conduire à la clinique pour voir son père.

« Déjà, hier après-midi, expliqua-t-elle, lors de ma visite, pendant que David vous faisait visiter Big Ben et l'abbaye de Westminster, j'ai remarqué quelques progrès. Peut-être en aura-t-il fait d'autres aujourd'hui ? Ah ! s'il pouvait nous donner le signalement de son voleur !... Mais surtout, ne parlez pas devant lui de l'agression d'hier. Il ne supporterait pas le choc. »

La clinique était assez proche pour qu'on puisse s'y rendre sans emprunter un de ces gros bus rouges, à deux étages, qui nous avaient tant amusés, la veille, et que nous nous étions juré de prendre au moins une fois avant notre retour à Lyon. L'établissement donnait sur un jardin d'un vert éclatant.

« Oh ! si daddy pouvait se rappeler », répéta encore Margaret en nous invitant à la suivre le long d'un couloir.

La chambre de son père se trouvait au rez-de-chaussée.

Assis dans un fauteuil, près de la fenêtre, l'inventeur regardait un jardinier tondre la pelouse.

« Te souviens-tu, daddy ? Hier je t'ai parlé des jeunes Français que David a eu la bonne idée d'inviter à Londres, ceux qui t'ont sauvé, à Lyon. Je te les amène... avec leur chien, qu'on a bien voulu laisser entrer.»

Harry Simson nous sourit aimablement. Il ne portait plus aucun pansement et ses traits reposés indiquaient qu'il allait mieux.

«Je vous reconnais, déclara-t-il. Je me rappelle très bien votre visite à l'hôpital de Lyon. Ma mémoire est en partie revenue. Malheureusement, je n'ai aucun souvenir de l'accident.»

Lui aussi parlait assez correctement le français, mais avec un accent encore plus prononcé que sa fille. Il s'intéressa beaucoup à Kafi et me posa toutes sortes de questions sur mon chien, mais quand Margaret insista une nouvelle fois sur le vol des plans, il soupira :

«Ne me tracasse pas avec cette triste affaire. Je suis bien assez malheureux moi-même de me voir dans cet état.»

Quand nous quittâmes la chambre, Margaret ne cacha pas son inquiétude pour l'avenir. Son père guérirait-il vraiment? Pourrait-il reprendre ses travaux, reconstituer les fameux plans qui représentaient des mois et des mois de recherches?

Nous revenions lentement vers Hanover Street, déçus nous aussi, malheureux de notre incapacité de l'aider, quand une averse nous surprit.

En quittant Lyon, nous avions pensé à beaucoup de choses, sauf à nos imperméables. Courant sous la pluie, nous arrivâmes à Hanover Street imprégnés de cette fine humidité anglaise qui, somme toute, n'était pas désagréable. A genoux dans le vestibule, le gardien astiquait le plancher.

« *Wipe your feet!* » lança-t-il d'un ton bourru.

C'était un homme d'une cinquantaine d'années. La veille, quand nous l'avions aperçu pour la première fois, nous lui avions trouvé une drôle de tête avec ses cheveux couleur de paille, son regard bleu métallique, perçant comme une vrille. Pour tout dire, il ne paraissait pas sympathique et Kafi tout à l'heure lui avait montré les crocs, quand nous descendions l'escalier.

« *Wipe your feet!* » reprit-il en haussant le ton.

Si nous n'avions pas très bien compris les mots, le geste, lui, était éloquent. Le concierge nous ordonnait d'essuyer nos pieds. Tout le monde s'exécuta, même Kafi, à qui j'avais appris, à Lyon, à se frotter le bout des pattes sur le paillasson d'entrée.

C'est alors que se produisit un incident qui allait vite devenir gros de conséquences. Nous passions devant le gardien qui frottait toujours son plancher quand je fus pris d'une irrésistible envie d'éternuer. Je sortis si précipitamment mon mouchoir que la fameuse montre anglaise tomba de ma poche, et glissa sur le plancher pour s'arrêter sous le nez du gardien. Je me baissai pour la ramasser, le gardien m'avait devancé. Il allait me la tendre quand il interrompit son geste. Pendant quelques secondes il fixa le petit objet d'un air ahuri. Puis, il me le rendit en me dévisageant et me regarda le remettre dans ma poche. Après quoi, il nous

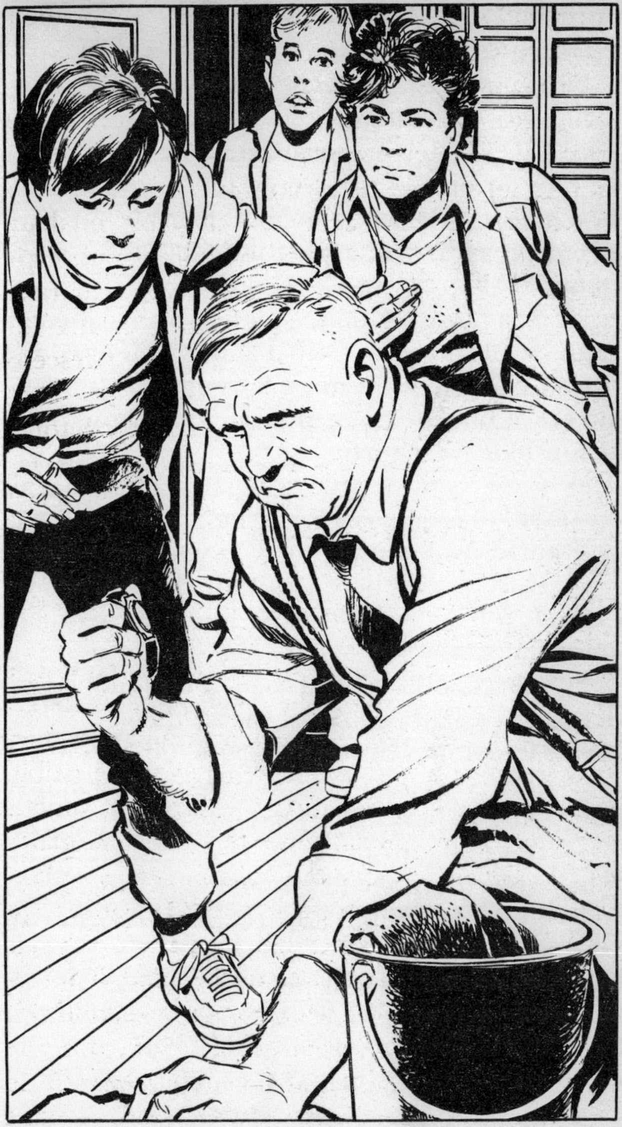

examina d'une curieuse façon, les uns après les autres, avant de se remettre à sa besogne.

Quelques instants plus tard, en me retournant, dans l'escalier, je vis que l'homme s'était arrêté de frotter et nous suivait des yeux, l'air de plus en plus bizarre, prêt à nous interpeller. Je n'étais pas le seul à avoir remarqué son attitude, car en arrivant au troisième, Mady, à qui rien n'échappait, dit vivement :

«Tu as vu, Tidou, quand le gardien a ramassé la montre, il l'a regardée d'une curieuse façon avant de te la rendre. Il a même ouvert la bouche pour dire quelque chose, mais aucun mot n'est sorti.

— C'est vrai, approuva Gnafron. On aurait dit qu'il la reconnaissait, qu'il était surpris de la voir entre tes mains.

— Et vous avez noté l'attitude de Kafi, ajouta Corget, il a tourné plusieurs fois autour de lui, en le flairant.»

Margaret, elle, n'avait rien remarqué. Je lui demandai ce qu'elle savait du gardien.

«Je le connais depuis toujours, dit-elle. Il est d'origine écossaise. C'est un vieux célibataire. Son nom est James Blackmoor.

— Il semble avoir un drôle de caractère. En tout cas, il n'a pas l'air commode.

— Ce n'est qu'une apparence. Il est un peu "soupe au lait", comme vous dites en France, mais, au fond, c'est un homme très bon.

— Est-il au courant des travaux de votre père?

— Il sait que daddy est un inventeur.

— Monte-t-il quelquefois à l'atelier?

— Je ne crois pas. Mais pourquoi ces questions ? Il vous intéresse tant ? »

Mais aussitôt, devinant que nous venions de le soupçonner d'être mêlé à l'affaire, elle prit un air horrifié.

« Oh ! vous ne pensez tout de même pas... simplement parce qu'il habite dans l'immeuble !

— Pour découvrir le coupable, fit Corget, il faut commencer par soupçonner tout le monde.

— Pas James Blackmoor. Jamais il n'aurait fait une chose pareille. Il a un petit défaut, son amour pour la bière anglaise, ce n'est pas une raison. Il n'est jamais ivre.

— Tu l'as toi-même reconnu, Margaret, ton agresseur est quelqu'un qui vous connaît, toi et ton père. Un gardien est bien placé pour suivre les allées et venues des locataires de l'immeuble. Ce James Blackmoor possède en double la clef de votre appartement, peut-être aussi celle de l'atelier.

— Non, répéta Margaret, ce n'est pas possible. James Blackmoor m'a connue toute petite. Quand je n'étais encore qu'une enfant, il m'achetait des sucettes. D'ailleurs, il n'est plus jeune, plus très robuste. Il n'aurait pu me jeter à terre avec cette force. Pourquoi pensez-vous à lui ?

— A cause de la montre. Tu as vu avec quelle insistance il l'a regardée en la ramassant. Il a même hésité à la rendre, et il n'a pas cessé de nous suivre des yeux, pendant que nous montions l'escalier.

— *My goodness !* vous pensez que cette montre lui a appartenu ? Pourtant, hier, Kafi n'a pas relevé sa trace dans l'atelier, preuve qu'il n'y est pas monté.

— Lui non, mais il aurait pu y envoyer quelqu'un d'autre, un complice.»

Presque fâchée de nous voir soupçonner le gardien, Margaret se tourna vers Mady et lui demanda ce qu'elle en pensait.

«Je suis ennuyée de te contrarier, Margaret, mais la scène de tout à l'heure m'a frappée. Moi aussi, j'ai eu l'impression que James Blackmoor reconnaissait la montre... et que Kafi, de son côté, retrouvait l'odeur du gardien. Il ne tourne jamais autour des gens de cette façon. Il faudrait vérifier que nous ne nous sommes pas trompés.

— Comment?

— En trouvant un prétexte pour redescendre chez le gardien avec Kafi, après lui avoir fait de nouveau sentir le bracelet de la montre.»

C'était exactement ce que je pensais. Margaret, elle, ne voulut rien entendre. Cependant, au bout d'un moment, elle se décida à m'accompagner, avec mon chien, sous prétexte de rapporter la clef prêtée la veille à David.

Le gardien n'était plus dans le vestibule. Margaret frappa à sa porte et, comme convenu, pour que j'aie le temps de suivre les réactions de Kafi qui venait de flairer une nouvelle fois la montre, elle entama une conversation, en anglais, avec Blackmoor.

Ma conviction fut vite faite. Après avoir tourné autour du gardien, mon chien releva la tête pour flairer avec insistance son poignet gauche, revenant à deux reprises près de moi comme pour me dire : « Aucune erreur, Tidou, c'est l'homme que tu me demandais de rechercher. » Tout en bavardant, Margaret, ellemême, avait parfaitement suivi ce manège.

« Vous aviez raison, fit-elle, bouleversée, quand nous nous retrouvâmes chez elle, cinq minutes plus tard. Il est possible que la montre ait appartenu à James Blackmoor. »

Sur quoi je repris :

« C'est même certain. D'ailleurs, au poignet gauche, le gardien porte une montre qui brille, comme une montre neuve, et dont le bracelet, lui, est certainement neuf.

— Oh ! *Lord !* soupira Margaret en se laissant tomber dans un fauteuil. Un homme qui a toujours été si gentil avec nous, si dévoué... Ce serait affreux ! »

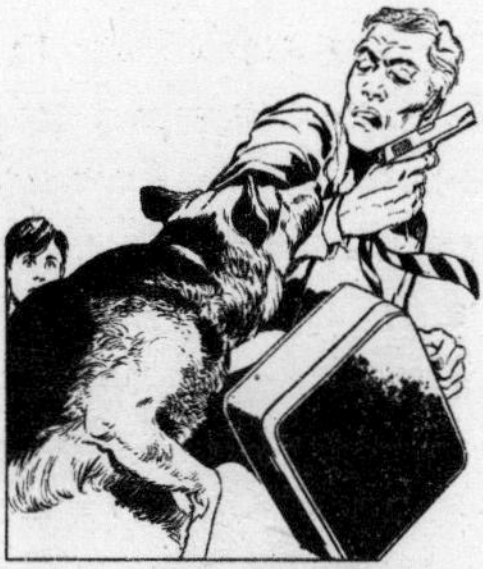

Chapitre 8

# La bière anglaise fait parler

Bouleversée par cette découverte, Margaret essayait, malgré tout, de défendre le concierge.

« Vous vous trompez, répétait-elle, il n'est pour rien dans le vol des plans et mon agression de la nuit dernière.

— Cependant, fit Gnafron, tu admets que cette montre est la sienne.

— Il a pu la prêter à quelqu'un, ou on la lui a volée.

— S'est-il absenté au moment du voyage de ton père à Lyon ?

— Je ne me souviens pas.

— Pourtant, reprit Bistèque, quand un gardien n'est plus dans son immeuble, les locataires s'en aperçoivent, non ?

— Pas forcément. Londres n'est pas Paris ou Lyon. En France, les concierges gardent leur maison nuit et jour et il faut parfois les éveiller, le soir, quand on rentre tard. A Londres, les gardiens sont rares et ils ne restent pas en permanence chez eux. James Blackmoor se rend souvent chez sa sœur, dans le quartier de Haggerston, à l'autre bout de la ville.

— Qui le remplace quand il s'absente plusieurs jours ?

— Personne.

— Alors, qui distribue le courrier dans la maison ?

— Dans ce cas, la porte de James Blackmoor n'est pas fermée à clef. Les locataires prennent eux-mêmes leur courrier dans son petit livingroom.

— Drôle de gardien, fit Gnafron. On entre chez lui comme dans un moulin. Dans la journée, à quelle heure a-t-on des chances de ne pas le trouver dans son appartement ?

— Souvent, le soir, vers six heures, je peux même dire régulièrement, il va boire dans un *pub*.

— Un *pub*, demanda le Tondu, qu'est-ce que c'est ?

— Une sorte de café où on consomme surtout de la bière anglaise, très forte. Je vous ai dit que James Blackmoor avait un faible pour la bière.

— Alors, reprit Gnafron, pendant qu'il ira boire, nous essaierons de savoir si les plans sont chez lui ; ou à défaut, nous trouverons peut-être de la correspondance, des lettres de son complice lyonnais, si ce n'est pas lui qui est allé là-bas.

— Oh! protesta vivement Margaret, vous n'allez pas faire cela?

— Pourtant, il le faudra bien, rétorqua Corget. Réfléchis, Margaret. Si nous retrouvions les plans ou des indications qui permettraient de les récupérer... Préfères-tu avertir la police?

— Les plans du "système" ont été volés à l'étranger. Notre police ne s'intéresse qu'à ce qui se passe chez nous.

— Interpol pourrait intervenir.

— C'est peu probable. L'affaire n'est pas assez importante... et puis...»

Elle s'interrompit. Quelqu'un avait sonné à la porte.

Elle courut ouvrir. C'était David. Il venait nous chercher puisque nous devions prendre nos repas chez lui, En voyant Margaret toute pâle, il pressentit un nouveau drame.

«David! c'est épouvantable. Nos amis viennent de faire une découverte affolante. Le voleur des plans ne serait autre que le gardien.

— Blackmoor?

— Kafi vient de prouver que la montre tombée dans l'herbe, à Lyon, au moment de l'accident, était la sienne.»

Au tour de David d'être abasourdi. C'était trop invraisemblable. Comment cet homme toujours si gentil avec Harry Simson et sa fille aurait-il monté un coup pareil? Cependant, le coupable était un familier de l'inventeur. David réfléchit :

«Bien sûr, jamais je n'aurais pensé à lui, mais il boit volontiers et quand on n'a plus tout à fait la tête à soi...

— Oh! David! James Blackmoor n'est jamais ivre. Le soir, quand il rentre de son pub, il est toujours très correct. »

David fronça les sourcils.

« Je ne vois qu'un moyen de découvrir la vérité : parler à Blackmoor. »

Mady se récria :

« Tu n'y penses pas, c'est le plus sûr moyen de tout gâcher! Si, de loin ou de près, Blackmoor a participé à l'affaire, il se tiendra sur ses gardes, et adieu les plans.

— Il y a la façon de s'y prendre. Il m'est déjà arrivé d'inviter Blackmoor, au pub, en remerciement de petits services qu'il m'avait rendus. Je l'y entraînerai de nouveau, ce soir. Quand il n'aura plus tout à fait sa tête à lui, je le ferai parler.

— Est-ce prudent? fit Corget. Il sait que nous sommes français et il a vu la montre. Même sous l'effet de la bière, il comprendra que tu veux lui tirer les vers du nez.

— Les vers du nez? reprit David effaré.

— C'est une expression française qui signifie : faire dire par la ruse à quelqu'un ce qu'il cherche à cacher. »

David secoua la tête.

« Je connais les effets de la bière anglaise. Elle joue de très mauvais tours. Ce soir, j'inviterai James Blackmoor.

— Pourquoi pas tout de suite? dit vivement Gnafron, toujours impatient.

— Parce que ce n'est pas l'heure d'aller au pub. Fais-moi confiance, ce soir, à six heures, dans l'air lourd de fumée, je saurai faire parler

James Blackmoor sans qu'il s'en aperçoive ; mais pour l'instant, il est l'heure du lunch. »

Et, s'adressant à Margaret :

« Es-tu prête, *darling* ?

— Oh ! David, tes parents m'ont déjà invitée hier, je ne veux pas abuser.

— Tu es encore invitée aujourd'hui, avec nos amis. »

Quelques instants plus tard, nous descendions tous l'escalier. En bas, Blackmoor se tenait dans son petit living-room. Assis devant son poste de télévision, il regardait l'édition de midi du journal.

« Attendez-moi une seconde », fit David en frappant à sa porte.

Dérangé, le gardien fit d'abord la grimace mais, le mot *pub* à peine prononcé, un sourire illumina son visage ingrat.

« *All right !* fit David en nous rejoignant. C'est entendu, je passerai le prendre ce soir à six heures. D'ici là, je vous demande à tous de ne plus penser à rien. Venez vite, nous sommes en retard. »

Il était venu à pied, et c'est à pied que nous gagnâmes Regent Street. William Heddle et sa femme nous attendaient dans le petit salon attenant à la luxueuse salle à manger. Comme la veille, nous nous sentions gênés dans ce décor, peu fait pour des « gones » de la Croix-Rousse. Le maître d'hôtel, surtout, continuait de nous impressionner, avec son air digne, son habit noir, sa façon très raide de marcher, en tirant la jambe droite comme si elle était en bois. Droit comme un cierge, il apparaissait avec les plats qu'il déposait religieusement sur la table, exécutant une courbette devant la maîtresse de maison et se retirait, à reculons, jusqu'à ce qu'un brusque demi-tour l'emporte vers la cuisine.

Nous voyant suivre ses faits et gestes, Mme Heddle expliqua avec fierté qu'il était à son service depuis un mois et demi seulement, mais qu'elle n'avait jamais eu un *butler* aussi stylé.

« Il ne marche pas toujours ainsi, expliqua-t-elle dans un français presque correct. Le mois dernier, il a fait une mauvaise chute, dans un escalier, en allant dans le Yorkshire pour la mort de son père. »

Comme la veille, la conversation dévia rapidement sur le vol des plans du fameux « système ». En apprenant que le concierge de Margaret pourrait être mêlé à l'affaire, Mme Heddle se montra indignée.

« Quelle horreur ! Quelqu'un qui habite dans la maison ! Heureusement, s'il visite de nouveau le grenier, il ne trouvera rien. »

Et, s'inquiétant soudain des deux feuilles :

« Voyons, David, ces feuilles sont-elles vraiment en sécurité ? Où les avez-vous cachées ?

— Dans l'armoire de la chambre, au fond d'un tiroir, et j'ai glissé la clef derrière un livre de ma bibliothèque. Rassurez-vous, mère. Elles étaient encore à leur place ce matin. »

Le repas terminé, Margaret demanda la permission de se retirer.

Elle voulait retourner à la clinique passer un moment auprès de son père à qui elle n'avait guère tenu compagnie le matin. De son côté,

David devait se rendre dans une fabrique de chapeaux où une machine était en panne.

« Les ateliers sont dans les quartiers de Whitechapel, expliqua-t-il, près de la célèbre Tour de Londres et du fameux Pont sur la Tamise. Si vous voulez, je vous emmène.

— La Tour de Londres ! s'écria Mady. J'ai lu des choses affreuses sur cette prison. Et n'est-ce pas là aussi que sont conservés les joyaux de la Couronne ?

— *That's right!* Je vous ferai tout visiter. »

Nous prîmes donc la direction de Whitechapel, un quartier pauvre en bordure du fleuve. La visite des ateliers ne nous passionna guère. Nous pensions à bien autre chose qu'aux chapeaux melons. Pourtant, leur fabrication était curieuse. Des plaques de feutre étaient moulées, pressées sur des formes rondes surchauffées d'où s'échappaient des jets de vapeur. Pour nous amuser, David Heddle nous fit essayer plusieurs modèles. Mady pouffa de rire en voyant la cloche noire de Gnafron lui descendre jusqu'au nez. Quand au Tondu, que nous n'avions jamais vu qu'avec un béret, il était méconnaissable et Kafi le regarda en aboyant.

Mais Mady, impatiente de visiter la Tour de Londres, fit abréger les essayages et on quitta les ateliers, pour l'ancienne prison.

Il était déjà tard quand nous en sortîmes. Nous avions hâte de rentrer à Hanover Street.

« Tu n'oublies pas ton rendez-vous avec le gardien ? glissa discrètement Gnafron à D

— Je sais, mais il est cinq heures,

du thé. Personne, en Angleterre, ne manque jamais l'heure du thé. »

Malgré nos protestations, il nous emmena dans un *tea-room* et une serveuse apporta, outre le thé, une montagne de gâteaux, de toasts..., sans parler des coupes de beurre et de confiture. Une demi-heure plus tard, nous regagnions la voiture pour rentrer au centre de Londres. Tandis que David emmenait James Blackmoor, nous montâmes chez Margaret, revenue de la clinique. Mais elle était déçue de constater le peu de progrès de son état.

« Le docteur m'a dit, déclara-t-elle, que la mémoire pourrait lui revenir brusquement, au moment d'une forte émotion ; mais celui de Lyon m'avait déjà rassurée de cette façon. Je n'y crois plus guère. »

Nous attendîmes, chez elle, le retour de David. Plus d'une heure s'écoula.

« Je n'approuve pas beaucoup le procédé de David, fit la jeune fille. Il ne se conduit pas tout à fait en gentleman. Ce n'est pas honnête de profiter ainsi du faible de James Blackmoor pour la bière anglaise.

— Sans doute, fit Mady, mais c'est pour vous, pour retrouver les plans. »

Un long moment passa encore. David avait-il arraché des aveux au concierge ? L'avait-il conduit à la police ? Tout à coup, Kafi dressa l'oreille. Il venait d'entendre des pas dans l'escalier.

« Ecoute, fit la Guille, David n'est pas seul, Margaret. Il monte avec quelqu'un. »

Nous reconnûmes avec stupeur James Blackmoor. Le gardien avait un visage étrange, un visage bouleversé plutôt que celui d'un homme qui a trop bu. En apercevant Miss Simson, il se précipita vers elle, lui saisit les mains et se mit à parler très vite, sur un ton suppliant :

*« Dear Miss Simson !... I am so sorry !... I don't... »*

Nous ne comprîmes pas grand-chose à ce qu'il disait. Mais, à plusieurs reprises, je retins le mot *watch*, c'est-à-dire « montre ».

Il parla ainsi longtemps, d'une voix altérée, avec des larmes dans les yeux. Sa mine n'était plus rébarbative, mais malheureuse. Dans ses mains qui tremblaient, il serrait toujours celles de Margaret. Quand il eut fini, il se pencha vers la jeune fille et, paternellement, avec tendresse, l'embrassa. Après quoi, il sortit en trébuchant, pas en homme ivre à la recherche de son équilibre, mais comme un homme hagard, qui ne sait plus très bien ce qu'il fait.

« J'en étais sûre ! » s'écria Margaret, toute pâle, sitôt la porte refermée.

Puis, s'adressant à nous tous.

« Vous n'avez sans doute pas compris ce que disait James Blackmoor, mais vous avez deviné. Ce n'est pas lui le coupable. D'ailleurs, vous voyez, il ne parle pas un mot de français ; il n'a rien pu vous dire. Il affirme n'avoir jamais été en France et ne pas être mêlé à cette affaire.

— Pourtant, la montre, fit Gnafron.

— Il ne l'a pas nié : elle lui appartient, dit David. C'est beaucoup plus compliqué que vous le supposez. Asseyez-vous et écoutez. »

Il se laissa tomber dans un fauteuil et raconta la scène avec Blackmoor.

« Nous venions d'arriver au pub et buvions une pinte de bière, au comptoir. Je m'apprêtais à aiguiller la conversation sur ton père, Margaret, quand, d'un seul coup d'œil, je me suis aperçu que la montre de Blackmoor retardait de dix minutes. En plaisantant, je lui ai fait remarquer qu'il avait oublié de la régler sur Big Ben, comme tout Anglais qui se respecte. Il m'a répondu que sa montre, pourtant neuve, ne marchait pas très bien. Elle retardait de trois minutes par jour et il regrettait l'ancienne, perdue le mois précédent.

— Perdue, fit le Tondu, il a dit l'avoir perdue ?

— Naturellement, j'ai saisi l'occasion. En faisant semblant de m'intéresser à sa montre, je lui ai demandé comment il l'avait égarée. Ma question n'a pas paru le troubler. Il m'a raconté qu'il se trouvait dans ce même pub avec un ami ou deux. En frottant son poignet contre le rebord du comptoir, le bracelet passablement usé de la montre s'était coupé. Au lieu de mettre celle-ci dans sa poche, il l'avait posée sur le comptoir, pour mieux voir l'heure car, ce soir-là, il ne voulait pas rentrer tard. Mais, ayant bu un peu trop, il n'y avait plus pensé. Le soir, de retour chez lui, il s'était aperçu de son oubli. Trop tard. Ni le patron du pub ni les serveurs n'avaient rien trouvé. Alors, il avait acheté une nouvelle montre... mais qui ne valait pas l'ancienne.

— Vous ne pensez pas, continua la Guille, qu'il inventait une histoire, comme il jouait peut-être la comédie, tout à l'heure ?

— Certainement pas, car Blackmoor, et je vous traduis mot pour mot ses paroles, a poursuivi : « Vous me croirez si vous voulez, M. Heddle, mais mon ancienne montre, j'ai cru la reconnaître ce matin entre les mains d'un des jeunes Français qui logent chez Miss Simson. Celui qui possède un si beau chien en a laissé tomber une, à mes pieds, en sortant son mouchoir, la même montre, avec le même bracelet de cuir. J'ai failli lui demander où il l'avait trouvée. Après tout, c'était peut-être la mienne. J'ai cru l'avoir oubliée au pub, elle était ailleurs. J'avais encore trop bu de cette damnée bière, ce soir-là. Je ne savais plus où j'avais la tête. »

— Evidemment, soupira Mady, l'explication n'avait pas l'air déguisée. Alors, qu'est-ce que tu lui as dit ?

— Quand j'ai eu la conviction de sa sincérité, à mon tour, j'ai dit la vérité en lui apprenant que sa montre avait été retrouvée à Lyon, sur les lieux de l'accident.

— Comment a-t-il réagi ?

— Il a tout d'abord ri de bon cœur, croyant à une plaisanterie. Puis brusquement, il a pensé qu'on le soupçonnait. Il a pâli, sa voix s'est troublée. Il a posé la main sur mon bras en disant : "Oh ! M. Heddle, vous ne me croyez pas capable d'une chose si affreuse ? Je connais Miss Simson et son père depuis des années. J'ai vu Miss Margaret toute petite, haute comme ça et je l'ai fait sauter sur mes genoux. Non, elle ne peut pas me soupçonner. Ce serait horrible !... Je veux la voir... tout de suite." Voilà quelle a été sa réaction et le malheureux, qui aime tant la bière, n'a même pas vidé son verre. Il a voulu m'accompagner ici pour se justifier. Vous comprenez, à présent, le sens de la scène de tout à l'heure. Si, sur le moment, elle ne vous a pas convaincus, vous ne pouvez plus l'accuser.

— Oui, fit le Tondu, en se grattant la tête sous son béret. Blackmoor n'est certainement pas coupable. N'empêche que sa montre a été entre les mains de l'agresseur de ton père, Margaret... et que cet homme a un complice à Londres, celui qui t'a ligotée dans le grenier.»

Ainsi, nous avions suivi une fausse piste mais tout n'était pas perdu. James Blackmoor était innocent et il pouvait nous aider. Pour se justifier et par affection pour Margaret, il le ferait certainement.

«Il faut le questionner, déclara Mady. Il nous dira avec qui il buvait, le soir où il a laissé traîner sa montre sur le comptoir. Il s'agissait peut-être d'un faux ami, d'un individu qui l'invitait pour obtenir des renseignements sur ton père, Margaret, et qui, par-dessus le marché, lui aurait volé sa montre.

— Très juste, Mady, approuva le Tondu. Enfin, je te reconnais, avec tes intuitions. Descendons chez Blackmoor!»

Chapitre 9

# Un certain Peter Bradson

Dix minutes plus tard, nous descendions chez le gardien, avec Margaret et David comme interprètes, puisque Blackmoor ne parlait pas un mot de français et que notre anglais, à nous, était plutôt rudimentaire.

Surpris de cette irruption dans son petit appartement, le malheureux prit une mine décontenancée, croyant que nous allions encore l'accuser d'autre chose.

« Rassurez-vous, lui dit vivement Margaret, nous venons seulement vous demander votre aide. Vous pouvez nous être utile pour découvrir le coupable.

— Soit ! soupira le concierge, si vous voulez. Posez-moi toutes les questions que vous voudrez.

— Etiez-vous au courant des travaux de mon père ? Saviez-vous qu'il venait d'inventer un nouveau métier capable de révolutionner la broderie sur soie?

— Oui, je le savais. Votre père s'arrêtait quelquefois chez moi, pour bavarder. Il m'avait parlé de son invention. Quelques jours avant son voyage en France, il m'a dit que s'il faisait fortune, il me saurait gré des petits services que je lui rends.

— Et vous en avez parlé à vos amis, ceux que vous rencontrez au pub?»

Le gardien prit un air gêné.

«Excusez-moi, Miss Simson, il se peut que j'en aie parlé. Dans un pub, on ne fait pas toujours attention à ce qu'on raconte... et cette damnée bière anglaise fait si facilement perdre la tête.»

A son tour, David demanda :

«Qui buvait avec vous, le jour où vous avez perdu votre montre?»

Blackmoor gratta sa pomme d'Adam, qu'il avait volumineuse, comme si ses souvenirs allaient sortir de là.

«Je peux dire seulement que c'était le 3 juin, le jour de mes cinquante-deux ans.»

Cependant, il réfléchit.

«Attendez!... oui, c'est cela, j'étais avec un nommé Peter Bradson.

— Un ami que vous voyez souvent?

— Un homme qui n'a jamais eu de chance dans la vie, alors comme moi, il se console parfois avec de la bière.

— Il a un métier?

— En ce moment, il travaille dans un restaurant, mais je sais qu'il a longtemps été employé dans le tissage.

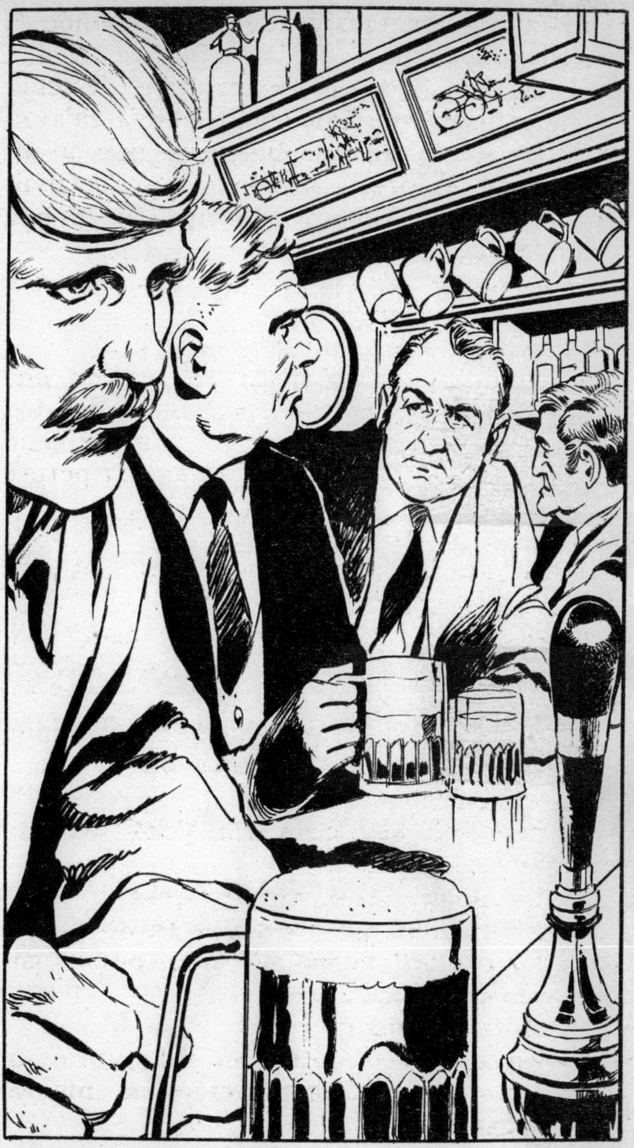

— Le tissage? reprit David soudain intéressé. Et vous lui avez parlé de l'invention de M. Simson?»

James Blackmoor baissa la tête.

«Il regrettait son ancien métier, alors vous comprenez. Il m'a raconté que, lui aussi, il aurait aimé inventer quelque chose.»

Puis, saisissant les mains de Margaret :

«Oui, je lui ai parlé de votre père, mais ce n'est pas lui qui a volé les plans, qui vous a attaquée dans le grenier. Peter Bradson est un honnête homme. La preuve, il m'a toujours rendu ce que je lui prêtais.

— Il a des ennuis d'argent?

— Il n'est pas très bien payé par son patron et il a une nombreuse famille, mais je vous jure qu'il est honnête. Ce n'est pas lui qui m'a pris ma montre. D'ailleurs, je me rappelle, à présent, il y avait beaucoup de monde au pub, et je crois bien que Thomas buvait avec nous.

— Thomas?

— Lui, je le connais depuis moins longtemps, quelques semaines seulement. Il travaille dans une banque et ne manque pas d'argent. Quand nous buvons ensemble, il paie plus souvent qu'à son tour.

— Revenons à Peter Bradson, reprit David. Vous dites qu'il travaille dans un restaurant?

— Pas très loin d'ici, dans le quartier de Soho, à deux pas de Piccadilly Circus, dans un restaurant français qui s'appelle *Le Cochon de lait.*

— Un restaurant français? se récria Margaret. Il parle français?

— Peut-être. »

Très intriguée, Miss Simson se tourna vers nous.

« Vous avez entendu ? Ce Peter Bradson travaille dans un restaurant français. Il parle donc votre langue d'une manière courante.

— Alors, demande-lui, Margaret, fit Gnafron, si Bradson s'est absenté de Londres le mois dernier. »

Blackmoor réfléchit encore et déclara :

« Non, il n'a pas quitté la capitale. Il s'est seulement absenté plusieurs jours à cause d'une de ses filles gravement malade. Il m'a même demandé de l'argent à cette occasion.

— C'était à quelle époque ?

— Vers le début ou la mi-juin, si j'ai bonne mémoire. »

J'échangeai un regard avec mes camarades. Peter Bradson avait quitté son travail juste au moment du vol à Lyon. Quelle coïncidence !

Par l'intermédiaire de David, Corget et Mady posèrent encore plusieurs questions au concierge, mais celui-ci avait dit tout ce qu'il savait. Il se contenta de répéter sa conviction que Peter Bradson n'était pour rien dans cette affaire. Il ne nous restait plus qu'à le remercier et à sortir.

« Cette fois, se réjouit David, j'ai l'impression que nous sommes sur la vraie piste. Je connais *Le Cochon de lait.* J'y ai dîné plusieurs fois avec des amis. Le patron est accueillant. Il me renseignera sur son employé. Je verrai s'il est le genre d'homme décrit par James Blackmoor et je saurai la date exacte de son absence. »

Puis, prenant les mains de Margaret :

«*All right, darling!* Tout va pour le mieux. Ne désespérons plus de retrouver les plans du "système". Dès demain matin, je cours à Soho. Pour l'instant, il est grand temps d'aller dîner à Regent Street.»

Il nous entraîna chez lui et, en cours de route, recommanda :

«Surtout, pas un mot à mes parents. Ma mère est très émotive. Elle a tendance à voir des gangsters partout. Elle croirait notre entreprise dangereuse.»

Durant tout le repas, il ne fut question de rien et William Heddle, passionné d'histoire, en profita pour nous faire un cours sur l'origine des chapeaux melons en Angleterre et se lamenter sur leur disparition prochaine.

Il était plus de dix heures quand, sous une averse, nous revînmes chez Margaret pour rejoindre notre grenier. Très excités par les événements, nous n'avions guère envie de dormir. Pourtant, la chaleur n'était pas incommodante. J'avais presque froid sous mes couvertures.

«Oui, tout va bien, commença Bistèque. Pour moi, c'est clair. Sous son air rébarbatif, Blackmoor est un naïf. Il s'est laissé "embobiner" par Bradson, un bon à rien qui a fait tous les métiers, et n'a pas hésité à lui rafler sa montre.

— Sans parler de l'argent qu'il doit lui soutirer, ajouta le Tondu. Vous avez remarqué qu'il en a emprunté au concierge, au moment où il s'est absenté. C'était peut-être pour payer son billet d'avion.

— Probablement, approuva la Guille. Jusqu'à présent, impossible de savoir s'ils sont plusieurs dans le coup, mais un fait est presque certain. C'est Bradson qui est allé à Lyon. Il parle couramment le français et il a travaillé dans le tissage. En présentant les plans, il était capable d'explications techniques que quelqu'un d'autre n'aurait pu donner. »

Enfin, nous nous endormîmes. Le lendemain, dès sept heures et demie, nous étions déjà debout. Quand, toilette faite, la bande descendit au troisième, Margaret et Mady préparaient le breakfast avec les mêmes délicieux œufs au lard que la veille... mais aussi le même porridge pâteux et gluant que Kafi fit disparaître avec beaucoup de discrétion.

Le petit déjeuner terminé, nous aidions au rangement de la vaisselle quand le téléphone sonna.

Margaret courut vers le récepteur.

« Allô!... Ah! c'est toi, David? Que se passe-t-il donc?... Oui, je les préviens. Bien, ils attendront ton retour. Fais bon voyage. »

Et, reposant l'appareil :

« David ne peut pas aller au *Cochon de lait* ce matin. Une machine vient de tomber en panne à la fabrique de feutre que possède son père à Colchester.

— Quand rentrera-t-il?

— Il fera son possible pour être de retour à midi, mais ce n'est pas certain. Colchester est à quatre-vingts kilomètres de Londres. »

Nous nous étions levés avec l'espoir d'avoir tout de suite des renseignements sur Bradson.

C'était la déception. Devrions-nous attendre jusqu'au lendemain ?

« Et pourquoi n'irions-nous pas nous-mêmes au *Cochon de lait* ? proposa Gnafron. Le patron est français, nous nous débrouillerons sans peine.

— En effet, approuva Margaret, faites un tour à Soho. C'est un des plus curieux quartiers de Londres, et si près d'ici. Puisque vous n'avez pas besoin de Kafi, vous devriez me le laisser, je l'emmènerais de nouveau à la clinique. Mon père aime tellement les chiens. »

Je lui confiai donc Kafi et, suivant ses indications, nous gagnâmes Soho, un étrange quartier peuplé de cabarets, de dancings, de clubs et, surtout, de restaurants. Dans certaines rues ils se succédaient sans interruption : restaurants chinois, français, grecs, turcs, italiens. Malheureusement, nous n'avions pas l'adresse de celui que nous cherchions.

« Adressons-nous à un agent, fit Mady, une belle occasion de voir si nous prononçons l'anglais correctement. »

Le premier policeman qui passait, un *bobby* comme on appelle familièrement les agents à Londres, nous indiqua *Le Cochon de lait* dans une rue parallèle à celle que nous suivions. Nous le découvrîmes de loin grâce à son enseigne représentant un petit cochon rose et dodu à la queue en tire-bouchon. Neuf heures venaient de sonner. Le restaurant était désert.

« Tant pis, entrons, dit Gnafron. Nous laisserons Mady parler. Elle se débrouille mieux que nous pour interroger les gens. »

Nous attendions depuis quelques instants au milieu de la salle quand le patron apparut. Au premier coup d'œil, il reconnut des Français. Avec un accent du Midi aussi prononcé que le mien, il demanda :

« Qu'y a-t-il pour votre service, mes pitchounets ? »

Du coup, enlevant la parole à Mady, j'expliquai que nous cherchions des renseignements sur l'un de ses employés : Peter Bradson.

« Bradson ? C'est que... il n'est pas arrivé. Il ne prend son service qu'à dix heures et demie.

— Tant mieux, nous préférons qu'il ne soit pas là. Nous venons de la part de M. David Heddle.

— Ah ! le jeune David ! Je le connais ! C'est un bon client.

— Il n'a pas pu venir. Il voudrait savoir, et nous aussi, qui est au juste Peter Bradson. Pouvez-vous nous dire ce que vous savez de lui ?

— Bien sûr, d'autant plus que je n'ai pas à m'en plaindre. Bah ! il lève bien un peu le coude, comme on dit en France, mais ça ne lui arrive pas souvent.

— Parle-t-il le français ?

— Pas un mot, et je le regrette. Je l'aurais mis au service de la salle à manger au lieu de le laisser à la cuisine à éplucher les légumes ou faire la plonge.

— Depuis quand travaille-t-il chez vous ?

— Cela fait plus de deux ans. Il venait, je crois, de Liverpool. Le climat marin ne valait rien à ses enfants. Du moins, c'est ce qu'il m'a dit.

— Vous rappelez-vous s'il s'est absenté, au début du mois dernier ?

— Quelques jours seulement.

— Vous pourriez nous donner la date exacte ? »

Le restaurateur prit un registre, sous son comptoir, le feuilleta et précisa :

« Du 2 au 10 juin. Si ma mémoire ne me trompe pas, un de ses enfants était malade.

— Où habite-t-il ? »

Le patron du *Cochon de lait* rouvrit le registre qu'il venait de refermer pour chercher l'adresse de son employé :

« 7 Coalway Street. Si vous ne connaissez pas très bien Londres, c'est assez loin d'ici, dans le quartier des docks, mais c'est direct en métro. »

Et le restaurateur ajouta en riant :

« Seriez-vous venus en Angleterre pour jouer aux détectives ? Est-ce tout ce que vous désiriez ? Excusez-moi, mes pitchounets, mes fourneaux m'attendent. »

Il nous serra la main, m'adressa deux mots en provençal et nous laissa.

« Pas de chance, fit Mady en sortant du *Cochon de lait*. J'ai l'impression que nous suivons encore une fausse piste. Bradson n'a pas menti au gardien, ou il a menti aussi, et de la même façon, au patron du restaurant, ce qui serait surprenant. Un seul point reste à éclaircir : le vrai motif de l'absence de Bradson du 2 au 10 juin.

— Nous connaissons son adresse, dit le Tondu. Allons nous renseigner auprès de ses voisins. »

Il nous restait du temps avant midi. Cependant, le métro londonien nous inquiétait quelque peu car nous ne l'avions évidemment jamais pris.

«Tant pis, fit la Guille, c'est trop important. Nous nous débrouillerons!»

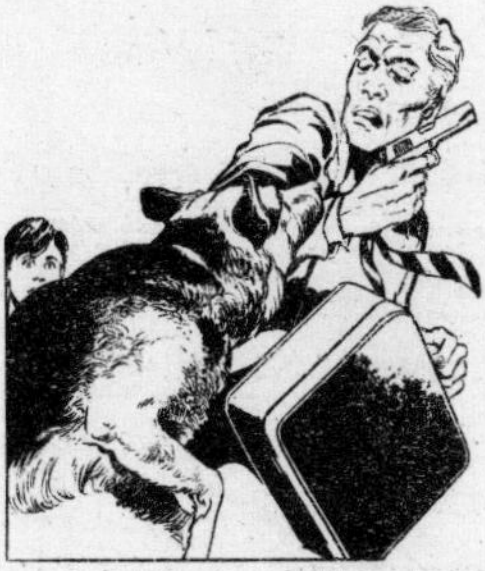

Chapitre 10

# Une « formidable » intuition

Non, le métro de Londres n'avait rien d'effrayant. Ce n'était, après tout, qu'un train comme les autres qui roulait sous l'immense cité, mais j'avais bien fait de ne pas emmener Kafi ; il n'y aurait pas été admis.

Une demi-heure plus tard, nous débarquions à la station indiquée par le restaurateur. Rien de commun entre ce populeux faubourg de Londres et la luxueuse Regent Street.

Là, pas de vieux messieurs en chapeau melon et fleur à la boutonnière mais des débardeurs, des matelots, des enfants plus ou moins dépenaillés.

Par chance, sur un plan du faubourg, Bistèque repéra tout de suite Coalway Street, tout près de l'endroit où le métro nous avait laissés. Dans cette petite rue, impossible de distinguer les unes des autres, autrement que par leurs numéros, les maisonnettes de brique qui la bordaient, tant elles se ressemblaient.

« A présent, comment on va faire ? fit le Tondu en grattant son crâne chauve sous son béret comme chaque fois qu'il était dans l'embarras.

— Je pense à une petite ruse, fit Mady. Je vais sonner à la maison voisine de celle de Bradson comme si je m'étais trompée. On me répondra qu'il habite à côté et j'en profiterai pour demander des nouvelles de sa fille, celle qui a été malade. Je verrai bien ce qu'on me répondra.

— Et si la personne qui t'ouvrira te dit qu'elle ne connaît pas les Bradson ?

— Si un de ses enfants a été très malade, cela doit se savoir, dans le quartier. »

Tandis que nous nous tenions à l'écart, Mady sonna au numéro 9. Une vieille femme vint ouvrir. Elle parut mal comprendre ce que Mady s'efforçait de lui expliquer en anglais car elle eut un air embarrassé. Enfin, elle désigna la maison voisine et expliqua encore quelque chose en tendant la main, cette fois, du côté opposé. Après quoi, sa porte se referma et Mady revint vers nous en courant.

« Ça y est ! J'ai le renseignement. Une des filles de Bradson a réellement été très malade. Elle a été soignée à l'hôpital Saint-Patrick, tout près d'ici.

— Donc, fit Gnafron découragé en fourrageant sa tignasse noire, sur ce point-là, non plus, Bradson n'a pas menti. »

Mais, se reprenant aussitôt :

« Après tout, ça ne l'empêcherait pas d'avoir été en France. Au contraire, la maladie de sa fille pouvait être un prétexte pour quitter son travail. Nous saurons peut-être, à l'hôpital, s'il est venu voir sa fille. »

Cinq minutes plus tard, nous arrivions devant Saint-Patrick. Mady, notre déléguée aux renseignements, eut la chance de tomber tout de suite sur une jeune secrétaire qui avait séjourné à Bordeaux et parlait assez bien le français. Elle se souvenait de la petite Elisabeth, hospitalisée pour une broncho-pneumonie, et que son père venait voir chaque jour pendant que la mère s'occupait des autres enfants.

Ainsi, James Blackmoor avait raison. Bradson, lui aussi, était certainement étranger à l'affaire. Le pauvre homme avait d'autres soucis en tête que de monter des coups de main.

Il ne nous restait plus qu'à rentrer au plus vite à Regent Street pour ne pas être en retard. Durant tout le trajet, dans le métro, personne ne souffla mot. Pourtant, j'en restais convaincu, le voleur des plans était un client du pub, un familier de James Blackmoor.

Il était plus d'une heure de l'après-midi quand la bande arriva à Regent Street. Qu'allions-nous dire à Mme Heddle, assez stricte sur l'heure des repas ?

« Tant pis, fit Mady, si elle nous questionne, disons tout bonnement la vérité. »

Mais Mme Heddle ne s'était pas inquiétée de notre retard. Pour attendre son fils, elle avait repoussé le lunch d'une demi-heure... en vain d'ailleurs, car David venait de téléphoner, annonçant qu'il ne pourrait pas rentrer à Londres avant l'après-midi.

« Mon fils s'excuse de ne pas vous tenir compagnie, dit-elle, il en est désolé. »

Chacun reprit sa place habituelle autour de la table ovale en acajou et Mady raconta notre expédition dans le quartier des docks.

« Oh ! s'écria Mme Heddle, vous êtes allés vous promener dans ces quartiers mal famés ? »

Et, nous voyant suivre des yeux une domestique en tablier blanc qui allait et venait, elle expliqua :

« Vous excuserez le service, aujourd'hui. Herbert, le maître d'hôtel, n'est pas venu ce matin. Je le suppose souffrant. J'ai dû le remplacer par la femme de chambre. »

Et le repas commença. Mais notre déconvenue nous avait coupé l'appétit. Nous devions nous forcer pour trouver excellente cette cuisine anglaise plutôt fade à notre goût. Tandis que Mady poursuivait le récit de notre expédition à l'autre bout de Londres, je ne cessais de suivre les allées et venues de la femme de chambre. Et tout à coup, comme celle-ci retournait à la cuisine avec un plat vide, une idée me traversa l'esprit, si subite, si effarante, que je m'arrêtai de manger, la gorge nouée.

« Qu'as-tu, Tidou ? fit la Guille en me voyant m'étrangler.

— C'est vrai, reprit Mme Heddle, vous êtes tout pâle, mon jeune ami. Vous vous sentez mal ? »

Oui, je me sentais mal, mais ce n'était pas la nourriture qui m'étouffait. Tous les regards braqués sur moi, je demeurai quelques instants comme paralysé. Enfin, dans un grand effort sur moi-même, je m'adressai à Mme Heddle.

« Excusez-moi. Il n'est pas convenable de se lever pendant le repas. Serait-il tout de même possible d'aller voir dans la chambre de votre fils si les plans sont toujours dans l'armoire ? »

Instantanément, les visages changèrent d'expression.

« Quoi ? se récria M. Heddle, vous voulez dire, mon ami, qu'ils n'y seraient peut-être plus ?

— Ils s'y trouvaient encore hier, reprit vivement sa femme, incrédule. Souvenez-vous, pendant le repas, mon fils a affirmé les avoir vus, le matin, en ouvrant l'armoire.

— En effet, Mme Heddle..., mais c'était hier. »

La bouche ouverte de stupeur, Mady se demanda si je ne perdais pas la tête et le Tondu se gratta furieusement le crâne. Il y eut quelques secondes de silence, puis le père de David se leva.

« *All right!* Allons tout de suite voir ! »

La chambre de son fils était située au bout de l'appartement. Il se dirigea gravement vers la bibliothèque et, après quelques tâtonnements, découvrit la clef derrière un volume des œuvres complètes de Shakespeare.

« Vous voyez, mon ami, me fit Mme Heddle sur un ton de reproche, la clef est bien à l'endroit indiqué par mon fils. Par conséquent, rien n'a été touché. »

Je ne répondis pas. Son mari s'avança vers

l'armoire, en ouvrit les deux battants, puis introduisit la petite clef dans la serrure de l'unique tiroir. Soudain, ses traits se contractèrent.

« *My God !...* Les plans !... Ils ne sont plus là ! »

Huit paires d'yeux se braquèrent de nouveau sur moi.

« Tidou ! s'écria Mady en me saisissant le bras. Comment as-tu su qu'ils avaient disparu ? Comment un voleur se serait-il introduit ici ?

— Il pouvait entrer tous les jours dans cette chambre, le plus simplement du monde.

— Quoi ? Le voleur entrait chez nous comme il le voulait ? reprit Mme Heddle horrifiée. Moi qui ai toujours eu si peur des gangsters !...

— Rassurez-vous, madame, il n'avait pas l'air d'un gangster. D'ailleurs, vous ne le reverrez certainement plus.

— Mais qui était-ce ?

— ... Votre maître d'hôtel ! »

Chapitre 11

# Le maître d'hôtel

Pendant quelques secondes, Mme Heddle parut littéralement assommée comme si le plafond de la chambre venait de tomber sur sa tête. Puis, reprenant son souffle, elle s'écria :

« Non, ce n'est pas vrai! Herbert est un homme correct, presque un gentleman. Les plans ne sont plus dans le tiroir, tout simplement parce que David les a cachés ailleurs.

— Excusez-moi de vous contredire, madame Heddle, mais ce n'est guère vraisemblable. Si le tiroir ne renfermait plus rien de précieux, votre fils n'avait aucune raison de replacer la clef derrière les livres de la bibliothèque.

— En effet, fit son mari, David n'a pas l'habitude de cacher ses clefs. Mais pourquoi soupçonner le maître d'hôtel? Il n'est pas le seul domestique dans la maison.

— Oui, Tidou, reprit Mady, pourquoi lui? Vite, explique-toi!

— Tout à l'heure, quand j'ai appris que, sans

motif, il n'avait pas pris son service, ce matin, j'ai eu comme un choc. Aussitôt, j'ai fait plusieurs rapprochements.

— Quels rapprochements? demanda vivement Mme Heddle.

— Ne s'est-il pas absenté, le mois dernier, pendant plusieurs jours?

— Je ne vois pas le rapport. Son père venait de mourir. Il était normal de prendre plusieurs jours de congé pour l'enterrement.

— Etes-vous sûre qu'il a réellement perdu son père?

— Oh! s'indigna presque Mme Heddle, pourquoi en douter? Il a reçu un télégramme et me l'a montré.

— En Angleterre comme en France n'importe qui peut probablement envoyer un télégramme. Rien ne prouve qu'il ne l'ait pas lui-même expédié.»

Et, à mes camarades :

«Il a dit avoir fait une chute, pendant son absence, or, souvenez-vous de l'accident, à Lyon. L'homme qui accompagnait le père de Margaret a pu être blessé, lui aussi. On sort rarement indemne d'une voiture qui a fait plusieurs tonneaux. Il l'était même certainement d'après l'ingénieur de la manufacture. "Une drôle de démarche", ce sont les mots qu'il a employés. Autrement dit, l'homme boitait. Et ce n'est pas tout. Toi, Gnafron, qui étais avec moi, tu te souviens certainement d'autres détails du signalement : un homme plutôt grand, d'un blond roux, avec un visage anguleux... comme le maître d'hôtel.

— Non, protesta vivement Mme Heddle, ce signalement ne signifie rien. Des millions d'Anglais ont les cheveux blonds et les traits accusés. »

A quoi je répondis :

« Excusez-moi, madame Heddle, mais celui-ci boitait et bon nombre d'Anglais ne parlent pas notre langue. Votre maître d'hôtel parlait certainement le français.

— Qu'en savez-vous ? Il ne prononce jamais un mot, pendant son service, ni en anglais, ni en français.

— Hier et avant-hier, j'ai remarqué qu'il comprenait ce que nous disions. Il a même souri à une plaisanterie de Bistèque.

— C'est vrai, approuva Mady. Il suivait ce que nous disions. Mais pourquoi aurait-il attendu jusqu'à présent pour voler les deux feuilles, s'il savait où les trouver ?

— Justement, il ignorait la cachette. Il ne l'a su qu'hier. Et c'est ici même qu'il l'a appris.

— Ici ? se récria Mme Heddle avec effroi. Quelqu'un, dans la maison, l'aurait donc renseigné ? C'est impensable !

— Excusez-moi encore, c'est vous-même qui la lui avez révélée, hier, au moment où vous avez fait préciser à votre fils l'endroit où étaient les plans. Le maître d'hôtel apportait un plat à ce moment-là, et comme il comprend le français !... »

La pauvre femme poussa un cri d'horreur.

« Epouvantable !... Ainsi, pendant deux mois, j'aurais été servie par un... par un... »

Elle ne trouva pas le mot ou n'osa pas le prononcer et se laissa tomber dans un fauteuil.

Alors, son mari et mes camarades, ébranlés par mes arguments, s'inquiétèrent de savoir comment le maître d'hôtel, s'il était vraiment le coupable, s'était procuré la montre de Blackmoor. J'expliquai qu'à mon idée il connaissait le concierge mais ne lui avait pas dit son vrai nom. Peut-être s'agissait-il de ce nommé Thomas qui buvait avec Bradson et Blackmoor, le jour de la disparition de la montre. Et j'ajoutai :

« C'est probablement lui aussi qui a ligoté Margaret dans le grenier. Ce qui expliquerait pourquoi il n'a pas fait entendre le son de sa voix. Elle le connaissait trop bien.

— Quoi ? se récria Mme Heddle, en bondissant de son fauteuil, Margaret a été attaquée ? »

Dans mon émotion, j'avais oublié que, devant le chapelier et sa femme, nous n'avions pas parlé de l'agression. Tant pis ! D'ailleurs, à présent, mieux valait tout dire. Je racontai ce qui était arrivé à la fiancée de leur fils et ils en restèrent décontenancés.

« Pourquoi n'a-t-elle pas averti la police ? dit vivement William Heddle. Je m'en occupe immédiatement. »

Il nous entraîne vers le salon et, sur le cadran du téléphone, compose un numéro.

« Allô !... Scotland Yard ? »

Très vite, en anglais, il explique ce qui se passe chez lui mais, à l'autre bout du fil, une voix l'interrompt. William Heddle fronce les sourcils et hausse le ton. Finalement, il raccroche nerveusement le récepteur, et, tourné vers nous :

« Malchance ! Une importante manifestation de dockers a lieu en ce moment sur le port. La police est sur les dents. Il n'est pas sûr qu'un superintendant puisse venir tout de suite.

— C'est pourtant urgent, fait Gnafron. Si le maître d'hôtel est vraiment le coupable, il doit penser qu'on le soupçonnera dès la découverte du vol. Quel est son nom exact ?

— Herbert Murray.

— Son adresse ?

— Il nous en a donné une : 12 Green Street à Lowfield.

— Est-ce loin ?

— De l'autre côté de la Tamise.

— Il faut tout de suite courir là-bas, vérifier s'il habite réellement là... ou s'il n'a pas déjà déménagé.

— Je suis désolé, dit le chapelier, il vous faudra attendre le retour de David. Ma mauvaise vue ne me permet pas de conduire une voiture.

— Ne vous inquiétez pas, Monsieur Heddle, fait le Tondu, nous nous débrouillerons. Comment filer au plus vite à Lowfield ?

— Je crois qu'un des bus qui passent à Piccadilly Circus dessert ce faubourg. Oui, c'est cela, le numéro 35. »

Je prie alors Mme Heddle de me procurer un vêtement ayant appartenu à Murray pour le faire flairer à mon chien. Elle s'extirpe à grand-peine du fauteuil où elle s'est de nouveau laissée choir, dans le salon, et se précipite vers l'office. Elle en revient avec l'habit noir que le maître d'hôtel-gentleman endossait pour son service. Elle a également trouvé ses gants blancs. Sans hésiter, je choisis les gants, moins encombrants, mieux imprégnés de l'odeur.

Alors, nous dévalons l'escalier et courons vers Hanover Street chercher Kafi que Margaret a gardé toute la matinée. En apprenant que le voleur serait le distingué maître d'hôtel des Heddle, elle reste suffoquée et demande des explications.

« Pas le temps, Margaret, fait Mady. Il faut que nous filions au plus vite à Lowfield. »

Et nous voilà repartis en courant vers Piccadilly Circus. Nous avons à peine le temps d'atteindre l'important carrefour qu'un gros bus rouge à deux étages, un 35, s'arrête le long d'un trottoir. Au moment où nous nous précipitons pour monter à l'intérieur, le receveur nous repousse, poli mais énergique :

« *Sorry !... No dogs !...* »

Les chiens ne sont pas admis dans les autobus !... et nous n'aurons pas plus de chance avec le métro.

« Tant pis, allons à pied, propose Bistèque.

— Tu n'y penses pas, réplique Mady. Lowfield est de l'autre côté de la Tamise.

— Alors, prenons un taxi !

— Il nous en faudrait deux, nous n'avons pas assez d'argent sur nous. »

Décontenancés, nous cherchons une solution quand la Guille se frappe le front :

« Attendez ! je viens d'avoir une idée... Camouflons Kafi avec l'imperméable du Tondu. »

Le Tondu est, en effet, le seul de nous sept à avoir emporté de Lyon un vêtement de pluie.

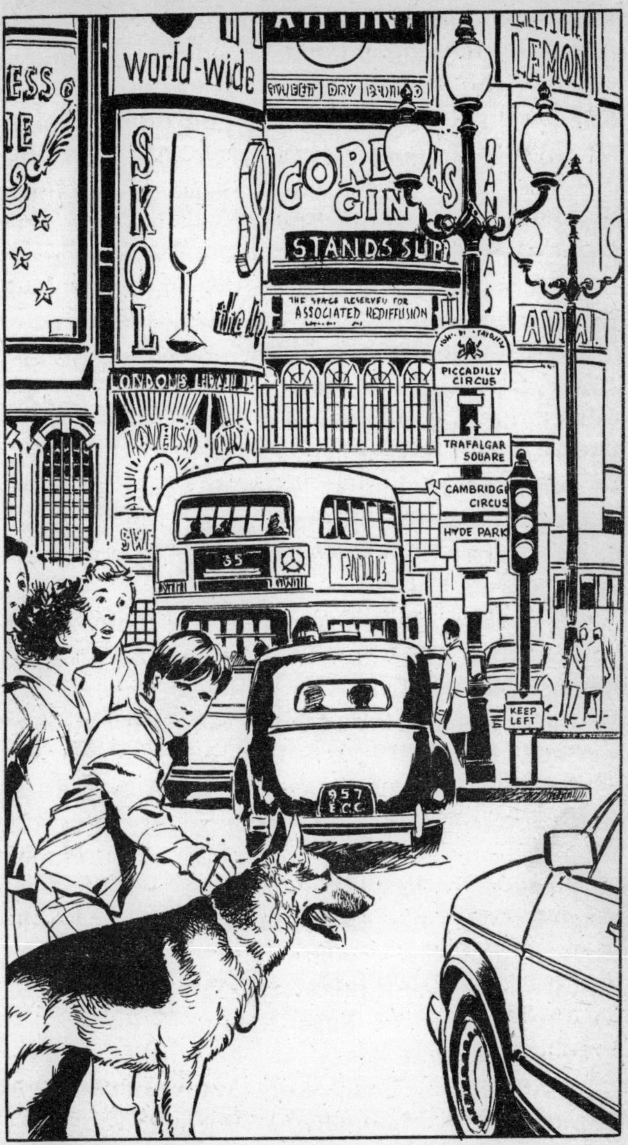
world-wide
LEMON
SKOL
DRY
GIN
THE SPACE RESERVED FOR
ASSOCIATED REDIFFUSION
PICCADILLY
CIRCUS
TRAFALGAR
SQUARE
CIRCUS
HYDE PARK
KEEP
LEFT
957
ECC

Il se dépouille de son imperméable et, tant bien que mal, avec un bout de ficelle que Gnafron trouve dans sa poche, j'empaquette mon pauvre Kafi en lui laissant juste un peu de jour pour respirer. Au moment où arrive un deuxième bus, nous nous présentons sans hésiter devant le marchepied. Nous voyant si lourdement chargés, le receveur écarte les autres voyageurs pour nous laisser passer les premiers. Brave Kafi! Il a compris qu'il ne devait pas bouger d'une patte, et il se laisse porter comme un vulgaire paquet de linge sale.

Et l'autobus démarre. En plein après-midi, la circulation n'est pas très dense, mais les arrêts se suivent, fréquents. Nous aurions le temps d'admirer Londres à loisir; mais nous pensons à bien autre chose. Pourvu que Murray soit encore chez lui!

Le voyage est interminable. La Tamise traversée, il se poursuit sur la rive droite et nous laissons derrière nous la fameuse tour de Big Ben avec son horloge géante qui donne l'heure à toute la ville.

«Lowfield?» demande pour la troisième fois Mady au receveur qui ne cesse de jeter des regards soupçonneux sur notre volumineux paquet.

«*Not yet!...* pas encore», répond invariablement l'employé.

Enfin, au bout d'un quart d'heure, celui-ci lui touche l'épaule du doigt.

«*Lowfield, next stop!*»

«Prochain arrêt», traduit Mady, décidément la plus douée en anglais.

L'autobus à peine arrêté, nous sautons sur le trottoir et je m'empresse de déballer Kafi qui jaillit de l'imperméable comme un diable d'une boîte. Il s'agit, à présent, de trouver Green Street au plus vite. Un vieux monsieur à qui Gnafron s'est adressé tend un doigt.

«*Next street but one, on the left.*»

Gnafron n'a rien compris... moi non plus, mais Mady, toujours elle, traduit :

«Prochaine rue sauf une sur la gauche... Ça doit vouloir dire la deuxième rue.»

En effet, au second carrefour, une plaque indique Green Street, une voie étroite, bordée de maisons basses, en brique, comme celle de Bradson. Le numéro 12 est une sorte d'hôtel qui porte le nom de *Tulip Home* : «Pension des Tulipes».

«Pour commencer, dit Corget, demandons simplement si un nommé Herbert Murray habite bien ici.»

La porte d'entrée est ouverte. Nous pénétrons dans un petit hall terminé par un escalier qui monte au seul et unique étage. Une vieille dame aux cheveux blancs, toute menue, vient à notre rencontre, et demande en anglais, bien entendu, ce que nous voulons. Au nom de Murray, elle pointe un doigt vers le plafond, pour nous indiquer une chambre, au premier. Mais, en même temps, elle secoue la tête.

«*Mr. Murray is away.*»

Ce que nous traduisons par : Murray est absent. Mais que signifie exactement «absent»? Le maître d'hôtel est-il sorti pour la journée? A-t-il définitivement quitté la pension en emportant ses affaires? Une laborieuse discussion s'engage avec la vieille Anglaise. Nous finissons par comprendre que Murray a quitté le *Tulip Home*, ce matin, avec ses bagages et qu'il n'a pas laissé d'adresse.

«Il fallait s'y attendre, soupire Gnafron découragé. Le fil de la piste est rompu. Il faudrait un miracle pour le retrouver!»

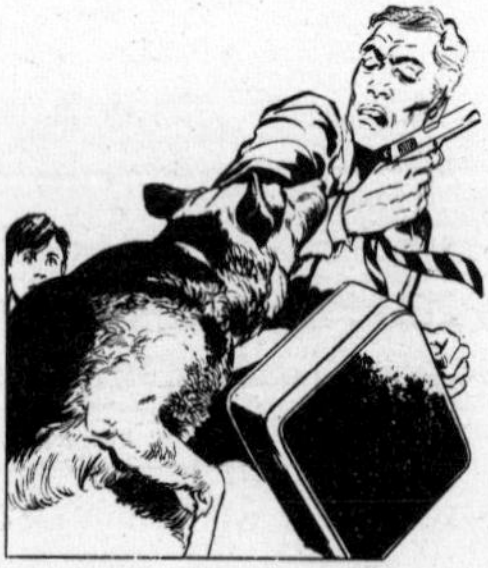

Chapitre 12

# Le « Tulip Home »

Le fil de la piste est rompu mais, par sa fuite, Murray a fait la preuve de sa culpabilité. Pourquoi aurait-il déménagé, juste ce matin, si ce n'était par crainte d'être retrouvé ?

Qu'est-il devenu ? En possession des plans, au complet, a-t-il pris le train ou l'avion pour la France ? En attendant de partir, se cache-t-il quelque part dans Londres ?

Le bouillant Gnafron trépigne, clamant que toute la bande, à part moi, a été stupide de ne pas penser plus tôt au maître d'hôtel.

« Ça crevait pourtant les yeux, bougonne-t-il. Mais que peut la police à présent ? Autant chercher une aiguille dans une botte de foin. »

Cependant, brusquement, la chance tourne de notre côté. Nous revenons sur nos pas pour prendre l'autobus quand la Guille, qui marche devant moi, se retourne brusquement et nous repousse vivement en arrière en s'écriant :

« Vite ! cachons-nous ! »

Sans chercher à comprendre, nous nous précipitons vers le premier refuge venu : une petite cour dont la grille est entrouverte.

« Je crois que c'était Murray, fait la Guille haletant. Aplatissons-nous contre le mur ; il vient dans notre direction, sur l'autre trottoir. »

Retenant notre respiration, nous attendons. Est-ce bien Murray ? Que reviendrait-il faire dans un quartier qu'il a fui ? Il est trop intelligent pour ne pas comprendre le danger de réintégrer le *Tulip Home.*

Tout à coup, une silhouette apparaît, en face. Aucun doute, c'est lui. Il semble effectivement retourner à la pension.

« Il a dû oublier quelque chose d'important, murmure Bistèque.

— Ou nous avons mal compris la logeuse, reprend le Tondu. Il n'était pas parti définitivement.

— Peu importe. Surveillons-le de près. »

Sitôt l'homme disparu à nos yeux, nous nous risquons à l'angle de la cour et, par précaution, je fais sentir un des gants blancs à Kafi. Malgré sa demi-infirmité, Murray marche d'un bon pas. Devant le *Tulip Home*, il s'arrête, jette prudemment un regard à la ronde, et s'engouffre dans le vestibule.

« C'est le moment ! fait Mady. Appelons un policeman !

— A condition d'en trouver un, réplique Gorget. Nous n'en avons pas vu dans le quartier... et il arrivera trop tard. L'homme ne va sûrement pas s'éterniser à la pension.

— Alors, pas d'hésitation, décide Gnafron,

bloquons le *Tulip Home* jusqu'à l'arrivée d'un bobby. Toi, Mady, qui te débrouilles bien en anglais, tâche d'en trouver un et décide-le à te suivre... Emmène la Guille avec toi ; il vaut mieux être à deux. »

Tandis que nos camarades s'éloignent, nous rasons les murs en direction du *Tulip Home.* Nous voyant reparaître, la logeuse ne cache pas sa surprise.

« Herbert Murray est ici, fait Corget en anglais. Nous venons de le voir entrer. Qu'est-il venu faire ? Vous nous aviez dit qu'il avait déménagé. »

Sa prononciation laisse à désirer et la vieille dame comprend mal. Alors, à sa façon, le Tondu reprend la question. La logeuse, cette fois, semble inquiète, Murray l'aurait-il menacée de représailles si elle dénonçait sa présence dans cette maison ?

Toujours est-il que la vieille dame nous invite avec insistance à sortir. A notre tour, nous faisons semblant de ne pas comprendre. Soudain, tandis que Gorget essaie de lui expliquer que nous attendons l'arrivée d'un policeman, Kafi, qui, après avoir flairé le gant tout à l'heure, ne demande qu'à suivre une piste, tire violemment sur sa laisse et m'échappe. Sans hésiter, il bondit vers l'escalier. Je me précipite pour le rattraper. Au moment où, sur la dernière marche, je saisis sa lanière, une porte s'ouvre sur le palier. Le temps d'un éclair, j'aperçois le maître d'hôtel qui s'apprêtait à sortir. L'homme change de couleur, prend un air affolé et referme vivement la porte à double tour. Il m'a reconnu. En tout cas, il ne peut pas ne pas avoir reconnu Kafi. Comme un fou, je dévale l'escalier :

« Murray !... Il m'a vu !... Il va chercher à se sauver. »

Et, à la logeuse :

« Peut-on sortir de sa chambre autrement que par la porte du palier ? »

Naturellement, la vieille dame ne comprend pas. Elle s'inquiète seulement un peu plus de ce qui se passe chez elle.

« Votre pensionnaire n'est qu'un voleur, un bandit, un gangster », répète Corget.

Gangster ! Elle n'a retenu que ce mot et nous regarde, hébétée. Ah ! si Mady pouvait arriver tout de suite avec un bobby. Gnafron enrage.

« Un policeman ! Vite un policeman ! »

Tout à coup, il aperçoit le téléphone dans l'appartement de la vieille dame. Dernière ressource, il se précipite vers l'appareil pour essayer, comme William Heddle, d'atteindre Scotland Yard. Mal lui en prend. Voyant ce garçon s'introduire de force chez elle, la logeuse se méprend. Croyant sans doute avoir affaire à de jeunes rôdeurs étrangers, elle appelle de toutes ses forces :

« *Help !...* Au secours ! »

Des pensionnaires accourent. L'un d'eux, un vieux monsieur distingué qui, heureusement, parle assez bien le français, nous demande ce qui arrive. Corget explique que, sans s'en douter, sa logeuse héberge un dangereux malfaiteur et que deux de nos camarades sont à la recherche d'un policeman.

« Un malfaiteur ? reprend le vieux monsieur suffoqué. Vous connaissez son nom ?

— Herbert Murray !

— *My goodness !...* Un homme si correct... Vous avez des preuves ?

— Nous sommes certains qu'il a commis un vol à Regent Street et probablement une agression.

— Si vous manquez de preuves formelles, la police n'interviendra pas. La police anglaise n'agit pas comme la vôtre. On n'arrête jamais quelqu'un sur de simples soupçons.

— Oh ! proteste Bistèque, puisque nous... »

Il n'achève pas. Un étrange bruit vient d'ébranler la maison, un bruit venu d'on ne sait où, peut-être du premier. Avec Kafi, qui ne demande qu'à suivre la piste, nous nous précipitons vers l'escalier. A coup sûr, quelque chose vient de se passer dans la chambre de Murray. L'oreille tendue, nous nous approchons de la porte. Rien, la pièce paraît vide.

« Essayons d'entrer », propose Gnafron.

Doucement, il fait tourner la poignée de la porte. Celle-ci est fermée à clef, comme il fallait s'y attendre. Le Tondu veut l'enfoncer d'un coup d'épaule ; le vieux monsieur intervient vivement.

« Surtout, ne fais pas une chose pareille. Vous pourriez tous avoir de graves ennuis. »

Heureusement, au même moment, nous parviennent les voix de Mady et de la Guille. Ils ont trouvé un bobby, un grand gaillard haut de deux mètres, qui bredouille seulement quelques mots de français. Le vieux monsieur lui traduit ce que nous venons d'expliquer. L'agent déclare qu'il n'a pas le droit de fouiller un domicile, même quand ce n'est qu'une chambre de pension de famille. Poliment, il se contente de frapper à la porte.

« C'est évident, il ne répondra pas, fait Gnafron excédé. D'ailleurs, je mettrais ma main au feu qu'il a filé au moment où nous avons entendu ce bruit, tout à l'heure. »

Embarrassé, le policeman soulève son casque et se gratte la tête. Comment pénétrer dans cette chambre sans enfreindre la loi ? Soudain, une idée lui vient. S'il n'a pas le droit, en tant que policier, de pénétrer chez quelqu'un qui refuse d'ouvrir, la logeuse, elle, peut le faire, ne serait-ce que pour mettre de l'ordre dans la pièce. Elle doit d'ailleurs avoir en double la clef de cette chambre. Il invite donc la vieille femme à descendre chercher cette clef et à ouvrir elle-même..., ce qu'elle fait d'une main tremblante.

« Personne ! » crie Gnafron, en se précipitant dans la pièce.

Par où l'homme s'est-il sauvé ? L'unique fenêtre donnant sur la rue est restée fermée. Mais, poussant la porte du cabinet de toilette, le Tondu s'écrie à son tour :

« Il s'est sauvé par ici !... »

Au fond du réduit, plusieurs lames du vieux plancher ont été arrachées. L'homme s'est laissé tomber par le trou jusqu'au rez-de-chaussée. C'est le bruit de sa chute que nous avons entendu tout à l'heure. Cette fois, le bobby réagit. Il réclamait un flagrant délit, le voici : dégradations à l'intérieur d'un immeuble. Il est en droit de demander des comptes à leur auteur.

Alors, au risque de défoncer les marches branlantes, il dévale l'escalier en nous invitant à le suivre.

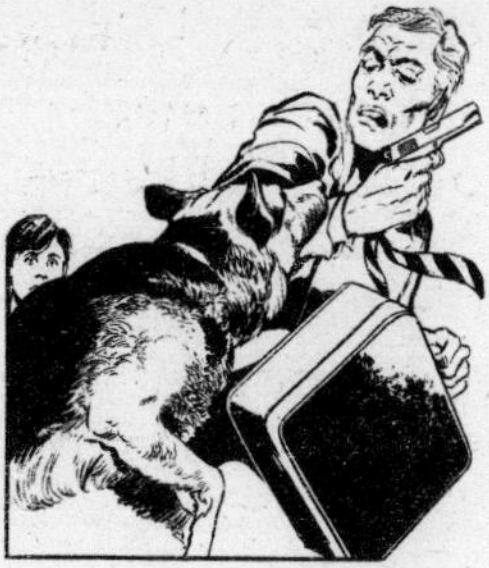

Chapitre 13

# Bravo, Kafi!

Naturellement, aucune trace de Murray dans la buanderie où il a atterri... mais une porte donnant sur une courette est restée grande ouverte. L'homme s'est échappé par là. Il suffit de voir Kafi se précipiter au bout de la cour, et se dresser contre le mur de clôture, pour s'en convaincre.

« Quoi ? fait le policeman en regardant mon chien, il est capable... de... de... »

Ne trouvant pas le mot français qu'il cherche, il renifle fortement en humant le dessus de sa main.

« Oui, fait Mady, nous l'avons dressé comme un chien policier. Il peut suivre une piste, très loin. »

Et pour en persuader le bobby, je sors les gants blancs, en expliquant qu'ils ont appartenu au pensionnaire du *Tulip Home.*

« *All right!* fait l'agent. Suivons votre chien. »

Le mur de brique, haut de deux mètres à

peine, se laisse facilement escalader, même par Mady à qui le policeman fait la courte échelle. De l'autre côté de la clôture, court une ruelle qui dessert les petits jardins de la rangée de maisons. La truffe au ras du sol, la queue battante, Kafi nous entraîne jusqu'à son extrémité, c'est-à-dire à l'endroit où elle débouche sur une rue perpendiculaire à Green Street.

« Attention, Kafi ! Ne nous égare pas ! »

Tirant toujours sur sa laisse, mon chien ne marque aucune hésitation. La chaussée traversée, il suit le trottoir d'en face. Puis, au bout d'une centaine de mètres, il s'arrête et ne sait plus quelle direction prendre.

« Regardez ! fait le Tondu, nous sommes sous un panneau d'arrêt d'autobus. Murray a couru ici en attendre un. La piste est coupée. »

En effet, Kafi va, vient sur le trottoir et me regarde d'un air lamentable. A tout hasard, cependant, je l'invite à s'écarter du poteau et, tout à coup, il tire de nouveau sur la laisse. Il m'attire vers la droite, c'est-à-dire dans le sens de marche de l'autobus. A-t-il retrouvé l'odeur de l'homme même si celui-ci poursuivait son chemin en voiture ? Je ne doute pas des possibilités de Kafi. Tout de même, la prouesse serait par trop extraordinaire. Mais, soudain, Mady s'écrie :

« Je crois comprendre, Tidou. L'homme s'est arrêté près du poteau pour attendre un bus, mais aucune voiture n'arrivait. Pris de peur, il a préféré poursuivre son chemin à pied jusqu'au prochain arrêt où il se sentait plus loin de Green Street.

— Très juste, Mady, approuve Bistèque. Malheureusement, à l'arrêt suivant, la trace sera définitivement perdue.

— Allons quand même jusque-là. »

Et nous voici repartis derrière mon chien. Cependant, le bobby, lui, commence à s'inquiéter.

« Vous croyez que votre chien ?... si loin ?... »

A grandes enjambées, sans courir, lui, il nous suit et, quatre cents mètres plus loin, nous apercevons un nouveau panneau d'arrêt pour les autobus.

Je freine l'ardeur de Kafi, certain de le voir encore embarrassé. Pas du tout. Sans prendre le temps de flairer à droite et à gauche, il continue son chemin.

« Tant mieux ! fait le Tondu. Cela prouve que Murray n'a pas non plus pris l'autobus ici parce que cela n'en valait plus la peine... Autrement dit, il n'allait pas très loin d'ici. Continuons. »

Cette fois, le policeman renonce à nous croire. Il comprend mal nos explications et se demande si nous ne sommes pas en train de lui faire faire le tour de Londres à une allure de marathon. Mady a toutes les peines du monde à le décider à continuer la poursuite.

« Regardez notre chien, insiste-t-elle, il n'a pas perdu la piste. Je vous le répète, c'est un chien extraordinaire. »

Nous dépassons ainsi un nouvel arrêt d'autobus que Kafi semble ignorer. Depuis Green Street, nous avons parcouru plus d'un kilomètre quand enfin mon chien s'arrête. Pas de panneau d'arrêt d'autobus à cet endroit, mais un passage pour piétons, tracé sur la chaussée.

« Nous touchons au but, affirme Mady. L'homme a piétiné quelques instants ici pour attendre un arrêt du trafic afin de traverser la rue. Or, en face, aucun carrefour. Par conséquent, il n'a pas changé de direction pour prendre une autre rue. Conclusion, nous sommes proches de l'endroit où il se rendait. »

Le raisonnement est subtil, trop difficile à expliquer au policeman qui, à présent, se contente de suivre sans chercher à comprendre.

Pourtant, Mady a raison. A peine a-t-il fait cinquante mètres sur l'autre trottoir, que, brusquement, Kafi oblique vers une maison et s'arrête devant la porte.

Est-ce un hasard ? L'immeuble abrite encore une pension de famille qui porte, elle aussi, un nom de fleur : *Daisy Boarding House* : « Pension des Marguerites ».

« C'est bien ça, dit la Guille. Son coup fait, il ne savait où se cacher. Il a cherché une maison du même genre. »

Le policeman, lui, reste sceptique, persuadé qu'un chien, même parfaitement dressé, n'aurait pu suivre sans se tromper une aussi longue piste. Il se décide tout de même à sonner. La porte s'ouvre sur une vieille petite dame qu'on prendrait pour l'autre logeuse sans les lunettes d'écaille qui chevauchent son nez.

A la vue de ce policeman, deux fois plus haut qu'elle, elle s'inquiète de ce qui a bien pu motiver la venue d'un agent. Notre bobby lui demande courtoisement si, parmi ses nouveaux pensionnaires, elle ne compte pas un nommé Herbert Murray.

« Murray ? répète la vieille femme en secouant la tête. Je n'ai pas de Murray chez moi. Je n'en ai même jamais eu. »

Mon chien, lui, qui me tire vers l'escalier, au fond du vestibule, semble prouver le contraire. S'il ne tenait qu'à moi, je m'empresserais de le suivre mais, nous venons de le voir, la police anglaise prend toutes sortes de précautions avant d'agir.

« La pension n'occupe sans doute pas entièrement l'immeuble, fait Bistèque, l'homme s'est peut-être réfugié chez quelqu'un d'autre, chez un complice.

— Ou il a donné un faux nom », reprend Gorget.

Poliment, le bobby invite la logeuse à lui montrer le registre sur lequel elle est tenue de consigner l'identité de ses pensionnaires avec les dates d'arrivée et de départ.

« Entrez ! dit la vieille dame. Vous le consulterez dans le living-room, vous serez plus à l'aise. »

Nous pénétrons dans une pièce encombrée de bibelots et, sans doute pour que personne, parmi les habitants de l'immeuble, ne sache que la police enquête chez elle, la logeuse referme avec précaution la porte derrière nous.

« Regardez tout de suite à la dernière page », fait Mady.

Penchée sur le livre, à côté du bobby, elle relève le dernier nom, inscrit le matin même : Harold Marland.

« C'est lui ! s'écrie-t-elle. Il a pris un autre

nom... mais en gardant les mêmes initiales, peut-être à cause de son linge marqué d'un H et d'un M.

— Hein?... Que dites-vous?» fait le bobby. Mady n'a pas le temps de traduire son explication. Brusquement, mon chien vient de tirer sur sa laisse en direction de la porte.

Kafi a entendu du bruit dans le vestibule!

Nous nous précipitons... juste à temps pour voir la porte donnant sur la rue se refermer. Ni le Tondu ni moi ne parvenons à la rouvrir. La vieille dame doit elle-même intervenir pour faire fonctionner l'antique système de verrouillage. Le premier, Gnafron bondit dehors et pousse un cri :

«Murray!...»

Malgré sa jambe raide et la valise qui l'encombre, le maître d'hôtel a pris de l'avance. Il nous avait certainement vus entrer. Dès qu'il a su que nous étions dans l'appartement de la logeuse, il est descendu à pas de loup pour prendre la fuite. Cette fois, le bobby n'hésite plus. Nous nous élançons derrière lui.

«Toi, Mady, fait le Tondu, reste en arrière. On ne sait jamais ce qui peut arriver.»

Il ne croit pas si bien dire. En effet, alors que nous ne sommes plus qu'à trente mètres de lui, le fuyard se retourne et brandit un revolver.

«Attention!» crie la Guille.

Un coup de feu claque, puis un second. Instinctivement, nous nous sommes plaqués contre une maison. Personne n'a été touché. Du geste, le bobby nous invite à rester où nous sommes, puis il s'élance de nouveau vers le maître d'hôtel qui s'est remis à courir. Mais, c'est plus fort que nous. Nous repartons nous aussi.

« Qu'est-ce qu'il attend pour tirer, le policeman, puisqu'il est en danger ? fait le Tondu.

— Les policiers anglais ne sont jamais armés, répond Corget. Margaret l'a dit. »

Cela n'empêche pas notre courageux bobby de continuer sa poursuite. Une seconde fois, le bandit se retourne pour faire feu.

« Le lâche ! enrage Gnafron. Il va finir par l'abattre. »

Mais, tout à coup, je pense à Kafi. A Lyon, avec un pistolet à amorce, je lui ai appris à se méfier des balles et à se protéger d'un tireur en courant par bonds désordonnés comme un lièvre. Je me penche vivement vers lui et lui fais signe, avec la main, qu'il doit aller désarmer l'homme en courant en zigzag.

« Va, Kafi !... et ne le lâche plus. »

Mon chien part en flèche, d'abord tout droit. Puis il exécute de grands bonds à droite, à gauche. Il rattrape le bobby et le dépasse. Encore quelques mètres et il rejoindra le fuyard. Murray l'a vu, mais ne se méfie de rien, car Kafi, au lieu de lancer son attaque de front, fait semblant de dépasser l'homme qui vient de se retourner une fois de plus pour tirer. Mon cœur bat à tout rompre. Cette fois, le bobby est si proche que le bandit ne le manquera pas.

Mais, au même moment, d'un bond fantastique, Kafi se jette sur le bras du tireur. Le coup est parti quand même... cependant, une fraction de seconde trop tard. Déviée, la balle atteint seulement le bobby à la cheville. Sa course stoppée, le policeman vacille et s'affaisse sur le trottoir, tandis que Kafi, acharné à secouer le bras droit du tireur, réussit à faire tomber l'arme.

« Plus rien à craindre! hurle Corget. Allons-y! »

Aux prises avec Kafi, l'homme essaie de se défendre avec sa valise en guise de bouclier. Peine perdue. D'ailleurs, nous sommes là, rejoints par des passants. Tandis que Mady se précipite avec des gens du quartier, pour secourir le blessé, la lutte se poursuit pour maîtriser le maître d'hôtel. Elle ne sera pas longue car le plus dangereux de la besogne, c'est Kafi qui l'a accompli. Saisi de toutes parts, le stylé maître d'hôtel de Mme Heddle comprend vite l'inutilité de toute résistance. Et, ironie, c'est Kafi, à présent, qui doit le défendre contre la fureur des témoins du drame.

Enfin, une ambulance surgit, se frayant à coups de sirène un passage à travers la foule qui grossit de minute en minute. Deux infirmiers et un médecin entourent le blessé, qui a réussi à se relever, et se tient debout sur un pied. Il ne paraît pas trop souffrir, heureusement.

« *Thank you!* » nous fait-il en s'efforçant de sourire.

Puis, cherchant Kafi des yeux :

« Votre chien?... Où est-il?... Il m'a sauvé la vie... Je veux le remercier. »

Avant d'être hissé dans l'ambulance, il caresse Kafi en répétant :

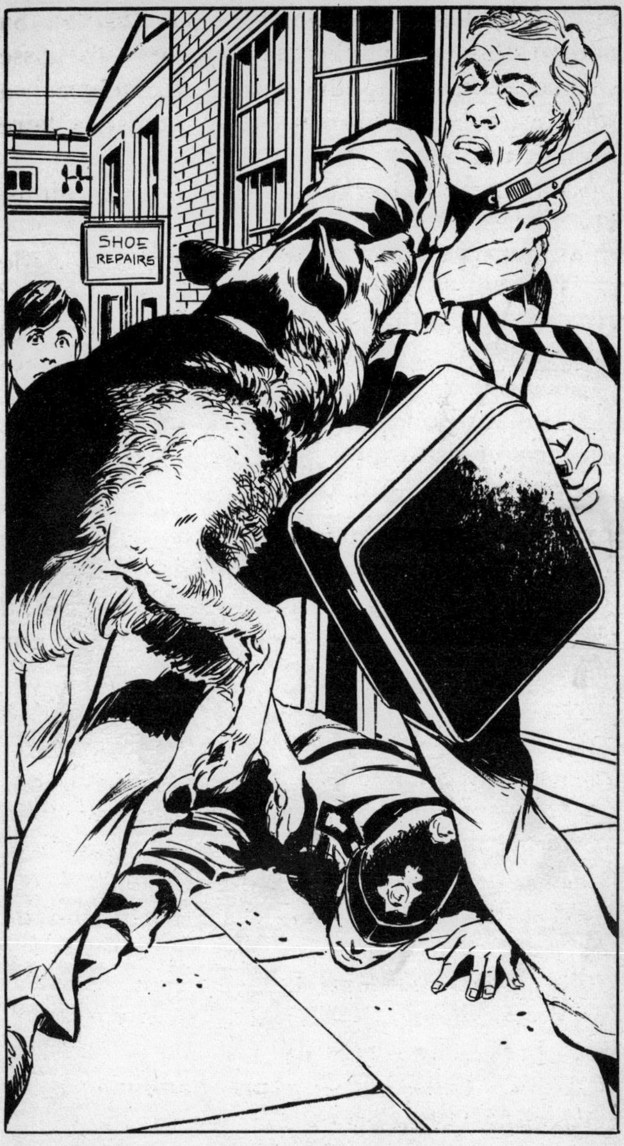
SHOE
REPAIRS

«*Thank you, my good fellow!...* Merci, mon copain!»

Mais, à peine sommes-nous revenus de nos émotions que deux nouvelles voitures débouchent dans la rue, des voitures de la police, celles-ci. Tandis que la première emmène le prisonnier, un policier en civil nous invite tous à monter dans la seconde, avec Kafi.

«Où nous conduit-on? demande Mady, encore toute pâle.

— A Scotland Yard!»

Scotland Yard!... Le fameux Scotland Yard des romans policiers qui me donnaient le frisson, le soir, dans mon lit, à Lyon. Ah! si jamais j'avais pensé qu'un jour...!

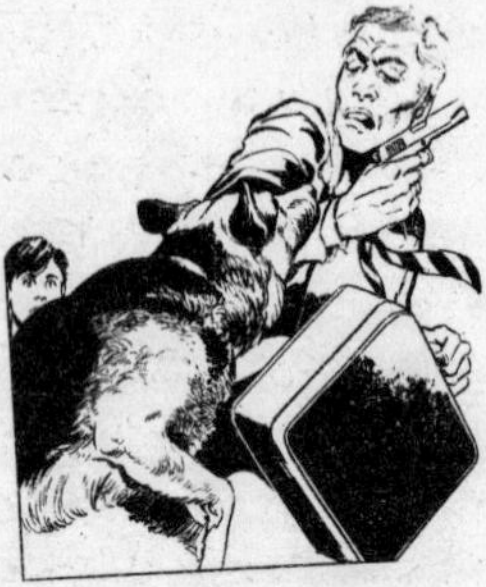

Chapitre 14

# Scotland Yard

Le grand pont de Westminster traversé, notre voiture oblique à droite vers les quais, puis exécute un savant virage avant de stopper devant un immense bâtiment tout neuf : le nouveau Scotland Yard qui, depuis peu, remplace l'ancien siège de la police londonienne.

Le policier en civil qui nous accompagne, et que tout le monde appelle respectueusement « monsieur le superintendant » (l'équivalent sans doute d'un commissaire), nous invite à descendre et à le suivre. Par un ascenseur, nous arrivons au sixième étage dans un vaste bureau bien éclairé, orné d'un grand portrait de la reine. Murray est déjà là, encadré de deux bobbies, encore plus grands que le nôtre. Impassible, il a repris son air digne de maître d'hôtel stylé et nous regarde sans sourciller.

Impressionnés par les lieux, nous nous faisons tout petits, et Kafi a l'air de se demander s'il a été bien inspiré en déchirant les vêtements de celui qui allait et venait, majestueux, dans la salle à manger de Regent Street.

Le superintendant nous fait placer à gauche de son bureau, tandis que les deux gardes du corps amènent Murray devant lui. Nos identités déclinées, nous sommes invités à décrire la scène au cours de laquelle le *constable* (c'est le vrai nom d'un agent de police, en Angleterre) a été blessé. Avide de détails précis, le superintendant pose question sur question, d'un ton sec qui nous intimide.

Plutôt que de parler tous à la fois, nous laissons Corget décrire les événements, ce qui n'est pas facile. Heureusement, il le fait en français, car un jeune interprète a été appelé. Par moments, le superintendant fronce les sourcils et, se tournant vers l'interprète, lui demande s'il ne se trompe pas dans sa traduction, tant cette affaire de plans volés paraît invraisemblable.

« Voyons, fait-il, cet homme aurait pris de tels risques pour les plans d'un simple métier à broder ? C'est incroyable !

— C'est que, intervient Mady, l'industriel de Lyon était très intéressé par le projet. Nous l'avons vu. Il en offrait une grosse somme. Le maître d'hôtel savait qu'il pouvait en retirer une fortune. »

Et, désignant la valise de Murray, déposée sur le bureau :

« Les plans, vous les trouverez probablement dans ces bagages. »

Le superintendant regarde durement Mady, signifiant qu'il n'aime pas recevoir d'ordres. Cependant, il commande à un policeman de vérifier le contenu de la valise verte dont Murray se servait comme d'un bouclier contre les attaques de Kafi. Le *constable* en retire du linge, entassé à la hâte, des objets de toilette, mais rien de plus. Nous nous regardons, atterrés. Interrogé, le maître d'hôtel feint l'ignorance. Il n'a jamais entendu parler de ces plans.

« Il ment ! proteste avec énergie Gnafron. Les deux feuilles, celles qui manquaient au voleur, ont disparu pendant que cet homme se trouvait chez M. William Heddle. La veille, il avait appris où elles se trouvaient. Il les a prises dans le tiroir d'une armoire. »

Cette assurance, qu'aucune preuve ne justifie, ne plaît guère au superintendant qui invite sèchement Gnafron à ne donner que des faits contrôlables. Cependant, il demande à Murray dans quelles circonstances il a quitté son service, la veille, chez les Heddle.

« J'étais souffrant, explique le maître d'hôtel. Je regrette de n'avoir pu prévenir Mme Heddle ; ma logeuse ne permettait pas qu'on utilise son téléphone.

— Alors, pourquoi vous sauviez-vous, si vous n'aviez rien à vous reprocher... et pourquoi avez-vous été pris de panique au point de tirer sur un policeman ?

— La peur, monsieur le superintendant, simplement la peur. Je... je regrette ce que j'ai fait. D'ailleurs, je ne le visais pas, je voulais seulement l'obliger à abandonner sa poursuite.

— Il ment ! s'écrie Gnafron. Les plans ne sont pas dans sa valise parce qu'il a quitté la pension précipitamment. Il les avait dans sa chambre ; il n'a pas eu le temps de les récupérer.

— Oui, monsieur le superintendant, dis-je à mon tour. Il faudrait visiter cette chambre. Si les plans y sont, mon chien saura les trouver, comme il a retrouvé la piste du voleur et l'a suivie sur plus d'un kilomètre. »

Le commissaire réprime un mouvement d'humeur, mais visiblement, mon chien l'intéresse. Finalement, il désigne deux agents pour m'accompagner, avec Kafi, jusqu'à la pension.

Un quart d'heure plus tard, la voiture nous dépose devant la porte de la logeuse qui, affolée, se demande quel bandit se cache encore chez elle. Nous grimpons aussitôt dans la chambre de Murray, au second. L'homme n'a pas eu le temps de rassembler toutes ses affaires. Du linge, un parapluie, une paire de chaussures ont été oubliés. En revanche, aucun papier dans les tiroirs d'une armoire et d'une commode à dessus de marbre. Alors, aussi robustes que des déménageurs, les policemen déplacent tous les meubles, espérant découvrir quelque chose. Rien... et rien non plus derrière les tentures de la fenêtre. Dernière cachette possible : les papiers peints, décollés par endroits. L'homme aurait pu glisser les feuilles entre la vieille tapisserie et le mur. Nous promenons nos doigts partout, en vain.

Mais, tout à coup, en me retournant, je vois Kafi rôder autour de la commode. Qu'a-t-il flairé ? L'un après l'autre, j'enlève du meuble les tiroirs déjà visités.

« Tu te trompes, Kafi, il n'y a rien. »

Pourtant, mon chien insiste. La tête relevée, il flaire avec application le dessus de la vieille commode. Une idée me traverse l'esprit. Par gestes, je fais comprendre aux policemen que j'aurais besoin d'un tournevis.

*« Yes! »* me fait l'un des deux hommes en sortant son couteau, muni de plusieurs lames et petits outils.

Délicatement, j'entreprends d'enlever les quatre vis qui maintiennent le marbre. La plaque à peine déplacée, je pousse un cri de triomphe.

« Les plans! »

Les feuilles paraissent au complet. Il y en a onze au total. Ahuris, émerveillés par le flair de Kafi, les deux bobbies flattent mon chien qui frétille de la queue, conscient d'avoir fait une importante découverte.

Il ne nous reste plus qu'à rentrer à Scotland Yard. A une vitesse folle, la voiture nous ramène sur les bords de la Tamise. Le premier, je fais irruption dans la salle et m'arrête sur le seuil, surpris d'y découvrir Margaret et David qui, je l'apprendrai plus tard, ont été avertis en mon absence par téléphone. En apercevant les plans, Margaret se précipite pour les compter.

« Oui, ils sont tous là! »

Cette fois, le commissaire se décide à nous prendre au sérieux. Devant la façon dont Kafi a retrouvé les feuilles sous le marbre, il reste confondu et lance à mon chien un regard plein d'admiration.

« La preuve est faite, lance-t-il à Murray, et

nous comprenons, à présent, pourquoi vous n'avez pas emporté ces plans en fuyant. Les enlever de leur cachette vous aurait pris trop de temps. Mais vous ne désespériez pas de les retrouver un jour.»

Le maître d'hôtel ne peut plus nier. Alors, changeant de tactique, il rejette la responsabilité du vol sur un complice.

«Ces plans m'ont été remis par un ami, explique-t-il.

— Quel ami?

— Le gardien de Harry Simson. C'est lui qui a tout organisé.»

Une soudaine colère monte au visage de Margaret.

«Oh! c'est trop fort! Je connais James Blackmoor, monsieur le superintendant. C'est un honnête homme. Il était au courant des travaux de mon père mais il n'aurait jamais monté un coup pareil. S'il est complice, c'est sans le vouloir. Le maître d'hôtel lui a extorqué des renseignements sur l'invention.

— Il faut que nous entendions cet homme, déclare le superintendant.

— Je le souhaite, approuve Margaret. Et il faudrait aussi que vous entendiez mon père.

— Vous avez dit qu'il était dans une clinique, et qu'il a perdu la mémoire.

— Ce matin, quand je l'ai quitté, il allait mieux. Je suis certaine que s'il revoyait son agresseur, il se souviendrait de lui. Me permettez-vous d'aller les chercher tous les deux?

— *All right!*» approuve le commissaire.

Il fait signe aux deux bobbies qui m'ont

accompagné de suivre la jeune fille et de l'emmener, au plus vite, dans la voiture de la police. Puis, faute de pouvoir tirer un mot de l'impassible maître d'hôtel, il nous demande de reprendre l'affaire, depuis le début, pour se faire une idée du rôle joué par Murray.

Mais le silence se fait de nouveau dans la salle. Margaret vient d'arriver, avec son père, au regard encore vague et James Blackmoor, visiblement troublé. L'instant est impressionnant. Lentement, appuyé au bras de sa fille, Harry Simson s'avance. A la vue de Murray, il s'arrête. Pendant quelques secondes il fixe étrangement le maître d'hôtel puis tend vers lui un doigt tremblant.

« C'est lui! s'écrie-t-il soudain. C'est lui! »

L'émotion a été si forte que l'inventeur chancelle, très pâle, prêt à défaillir. Un policeman lui apporte une chaise. Ainsi, les médecins avaient raison, il a suffi d'une violente émotion pour renouer, dans l'esprit du blessé, les fils coupés de la mémoire.

« C'est lui, reprend l'inventeur, le doigt toujours tendu. Je me souviens, à présent, je me souviens de tout... »

Le moment est poignant. La main sur l'épaule de son père, Margaret a les yeux pleins de larmes et le superintendant, lui-même, cache mal son émotion. Donnant à Harry Simson le temps de se remettre, le commissaire s'adresse à Blackmoor.

« Murray vous a accusé d'être son complice. D'après lui, c'est vous qui auriez monté cette affaire. Qu'avez-vous à répondre? En tout cas, un fait est certain, votre propre montre a été trouvée en France, à Lyon, sur les lieux de l'accident.

— Oh! monsieur le superintendant, bredouille le gardien, je vous jure que... que...»

Il n'achève pas. Paralysé par l'indignation, il s'effondre sur une chaise.

«Laissez ce pauvre homme tranquille, dit alors Harry Simson, dont le visage a retrouvé des couleurs. Je réponds de son honnêteté. Vous comprendrez mieux quand je vous aurai tout expliqué.»

Le père de Margaret passe la main sur son front, respire profondément et commence :

«Voilà, monsieur le superintendant, comment les choses se sont passées.»

Nous nous serrons autour de l'interprète pour ne pas perdre un mot de sa traduction.

«Oui, reprend Harry Simson, je reconnais cet homme et mes souvenirs, croyez-moi, sont redevenus parfaitement clairs. Cet individu était monté dans le même avion que moi, au *London Airport.* Je ne l'avais évidemment pas remarqué, puisque je ne l'avais jamais vu. A l'arrivée, les formalités terminées, j'allais monter dans la voiture qui m'attendait, quand il s'est présenté, d'une manière très correcte, disant qu'il avait retenu, lui aussi, une voiture sans chauffeur mais qu'il ne l'avait pas trouvée sur le parking. Sans méfiance, je lui ai proposé, comme il s'y attendait, de l'emmener jusqu'au centre de la ville. Il s'est assis à mon côté et j'ai démarré. Il m'a alors expliqué que, représentant d'une importante fabrique de tissus de Manchester, il venait pour affaires à Lyon et que la valise qu'il tenait sur ses genoux contenait des échantillons. Puis, tout à coup, alors que nous traversions un endroit désert, il dit vivement :

« "Attention! ralentissez! la route est barrée devant nous." Oui, ce sont bien ses paroles exactes. Je me suis penché en avant pour découvrir l'obstacle que je ne voyais pas. Au même moment, j'ai reçu un violent coup sur la tête. Instinctivement, au lieu de me protéger, je n'ai pensé qu'à reprendre le volant que j'avais lâché. Un second coup, plus fort, m'a fait perdre connaissance... Quand je suis revenu à moi, j'étais dans une chambre d'hôpital, tous souvenirs effacés. Mais à présent, monsieur le superintendant, ma mémoire est revenue, parfaitement limpide. Cet homme est bien mon agresseur... et il se trouvait dans le même avion. Il savait donc que je partais en France ce jour-là et pour quelle raison. »

Aussi bouleversés que Margaret et David, nous n'avons pas perdu un mot de la traduction.

« Cher daddy, murmure la jeune fille, en embrassant son père, je savais qu'un jour tu redeviendrais comme autrefois. »

Cependant, laissant Harry Simson se remettre de cette longue explication, le superintendant se retourne vers le gardien qui continue de baisser la tête, accablé.

« Nous voulons bien admettre, Blackmoor, que vous n'êtes pour rien dans cette affaire, cependant, vous connaissiez l'accusé, et il était en possession de votre montre.

— Pardonnez-moi, monsieur le superintendant, je le reconnais, mais n'y suis pour rien. C'est... c'est la faute de la bière.

— De la bière?

— De la damnée bière anglaise. Mais je vous le jure, c'est fini; jamais plus je n'y goûterai.

— Expliquez-vous!

— C'est arrivé un jour dans un pub, près de Piccadilly. Cet individu s'ennuyait. Il m'a offert une pinte de bière pour lui tenir compagnie... et il m'a encore invité le lendemain... et les jours suivants. Vous comprenez, monsieur le superintendant...

— Je comprends que vous aimez boire et que vous ne refusez jamais un verre.

— Ah! si j'avais su que cet homme m'invitait pour me faire parler! Je le reconnais, je lui ai dit des choses que j'aurais dû garder pour moi. Il m'avait dit s'appeler Thomas, être employé dans une banque. Il buvait avec moi et un nommé Bradson le jour où j'ai perdu ma montre. A présent, je suis sûr, c'est lui qui m'a volé ma montre. Oui, c'est à cause de cette damnée bière.

— Suffit, coupe le commissaire, nous avons compris.»

Et, revenant à Murray :

«Ainsi, avant de tirer sur un policeman, vous aviez déjà commis une agression. Est-ce James Blackmoor qui vous avait signalé le voyage de M. Simson en France?»

Une fois de plus, nous nous rassemblons autour de l'interprète, anxieux de tout savoir.

Murray, qui se sent perdu à présent, pense

que le reste n'a plus beaucoup d'importance et, d'une voix sèche, il commence :

« Quand je suis arrivé à Regent Street, j'ignorais tout de cette invention. J'ai appris l'existence des plans en faisant mon service de la salle à manger. C'est alors que l'idée m'est venue... »

Il raconte alors que, un jour où Margaret déjeunait chez les parents de son fiancé, elle avait parlé du projet de son père de se rendre en France pour vendre ses plans. Il avait ainsi appris que Harry Simson comptait en obtenir une forte somme mais que, pressé par le besoin d'argent, il avait négligé de prendre d'abord un brevet d'invention, à cause de la longueur des formalités.

Toujours au cours de son service, Murray, qui s'était arrangé pour faire la connaissance de Blackmoor, avait appris la date fixée pour le départ de l'inventeur. N'ayant pas réussi à s'introduire dans le grenier pour s'emparer des plans, il avait décidé de commettre son vol au moment du départ pour la France, entre Hanover Street et l'aéroport. Là aussi, son projet s'était trouvé déjoué. Au dernier moment, il avait appris que Margaret accompagnait son père à l'aéroport. Jouant le tout pour le tout, il avait retenu une place à bord de l'avion, prenant soin, pour justifier son absence, d'expédier un télégramme à Mme Heddle. Et c'est ainsi que, dissimulé dans l'aérogare, il avait attendu l'heure du départ.

Il explique ensuite comment, avec un marteau dissimulé dans sa valise, il a assommé

Harry Simson, croyant avoir le temps de sauter de la voiture avant l'accident... Enfin, il reconnaît avoir, plus tard, ligoté la jeune fille dans le grenier dont il avait subtilisé la clef au concierge.

Son récit achevé, il nous lance un regard glacé et murmure entre les dents :

« C'est cette sale montre qui m'a trahi. Au lieu de la garder au fond de ma poche, j'aurais mieux fait d'en changer le bracelet de cuir et de la placer à mon poignet pour remplacer celle que j'avais perdue. Elle ne serait pas tombée dans l'herbe quand la voiture a basculé au bas du talus en me blessant à la jambe. »

Et il ajoute, décidé à présent à tout dire :

« Je n'aurais pas dû, non plus, revenir au *Tulip Home* chercher les faux papiers que j'avais oubliés entre deux briques de la cheminée.

— *All right!* fait le commissaire, les aveux nous suffisent. L'enquête reprendra plus tard, en présence du policeman sur lequel vous avez lâchement tiré. »

Et, aux deux agents qui encadrent le coupable :

« Emmenez cet homme! »

Toujours aussi raide, le maître d'hôtel est entraîné hors de la salle. Alors, Margaret laisse libre cours à son soulagement. Empruntant le mot favori du Tondu, elle s'écrie :

« C'est tout simplement formidable! »

Et, les mains tendues vers nous :

« Que je suis heureuse! Vous avez sauvé les plans et mon père est guéri. Jamais je ne vous montrerai assez ma reconnaissance... Je voudrais tellement faire quelque chose pour vous remercier!

— Vous tenez vraiment à nous remercier? fait Mady, l'air malicieux. Alors c'est bien simple. Donnez-moi votre main.

— Ma main?

— Pour la mettre dans celle de David, en vous souhaitant de vous appeler au plus vite Mme David Heddle.»

Interdite, Margaret regarde David et tous deux deviennent plus rouges que des pivoines. Finalement, ils tombent dans les bras l'un de l'autre sous le regard du superintendant, gêné par cet épanchement sentimental dans un lieu aussi grave.

«Oh! excusez-moi, fait Margaret en rougissant de plus belle, oubliant que le commissaire ne parle pas un mot de français, je suis si follement heureuse!»

Et, comme Kafi tourne autour d'elle, tout joyeux, elle se penche vers lui pour une caresse.

«Et toi, mon bon chien, quelle sera ta récompense?

— Du porridge, répond le Tondu en s'esclaffant. A présent, nous pouvons l'avouer, il adore le porridge. Chaque matin, en cachette, c'est lui qui finissait le nôtre.»

Et Margaret de sourire, la main toujours dans celle de David.

Les formalités terminées, le superintendant, qui a abandonné son visage sévère, tient à nous remercier, lui aussi, par un de ces vigoureux shake-hand venus tout droit du cœur. Au moment où nous quittons son bureau, il se penche vers l'interprète qui se tourne vers moi et traduit :

« M. le superintendant désirerait savoir si, par hasard, votre chien ne serait pas anglais.

— Kafi ?... Certainement pas... Pourquoi cette question ?

— Parce que les chiens policiers anglais sont les meilleurs du monde. Le vôtre a été si... si formidable ! »

Aucun compliment ne pouvait me faire plus grand plaisir. Vraiment, Kafi l'a bien mérité.

Et nous quittons Scotland Yard. Soudain, de l'autre côté de la Tamise, la fameuse horloge de Big Ben égrène six coups.

« Six heures ! fait David. Nous avons failli manquer l'heure du thé. Suivez-moi, nous allons tout de suite fêter ce grand jour dans un *tea-room* que je connais, tout près d'ici. Etes-vous assez remis, M. Simson, pour nous accompagner ?

— *All right!* répond en riant le père de Margaret. En retrouvant la mémoire, j'ai aussi retrouvé le goût du vrai thé anglais. Celui de la clinique était atrocement “défectueux”. »

Et, se tournant vers nous :

« Est-ce bien ainsi qu'on dit en France, mes amis ? »

Chapitre 15

# Épilogue

J'achève de donner un dernier coup de brosse à mes chaussures quand Kafi dresse les oreilles, au bruit de pas dans l'escalier. En bon chien policier, il a reconnu Mady. C'est elle, en effet, qui vient me chercher.

« Dépêche-toi, Tidou, les autres Compagnons sont déjà en bas. Ce serait dommage de manquer le train. »

Le temps de mettre mon manteau, de passer la laisse au collier de Kafi et je suis prêt. En bas, mes camarades, ont, comme moi, fait toilette. A force d'aspersions, Gnafron a réussi à dompter sa mèche rebelle et le Tondu arbore un béret neuf. Par les petites rues de la Croix-Rousse, nous descendons vers la ville.

« Quelle chance ! fait Mady. Après la grisaille de ces jours derniers, le temps est presque beau, en tout cas pas froid pour la mi-novembre. En arrivant de la Côte d'Azur, Margaret et David ne seront pas trop déçus par notre climat lyonnais. »

Car Margaret et David ont promis de s'arrêter à Lyon en revenant de Nice où ils ont fait leur voyage de noces. Leur train doit arriver à 15 h 58 à la gare de Perrache. Cette visite ravive nos souvenirs anglais et, tout en marchant, nous évoquons une fois de plus notre aventure londonienne : l'arrivée à l'aéroport, la découverte de Margaret ligotée dans son grenier, notre poursuite à travers la ville, l'interrogatoire à Scotland Yard. Nous sommes tous si bien repris par les événements que nous arrivons à Perrache, sans même savoir quelles rues nous avons empruntées. La pendule de la gare ne marque que 15 h 30. Encore une demi-heure à attendre, que c'est long!

Tout émoustillé, Kafi semble deviner qui nous attendons. Sur le quai, où nous passons tout de suite, Mady évidemment s'interroge sur la toilette de Margaret... et nous, les garçons, nous nous demandons si David aura conservé son chapeau melon, enseigne de la fabrique paternelle.

Enfin, un haut-parleur annonce l'arrivée du Vintimille-Paris. Une locomotive électrique apparaît au bout des voies. Alignés sur le quai, nous nous sentons tout émus. Le train s'arrête. Des portières s'ouvrent. Presque devant nous, un voyageur en pardessus clair et casquette aide une jeune femme en manteau de fourrure à descendre.

« Mais... ce sont eux! » s'écrie Mady.

Comment les aurions-nous reconnus? Ou plutôt, comment reconnaître David Heddle sous cette casquette à carreaux enfoncée jusqu'aux oreilles ?

« Hello ! Nous sommes si heureux de vous revoir », s'écrie le mari de Margaret en lâchant ses valises pour venir à nous.

Et, riant de nos mines ahuries :

« Bien sûr, vous me reconnaissez à peine avec cette casquette ! C'est tellement plus pratique que le chapeau melon. Tant pis pour la réputation de notre maison. A mon retour à Londres, je la garderai. »

Ravie de nous retrouver, Margaret nous embrasse de bon cœur et caresse Kafi qui lui fait fête.

« Ah ! mes amis, quelle joie de se retrouver à Lyon, tous ensemble, pour effacer le mauvais souvenir que j'avais gardé de votre ville. »

Puis, au sortir de la gare, levant les yeux vers le ciel :

« Et quel temps merveilleux, presque aussi beau que sur votre Côte d'Azur, n'est-ce pas, David ? Enfin, nous allons voir votre fameuse caverne. Est-ce très loin de la gare ?

— Assez loin, explique le Tondu. A cause de Kafi, nous ne pouvons pas prendre l'autobus, mais si vous voulez un taxi ?

— Un taxi ? se récrie Margaret en riant. Il nous faudrait plutôt un autocar, ou un de nos gros bus rouges que vous aimiez tant. Est-ce que nous ne pourrions pas faire le trajet à pied, en bavardant ? Qu'en penses-tu, David ?

— Mais certainement, Margaret, c'est une bonne idée. »

Et nous voici partis à travers Lyon que David trouve à son goût et que Margaret redécouvre avec d'autres yeux.

« J'étais si triste, soupire-t-elle, quand j'y suis venue. »

Tout en marchant sous le tiède soleil de cet après-midi de novembre, elle évoque une fois de plus l'accident de son père et notre enquête qu'elle qualifie encore de formidable.

« Oui, à présent, je suis heureuse, fait-elle, et je vous le dois. Sans vous, je me demande si je serais devenue un jour Mme Heddle. »

Nous la questionnons alors sur son père et elle nous apprend qu'il est en train de mettre au point une nouvelle invention, grâce à la somme importante obtenue par la vente du fameux « système ».

« Et le bobby blessé ? demande le Tondu. Tu en as des nouvelles ?

— Il est tout à fait guéri. Je suis allée le voir, chez lui. Il a affiché, dans son living-room, le portrait de Kafi, vous vous souvenez, la photo parue dans le journal après l'interview à Regent Street.

— Et James Blackmoor ?

— Il a juré de ne plus boire une seule pinte de bière anglaise... et il a tenu parole. »

Tout en bavardant, nous atteignons la place des Terreaux qui, avec sa fontaine et ses pigeons, rappelle à David un peu Piccadilly.

Enfin, nous abordons la rude montée de la Croix-Rousse.

« Vous serez déçue, fait Mady un peu gênée, notre caverne est un vieil atelier abandonné.

Elle n'a rien d'un confortable living-room. »

Mady a tort de s'inquiéter. En pénétrant dans notre caverne, nos deux Anglais se montrent ravis. Tout les amuse : les rondins de bois en guise de sièges, les vieux rideaux tendus contre les murs pour dissimuler les creux et les bosses, la lanterne suspendue au plafond, la table boiteuse calée par des briques.

« Et cette chose, demande Margaret en tendant le doigt. Qu'est-ce que c'est ? »

Cette « chose », comme elle dit, est un vieux fourneau déniché dans une cave. Mady explique qu'il peut servir, par exemple, pour chauffer de l'eau.

« Chauffer de l'eau ? s'étonne Margaret... Et pour quoi faire ?

— Tu ne devines pas ?

— Non !

— Alors, regarde ta montre. Il est cinq heures : l'heure du thé. Nous n'avons pas oublié les habitudes anglaises. Le Tondu et la Guille ont visité toutes les épiceries de la Croix-Rousse pour trouver du vrai thé des Indes, comme celui que tu bois chez toi.

— Oh ! du thé ! s'écrie Margaret en battant des mains. Tu entends, David, nous allons tous fêter notre rencontre autour d'une tasse de vrai thé. C'est... c'est formidable !... »

# Table

*IMPRIMÉ EN FRANCE PAR BRODARD ET TAUPIN*
*Usine de La Flèche, 72200.*
*Loi n° 49-956 du 16 juillet 1949 sur les publications destinées à la jeunesse.*
*Dépôt : mars 1989.*